COUNTRYFILE'
GREAT BRITISH
WALKS

100 unique walks through our most stunning countryside

Edited by **Cavan Scott**

GREAT BRITISH
WALKS

Key to map symbols

	Nature
	History
	Cycling trail
	Train journey
	Boat trip
	Accessible route
	Food
	Arts and culture
	Horse riding
	Country drive
	Walking route
	Great photo opportunity

CONTENTS

FOREWORD

Walking is one of the few activities that transcends age, profession, social demographic and sex. You can be a spry seven year old or a sprightly septuagenarian and enjoy walking. There is nothing more therapeutic than roaming across great expanses of wild wonderful countryside – although more and more people are regularly enjoying urban strolls, millions of people hit the hills every weekend up and down the country.

I'll never forget striding out across the Peak District with my dad Michael when I was a wee young thing. A keen walker and general outdoor devotee, he took me walking for the first time when I was about 6 years old; by the time I was 12 or 13 I was a fully fledged hiker – I had my own boots and everything! 'Sensible footwear' is not a term to be used excessively in my opinion, but it is pretty much all you need when it comes to perambulation. Race walking may be an Olympic discipline but luckily for all of us you don't need to be anywhere near Olympic status to participate effectively. And the benefits? Oh the joy that it brings! Someone once said 'A pedestrian is a man in danger of his life. A walker is a man in possession of his soul.'

But nourishing the soul hasn't always been easy. There is no denying we like a

> Breathtaking beauty and sheer drama combine at the lakes of Snowdonia in Wales

good fight on these fair isles; we fight for buildings to be saved, we're fighting for air travel to be abandoned and we even fought for our right to ramble. In April 1932 four hundred or so agitated walkers set out on an expedition up Kinder Scout, the highest point in Derbyshire. It was a march with intention rather than a gentle stroll; folk from the cities had grown tired of the restricted access to the countryside. Landowners covetously guarded their property back then and the Duke of Derbyshire was no exception.

The ramblers, fighting passionately for their right to roam, clashed with the gamekeepers instructed to defend the estate. Although victorious, the leader of the pack – a mechanic called Benny Rothman – was subsequently arrested along with a number of other figureheads, and was imprisoned for civil disobedience. This caught public attention and sparked a national debate about our right to rural access. This countryside squabble arguably paved the way for National Parks and can be claimed to be the foundation of our rambling freedoms.

The UK is laden with wonderfully wild, peaceful backdrops of extraordinary beauty, abundant with nature and wildlife – great arcs of stunning landscape waiting for you to explore. Take advantage. This book is full of fantastic proposals.

Happy walking.

JULIA BRADBURY

INTRODUCTION

We're spoilt in the United Kingdom. Within a relatively small group of islands we can experience a whole world of different landscapes, from the wilderness of the **Scottish Highlands** to the secluded coves of **Cornwall**. With so much variety, so many distinct regions, it beggars belief that all too often we take it for granted. Think what we have on our doorstep: the untamed expanse of the **Yorkshire moors**; the remote fells of the **Lake District**; the scarcely known peaks of **Northern Ireland**; the timeless beauty of the **Cotswolds**; the secret beaches of the **Welsh coast**; the winding waterways of **Norfolk**; the neat orchards of **Kent**. It seems a crime that so many of us fail to explore these four countries of ours and instead look beyond our shores for adventure and romance.

First Steps

Eighty percent of the population of the UK now live in urban areas, so it's vital that we keep in touch with our countryside. It isn't simply that a walk in the country can keep you fit physically: connecting with open spaces can be as good for your mind and spirit. It can relax you one minute, then stimulate and challenge you the next. Some scientists claim that humans were never meant to live in a city environment, that we were hardwired to be surrounded by nature. A spell in the countryside therefore restores the balance, cuts down stress, and even improves our levels of concentration.

So, what are we waiting for? Why aren't we spilling out of our cities of sharp lines, escaping the noise and bustle and running for the hills and valleys? Well, actually, we are. Government figures suggest that seven million of us walk in the countryside every single weekend, and that figure is growing year on year.

But what if you don't know where to start? What if you need a helping hand to find that ideal rural location, that view to die for? That's where this book comes in. In your hands you have 100 walks gathered from the BBC's *Countryfile Magazine*, each researched and mapped out by expert walkers, ramblers, hikers – whatever you want to call them, all people who know and love our countryside. There is something for everyone here, with every walk graded for its level of difficulty: easy for beginners (or those who just fancy a stroll), moderate if you want to push yourself that bit harder, or challenging for those who are after a bit of a, well, challenge. For each walk we've given an indication of the kind of terrain you'll encounter and an estimate of the time it will take, based on a leisurely pace and allowing for breaks and stops.

However, these are the technicalities and on page 10 we'll also run through some basic tips. But from the moment you pull on your boots and take your first step, you'll discover that there is much more to walking than grid references, times and distances to cover. People who are bitten by the rambling bug know that the route itself is only half the story. It's what you encounter along the way that matters.

› Striking views and historical treats at the Ochil Hills in Stirling

› Absorb one of nature's most thrilling wonders at Holkham Beach

Fresh Ideas

Every walk in this book promises new surprises, new experiences, new wonders to behold. Yes, there are spectacular views that will take your breath away (we've even popped in some handy photo-opportunity suggestions), but look closer and you'll discover amazing wildlife, fascinating history and, most importantly for some, new and exciting culinary delights. Each walk is categorised by themes to help match your day out with your interests or, hopefully, to develop fresh ones. There are walks that have been designed to show you nature of note, rambles to help you escape the city and step fully into nature, routes that take in a little arts and culture, and hikes that will reward you with the very best in local food and delicacies.

Local Treasures

Walking in the British Isles becomes so enthralling and – ultimately – addictive because as well as the dramatic changes in the landscape as you pass through one county after another, you have the wealth of our history and culture laid out before

you. Once you start to explore you begin to appreciate the wonderful distinctiveness of society here in our United Kingdom. An early clue is the accents you hear in the villages, the shifting dialects where a vowel is dropped here or added there, and each region brings its own unique words and phrases. Then come the local stories, some based on historical fact, some flights of fancy but all fascinating. These legends and tales have shaped our nation and inspired great works of art, from Arnold Bax's symphonic ode to Arthur and Guinevere to Arthur Conan Doyle's demonic *Hound of the Baskervilles*. And of course there's the food and drink. In a world dominated by facsimile high streets and copycat chain restaurants, a walk through the countryside delivers unique delicacies and good honest food to you on a plate, and even offers a decent drop in your glass. Your taste buds will love you forever.

So, yes, we are spoilt here in the United Kingdom. We have miles upon miles of countryside that can help improve you in body, mind and, some would even argue, soul. All it needs is that first step…

The Safe and Responsible Walker

There's nothing to be scared about when walking in the countryside, but there's no need to take risks either. After all, even the most challenging walk should be an enjoyable and fun venture that leaves you in one piece. We are encouraging people to walk to feel good, not risk life and limb. So, before we start, let's run through some of the safety basics. Even if you're a frequent walker, it's worth reminding yourself of them every now and then.

Be Safe

First up, get planning. If you're a beginner don't dive straight into a difficult or overly long route. There's no one to impress and nothing to prove. If you do decide to tackle a longer walk, make sure you've worked out various points along the way where you can 'escape' if you need to cut things short. Also, wherever possible, let someone know where you're going and don't rely on your mobile phone: network coverage isn't always great, especially in hill country. Ensure that before you set out, you have a map and a compass and know how to use them. Don't just rely on the maps in this book, they are intended for planning, not orienteering, and are no substitute for a proper detailed map when you're out walking.

Make sure you know what weather you can expect and take heed of any warnings from the Met Office. We're lucky here in the UK; we talk endlessly about the weather, but we don't experience much in the way of extremes. What we all know is that it can change within minutes, especially if you're in the middle of nowhere or clambering up a fell. So, especially if you're heading into hills or remote areas, make sure you have the following with you:

> A waterproof jacket
> Waterproof trousers
> Good walking boots or shoes with support for your ankles and good solid treads
> Good-quality thick socks (some walkers swear by wearing more than one pair of socks, but be warned, this can lead to more friction around your feet and therefore, more blisters!)
> A spare fleece or jumper: always go for several layers if you have to keep warm
> A waterproof rucksack, containing a litre water bottle and enough food for your walk

You may have noticed an emphasis on waterproof there, but this is Britain we're talking about! Keep an eye on the sky for rain, mist or fog, but remember that strong winds can be a hazard too, especially on hillsides. Obviously, if conditions are anything less than clement, make sure you have gloves and hat in your kit (40 per cent of body heat is lost through your head).

It has to be said, especially when walking on the lowlands in good weather, that you don't need a lot of expensive walking gear. Good boots are always a sound investment and it's always better not to wear jeans because wet denim takes a long time to dry out, which can lead to chafing. Generally avoid wearing cotton items as these can soon absorb sweat, making you clammy and uncomfortable. Opt for thin synthetic layers that wick moisture (to you and me that means taking it away from the skin and drying quickly).

Be Responsible

Walkers are usually a responsible lot. A happy knock-on effect of rambling is that the more you walk through our beautiful countryside, the more you care about it and the people who work, rest and play there.

    The general rule of thumb is to leave the countryside as you found it. Here are a few guidelines to being a responsible walker. Once again, they may seem obvious, but you'll be amazed how many people forget the basics:

> - **Don't go clambering over fences and walls that often can be easily damaged. Find the nearest stile or gate instead.**
> - **If you do pass through a gate, make sure you shut it behind you. Of course, there are some instances when they're supposed to be open, for example, to allow farm animals access to water, but in most cases country gates are meant to be closed.**
> - **If you're walking with your dog, keep them under control, which largely means having them on the lead or at the very least near to you.**
> - **Respect the wildlife around you. It's illegal to pick wild flowers, unless you have the landowner's permission. Besides, it's always better to leave beautiful blooms for your fellow walkers to enjoy, rather than to snaffle them for yourself.**

> The ancient ruins of Hadrian's Wall let the imagination run wild

> - **There is one thing you should definitely take home with you – your rubbish. Don't drop it and certainly don't bury it. Pop it in your bag and take it with you. For a little extra good karma, why not pick up litter that other people have so casually and carelessly discarded?**
> - **Safeguard any water supplies you may come across, making sure you never pollute streams, rivers, ponds or lakes.**
> - **Guard against any risk of fire, be it a stray cigarette or campfire. If you really need to boil a cup of coffee on the move, consider buying a portable stove, but again, take care.**
> - **If you're crossing a farmer's crops, walk in a single line or around the edge of a field to minimise the chance of damaging precious harvest.**
> - **Respect the privacy of people living in the countryside; you wouldn't like it if someone traipsed through your garden, pausing to peer through your windows. Remember this is where people live and work, not a museum or theme park.**

Walking in the Great British Countryside: a brief history

Today, we are able to enjoy the splendours of much of our countryside with a great level of freedom, but the path hasn't always been clear – hard battles have been fought and won to attain this right, and the struggle to balance free access and protection of the land goes on.

The Fight to Roam

'Four or five hundred ramblers, mostly from Manchester, trespassed in mass on Kinder Scout to-day. They fought a brief but vigorous hand-to-hand struggle with a number of keepers specially enrolled for the occasion. This they won with ease, and then marched to Ashop Head, where they held a meeting before returning in triumph to Hayfield.'

That is how the *Manchester Guardian* reported the Kinder mass trespass on Monday, 25 April 1932. Today we have so much freedom to enjoy the countryside it's hard to think of a time when men had to resort to violence for the right to roam across our green and pleasant land. Yet, little more than 75 years ago this is what happened on Kinder Scout, the highest point in Derbyshire, and those 400 Mancunian ramblers triggered a chain of events that led to us being able to walk the British countryside today.

So let's take ourselves back to the early 1930s to understand what led those civilians to leave the confines of the city and head into the Peak District in the first place. At the time, landowners jealously controlled who was allowed to walk across their property, desperate to maintain their hold on what was prime and profitable hunting and shooting ground. In the nearby industrial cities, factory workers and dockers looked at the hills with envious eyes, keen to breathe clean, fresh air at the weekend when they would be free of the shackles of work. But those who set out to explore would find themselves barred from the countryside they longed for and largely unable to escape the confines of the cities. The common land of previous generations was rapidly disappearing, whittled away during a series of Enclosure acts in the 18th and 19th centuries. Most moorland around the grimy, polluted industrial centres of northern England in the early 20th century was out of bounds. Bills to permit free access to mountainous areas had been fought in Westminster since 1884, but had failed every time, not least because many MPs were landowners with an interest in maintaining their grip on privilege. The future for ramblers looked bleak to say the least.

› Pure freedom: clear skies over seemingly endless green fields in Devon

> One of England's most beautiful areas, the Lake District has picture-perfect routes for any walker

In April 1932, members of the Lancashire branch of the Communist-inspired British Workers Sports Federation were thrown off Bleaklow, a dramatic gritstone hill north of Kinder Scout. Enough was enough. The right-to-roam movement, which began back in 1876 with the formation of the Hayfield and Kinder Scout Ancient Footpaths Association, wasn't moving fast enough. Frustrated by the official rambling organisations' lack of success, and with socialist fire in their belly, members of the local Federation decided to take matters into their own hands. At 2pm on Sunday, 24 April, led by a 20-year-old mechanic from Cheetham, Manchester named Benny Rothman, 400 walkers headed for the highest point of the Peak District. The idea was simple: safety in numbers. No landkeeper would be able to stop such a mob of determined hikers.

'It was possibly a naive idea that if enough ramblers went on a ramble, no group of keepers could stop them because there would be more ramblers than keepers,' Rothman told the BBC in 1980, recalling how they marched up the William Clough Gorge, to be met by a group of gamekeepers from the Duke of Derbyshire's estate. 'There must have been a dozen or slightly more brandishing their sticks and shouting "get back". Of course we just ignored them or pushed them aside until we got to the top.' The ramblers massively outnumbered the keepers and so were able to grab the keepers' sticks while others pulled off their belts and used them as whips to try to break through.

> Spot deer and wild boar in Nagshead, Gloucestershire's own contribution to Lord Nelson's navy

Other than bruises and scrapes there was little in the way of real injury, save for one keeper, a Mr E. Beaver, who was knocked unconscious and hurt his ankle in the scuffle.

You can imagine the group's satisfaction, having got past the keepers, to reach the plateau of Kinder Scout and be met by a band of fellow trespassers from Sheffield who had started for Kinder Scout that morning from Edale with the intention of meeting the Hayfield group. Triumphantly the ramblers returned the way they had come, splitting back into two groups for Edale and Hayfield. As they returned to their starting points, they were confronted with the police. Six leaders were arrested, including Benny Rothman, and the following day were charged with 'riotous assembly'. Rothman served four

months, but his act of civil disobedience had done the trick. The arrests and subsequent incarceration sparked the public's interest. Why were hard-working folk like Rothman being thrown into prison for wanting to enjoy the British countryside? Just over one hundred years after William Wordsworth had described the Lake District as 'a sort of national property, in which every man has a right and interest who has an eye to perceive and a heart to enjoy', the demand for free access to rural Britain was growing. The disparate rambling organisations started to work with rather than against one another, and a few weeks later more walkers gathered at Winnats Pass, between Castleton and Edale, for a second mass trespass. This time, their numbers had swollen to a thousand.

Picking up the Pace

The tide was turning. Within three years, the various rambling organisations had consolidated into the body we know today as the Ramblers, and Westminster revisited an idea first floated in 1931. The Addison Report had recommended to Parliament that Britain would do well to follow the example of its American cousins who had established Yellowstone, the world's first National Park, nearly 60 years previously. Dovedale in Derbyshire had been proposed as the first English National Park, but a change of government and the world's growing financial crisis put paid to those plans. The mass trespass put the National Park firmly back on the agenda.

In 1935, walker and writer Tom Stephenson published an article in the *Daily Herald* entitled 'Wanted: A Long Green Trail'. Inspired by America's 2,175-mile (3,500-km) Appalachian Way, the longest continuous footpath in the world, he asked why Britons couldn't enjoy a Pennine Way between the Peak District and the Cheviots, a trail he dubbed The Jubilee Way in honour of George V. 'Whatever the cost,' Stephenson wrote, 'it would be a worthy and enduring testimony – bringing health and pleasure beyond computation, for none could walk that Pennine Way without being improved in mind and body, inspired and invigorated and filled with the desire to explore every corner of this lovely island.'

Events began to pick up pace. On 26 May 1936, the Standing Committee on National Parks held their first meeting, and two years later published 'The Case for National Parks in Great Britain'. 'It is not a question of physical exercise only,' wrote G. M. Trevelyan in its foreword, 'it is also a question of spiritual enjoyment. It is a question of spiritual values. Without sight of the beauty of nature the spiritual power of the British people will be atrophied.'

Even during the Second World War the importance of the National Parks remained in the public eye and the Scott Report of 1942, although containing some bizarre recommendations including painting rural telephone boxes green to make them blend in with the fields, reinforced the need for rights of access. The war and its aftermath did, of course, slow down the process slightly and it wasn't until 17 April 1951 that the post-war Labour Government established the Peak District as the nation's first National Park, along with Dartmoor, the Lake District and Snowdonia. A year later the new Peak District National Park authority negotiated rights of access for Kinder Scout and, shortly after, Bleaklow. Those who had marched as trespassers in 1932 could now return with the weight of the law behind them.

The National Parks

As soon as Britain started establishing National Parks, it was as if they couldn't stop. The 50s saw a flurry of new parks, including the North York Moors and Pembrokeshire Coast in 1952, Exmoor and the Yorkshire Dales two years later, followed by Northumberland and the Brecon Beacons in 1956 and 1957 respectively. We then waited 32 years for a new park as the Broads joined the ranks in 1989. Six years later the 1995 Environment Act revised the purpose of the National Parks, charging them with the responsibility to conserve and enhance their natural beauty, wildlife and cultural heritage and to promote opportunities for us all to understand and enjoy the special qualities of these vital areas.

The advent of the 21st century has done nothing to stop the growth of the National Parks. A second cycle of designations kicked off in 2002 with Scotland's first ever National Park in the form of Loch Lomond and the Trossochs. The Scots would receive their second – the Cairngorms, Britain's largest park, some 40 percent larger than the Lake District – the following year.

William the Conqueror's ancient hunting ground of the New Forest was made a park in 2005 and in 2009 the South Downs, often dubbed the 'green lungs' of London, was announced as finally winning National Park status. This last addition to the list has brought much celebration from those who continue to campaign for creation of new parks; the area was first suggested as far back as 1947. It was initially rejected for being too cultivated, but now, as Environment minister Hilary Benn said when he announced the designation, will be 'protected for ever for the enjoyment of everyone'.

Combined, the National Parks now make up 12 percent of the land surface of Britain and are home to a population of over 300,000 people and more than 2,000 miles of public right of way. Many people mistakenly believe that these designated areas belong to the state but they do not. The majority of the land is still private, the property of individuals, farmers, corporations and conservation groups. The joy is that they are ours to explore. Is it any wonder that over 100 million people visit these natural breathing places of wilderness, beauty and adventure every year?

Shady paths, quiet glades and fascinating wildlife populate the Langdon Nature Reserve in Essex – home to over 30 species of butterfly

> The sweeping hills of Staffordshire form the perfect backdrop to a taste of the region's culinary delights

Something to CRoW About

The creation of the National Parks was only the beginning. On 24 April 1965, thirty years after Tom Stephenson published his dream of the long green track, Britain's first National Trail, the Pennine Way, was opened, stretching 268 miles (430 km) from Edale in Derbyshire to the Scottish border, and crossing three National Parks. Since then 14 other National Trails have been created in England and Wales, covering some 2,500 miles (4,000 km), as well as four Long Distance Routes in Scotland, adding a further 464 miles (746 km).

The biggest revolution in free access to the countryside came 35 years after the opening of the Pennine Way. The Countryside and Rights of Way Act of 2000 (known as the CRoW Act to its friends, and even some of its foes) finally granted walkers in England and Wales the right to ramble across uncultivated open countryside, or Access Land. This can be mountain, moor, heath, down, and registered common land or even private land that has been voluntarily dedicated for access by the owner. It also contained additional provisions for coastal land.

Nonetheless, you must always check that any land you're intending to walk through is covered by the Act. The phrase 'right to roam' is often confusing. It doesn't mean that we suddenly have the right to wander wherever we want, nipping in and out of private property willy-nilly, because the Act only covers areas designated as open countryside. Any new Ordnance Survey map you now buy makes Access Land clear, and you can also keep an eye out for signposts displaying the

Open Access symbol (left). A red line through the symbol, as you'd expect, indicates the end of Access Land. Full lists and further information are also available on the Open Access website at www.naturalengland.org.uk/openaccess

When you've found your new Access Land you can walk, climb and watch wildlife to your heart's content, although some restrictions still apply. These include:

- Driving or riding any vehicle across Access Land
- Using a vessel or sailboard on any non-tidal water
- Bathing in any non-tidal water
- Walking with any animal other than a dog (which themselves must be kept on a lead during lambing and the ground bird nesting season (1 March–31 July) or at any time of year near livestock)
- Lighting or tending a fire
- Intentionally killing or disturbing any wildlife
- Intentionally damaging or destroying any eggs, nests or plants
- Feeding livestock
- Hunting, shooting or fishing
- Using a metal detector
- Obstructing the flow of any drain or watercourse
- Neglecting to shut any gate, except where it is intended to be left open
- Engaging in any organised games, or in wild-camping, hang-gliding or para-gliding
- Engaging in any activity which is organised for commercial purposes

In some cases the owners will allow any or all of these activities on their land, but likewise they have the right to withdraw the permission without any notice at all.

In Scotland, things are slightly different. The Land Reform Act of 2003 and the Scottish Outdoor Access Code of 2004 gave everyone rights of access over most land and inland water throughout Scotland, provided they act responsibly. This opened the majority of the Scottish countryside for walking, cycling, horse riding and wild-camping. As in England and Wales, these rights don't apply to buildings, houses, schools, private gardens or land where crops are being grown.

Unfortunately, Northern Ireland has no rights of access or indeed any plans to pass its own version of the Act, but for the rest of the United Kingdom at least, the dream of those 400 ramblers who set out for Kindler Scout has come true. The countryside is largely ours to explore. Now all we have to do is get out there.

> A tour of Cornwall's coastline offers a glimpse of former glories

SOUTH WEST

The South West of England is a land of mystery and magic. From the pixies of the Cornish hills to the Arthurian mysticism of **Somerset**, the very landscape is steeped in the stuff of legend. You can't help but walk through history wherever you go, whether it's in the shadows of **Stonehenge** or **Avebury**, hunting for fossils along Dorset's Jurassic coast or following in the footsteps of Cornish smugglers.

The area is one of tremendous contrasts. Picture-postcard countryside and quaint villages roll one after another throughout Somerset and **Devon**, while the stunning 630-mile (1014-km) South West Coast Path, Britain's longest waymarked trail, takes in bustling ports, dramatic coves and glorious beaches

Even the South West's three great moors couldn't be more different, if you excuse the pun. The heathered slopes of **Exmoor** stretching across Somerset and north Devon contain evidence of the country's most ancient farmland, some older than the Domesday Book itself. Its rolling hills and combes, rich in woodland and pasture, are populated by Exmoor ponies and red deer, while the spectacular Exmoor sea cliffs-provide a rocky resting spot for seabirds. However, it's little wonder than Arthur Conan Doyle decided to let the demonic Hound of the Baskervilles loose on the stark, forbidding expanse of Devon's other moor: cold, bleak but breathtakingly beautiful **Dartmoor**. Of course, another fabled creature is said to stalk the wilds of north Cornwall: the beast of **Bodmin Moor**. Tiny in comparison to its near neighbouring moors, Bodmin's gentle sloping hills, offer a wild and windswept landscape.

When it comes to food and drink, the South West again serves up its fair share of legends. Jamaica Inn, immortalised by the pen of Daphne du Maurier is no work of fiction but an old staging post on **Bodmin**, and a welcome sight for walkers. There's the world-famous pasty, said to originate in Cornwall (though often contested by Devonians), head-spinning Somerset scrumpy cider and irresistible clotted cream tea – believed to have originated from Benedictine monks in **Tavistock** over 1,000 years ago. The once sleepy fishing habour of **Padstow** has been transformed by its cuisine, and is now bursting with the best seafood the region has to offer, thanks mainly to the efforts of celebrity chef Rick Stein.

Whether you feed your belly or your imagination in the South West, one thing is certain: once you're under the region's spell, you'll be bewitched forever.

Land's End Cornwall

Distance 4½ miles (6½ km) **Type** Moderate **Time** 3 hours

> The coastal scenery around Land's End is truly magnificent

This walk offers a chance to see **Land's End** as it should be seen: on foot from the coast path. Those who can remember when this spot was home simply to a hotel and the First and Last House tend to resent today's addition of cafes, shops and attractions, but there's no doubt that the coastal scenery around Cornwall's westernmost tip is magnificent. Stick to the **South West Coast Path**, which skims the edge of the

> The stunning Whitesand Bay is a real treat for walkers

development, and the latter is soon left far behind. This walk starts from the vast and beautiful expanse of **Whitesand Bay** at **Sennen Cove** and runs inland through fields to pick up

the coast path at **Nanjizal**, one of the most secluded beaches in the area, before returning to Sennen Cove along the coast.

▶ START

Park in the beach car park at the southern end of Whitesand Bay. Walk up the road; turn right at the first lane to walk along the top of the village, with fantastic 📷 views. Where the lane turns left, keep ahead as signed, and follow the footpath in a straight line across fields, aiming for a solitary house ahead and slightly right. Join the drive to **Treeve Moor House**; keep ahead to the A30. Cross the road carefully and then walk along the B3315 towards **Trevescan**.

1 1¼ MILES

Turn right opposite **The Little Barn Cafe** to pass through a cottage garden, and climb a Cornish stile. Keep ahead along the left side of fields to cross the farmyard at **Trevilley**, over a stile and on to a track. Turn right; where the track ends follow footpath signs through three fields, eventually reaching a gate on the edge of a gorse-filled valley. Turn right then follow the narrow path as it descends steeply to the 📷 coast path above Nanjizal (Mill Bay). This glorious spot is only accessible on foot and is perfect: no car park, no cafe, and it is ideal for picnics and

paddling (to access the beach, turn left on the path, then bear right).

2 2 MILES

Turn right along the coast path and follow a rocky path along the back of the bay before climbing on to **Trevilley Cliff**. Follow the cliff edge round **Pordenack Point** (look out for seals) and pass stunning rock formations such as the extraordinary arch of 📷 the **Armed Knight**, just off the coast. The path becomes increasingly worn as you approach Land's End. Follow the coast path signs – basically keep to the path nearest to the cliffs. Pass **Grebe Farm** on your right then follow the signs down steps and uphill eventually to pass the official Land's End signpost, which tells you that you are 874 miles away from John O'Groats.

3 3½ MILES

Follow the coast path over National Trust land on **Maen Cliff**, soon passing the remains of **Maen Castle**, an Iron Age fort. Pass the old coastguard lookout, with fabulous views of Whitesand Bay, then drop steeply down to Sennen Cove. Don't miss the harbour and the lovely **Roundhouse Gallery**, which shows local crafts and paintings, before walking along the front back to the car park.

Sennen Cove offers sweeping sands, the most westerly point on the English mainland and one of Cornwall's most magical beaches

KEY   ▶INFO

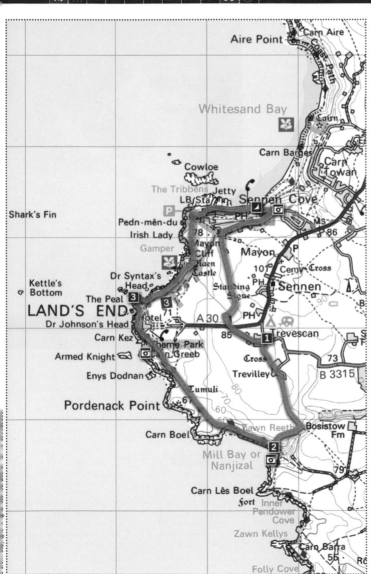

TERRAIN
Field paths and well-trodden coast paths.

HOW TO GET THERE
BY CAR: Sennen Cove is signed off the A30 and is also accessed via the B3306.
BY PUBLIC TRANSPORT: The First & Last bus service run from Penzance to Sennen Cove and Land's End.

MAP
Ordnance Survey Explorer Map 102.
Grid ref: SW 354 263

NEARBY EXCURSIONS
Geevor Tin Mine
Pendeen TR19 7EW
☎ 01736 788662
www.geevor.com
Open all year (not Sat) from 9am-5pm (3pm winter).

MORE INFO
Penzance Tourist Information
☎ 01736 362207

South West Coast Path
www.nationaltrail.co.uk
southwestcoastpath.com
www.swcp.org.uk

Visit Cornwall
www.visitcornwall.com

Route ━━━━

23

Kennall Vale Cornwall

Distance 3 miles (4.8 km) **Type** Easy **Time** 3 hours

This 20-acre woodland in Cornwall, managed by the Cornwall Wildlife Trust since 1985, is a hidden gem on the edge of the small village of **Ponsanooth**. Within the walled site is a treasure trove of Cornish mining history, dating back to 1812 when the site was used as a gunpowder factory, although the moss-covered ruins are now all that remain. The great wheels of the mills and the many leats used to carry water from the **River Kennall** are now home to the wildlife that flourishes here all year. During winter, the bare broadleaf trees allow light to spill into the valley – and the moss is ever-present, blanketing the granite boulders and ruins dotted around the reserve.

▶ START

The only entrance (and exit) is just off Park Road, marked with a Wildlife Trust (WT) sign, and leads straight into the wooded valley along a wide footpath. Ferns and ramsons line the surrounding area as well as beech, ash and sycamore trees. The WT have attached bird boxes to many of the trunks to provide fixed nests for chiffchaffs and other small birds visiting the valley. The trees were originally planted here by the **Kennall Vale Gunpowder Company** In the early 19th century to help retain a damp atmosphere and prevent any risk of explosion – although in 1838 a

massive explosion did occur, miraculously resulting in only one fatality and little damage to the overall site.

It's easy to navigate your way around the reserve; just stick to the pathway and have fun veering off course every now and then to inspect the ruins of the various buildings along the way. Highlights include the manager's house, the sulphur mills and the workshops in **Kennall Wood**, with more ruins higher up in the valley at **Roches Wood**.

1 | 1½ MILES

From the main pathway on the right you'll soon reach a footbridge with handrails that crosses to the other side of the valley, over a rushing river lined with mossy banks and boulders. Upstream you'll see a waterfall that 📷 is particularly impressive after rainfall and you may even glimpse a dipper.

2 | 2 MILES

The other side of the valley offers a chance to explore inside the ruins of the old sulphur mill. Stay on the panelled footbridges that run alongside the leats filled with water and you'll reach some steep steps leading down to the mill's entrance. The mill is without a roof but still has walls, window frames, an 📷 abandoned millstone and one large wheel, now host to mosses and insects.

› **The old milling machinery is covered in moss and teems with life**

Walk around inside and imagine the noise and energy that once filled this space, as the churning water drove the mill wheel and turned the heavy millstones.

3 | 2½ MILES

Higher up in the valley at Roches Wood stand decrepit ruins of the Gunpowder Company's newer buildings, constructed in 1844 when the company expanded in response to the thriving industry and

demand for gunpowder. It wasn't until 1880, with the invention of gelignite and dynamite, that the future of the company was under threat. The demand for gunpowder slumped in favour of nitroglycerine-based high explosives, and by 1910 production ceased.

After visiting all the ruins exit the reserve the way you came in. If you time it right you may spot a resident pipistrelle bat feeding on the wing.

Once a thriving gunpowder mine, **Kennall Vale** is now one of Cornwall's most important nature reserves and a perfect heritage trail

KEY

▶INFO

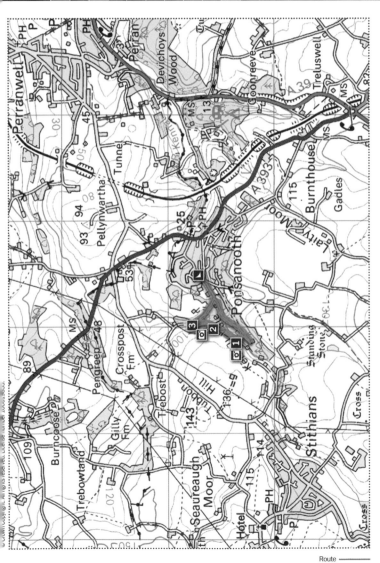

Route ————

TERRAIN
Woodland footpaths, panelled footbridges, some slippery stones, muddy if wet.

HOW TO GET THERE
BY CAR: Parking is limited, with no dedicated car park. Turn off the A39 onto the A393 for Ponsanooth. At Ponsanooth post office, follow the road up the hill as it narrows onto Park Road. Look for a Kennall Vale sign on right, only possible to see on foot. The entrance is beyond a private house.
BY PUBLIC TRANSPORT:
Firstbus run a regular service from Redruth to Ponsanooth, number 41, or 88 and 88B from Falmouth.
www.firstgroup.com

MAP
Ordnance Survey Explorer Map 104.
Grid ref: SW 753 375

NEARBY EXCURSIONS
Stithians Lake, near Redruth, Cornwall, TR16 6NW
Open year round for birdwatching, seasonal angling and sailing.
www.swlakestrust.org.uk

MORE INFO
Cornwall Wildlife Trust, Five Acres Allet, Truro TR4 9DJ
☎ 01872 273939
cornwallwildlifetrust.org.uk

Redruth Tourist Information Centre, Alma Place, Redruth TR15 2AT
☎ 01209 219048
www.visitcornwall.co.uk
www.cornish-mining.org.uk

25

Mitchell •

▶ ST AGNES

Redruth •

St Mawes •
Falmouth •

• Helston

St Agnes Cornwall

Distance 6 miles (9½ km) **Type** Moderate **Time** 4½ hours

▶ The South West Coast Path is a short walk from the campsite

▶ START

From the campsite go left then right into a National Trust car park and follow the path in the opposite corner. Soon you'll find the remains of **Wheal Coates** tin mine, a remnant of what was once a booming industry.

A steep, zigzagging path continues down below the main buildings to the spectacular old pumping house. Follow the coast path left to **Chapel Porth**, a popular beach for families and local surfers. The beach

▶ The sandy Trevaunance Cove is popular with surfers

cafe has a tasty menu, and is especially famous for Hedgehog ice creams. Cross the bridge to the right and follow a path heading inland up a sheltered valley.

Go through a wooden kissing gate on your left. Turn right along a farm track alongside a stream, buzzing with insects and brimming with wild flowers. Eventually go through another kissing gate, walk up a short track then turn right and, on reaching a lane, turn left. At the crossroads go left and take a path on the right, which climbs and narrows before splitting – take the steep path straight up across the open heathland, a stunning carpet of purple bell heather, to **St Agnes Beacon**.

1 2¾ MILES

From the beacon summit (192m above sea level), there is a fantastic 360° view down to **St Ives**, over to **Redruth** and up the coast to **Trevose Head lighthouse**. An information plaque directs you to local landmarks, including distinctive tin mine chimneys. Historically, fires were lit on the beacon to warn villagers of imminent attack. Take the path heading

in the direction of St Agnes. Turn left at a lane, signposted **Higher Bal**. After houses, walk over a stone stile and follow the footpath over fields until you reach the centre of the village. **St Agnes** is a year-round bustling village with galleries and craft shops. Don't forget to grab a traditional Cornish pasty from the bakery.

2 3½ MILES

Turn left on the main road, past the church and the famously quirky row of houses known as **Stippy Stappy**.

Follow **Quay Road** to **Trevaunance Cove**, passing the wonderfully inviting 17th-century **Driftwood Spars Hotel**. Left of the beach pick up the coast path and follow it back to Wheal Coates mine. At **St Agnes Head** look out for fulmars soaring around the cliffs and gannets diving out to sea. Notice the numerous capped mine shafts, evidence of the tin mining history. On reaching Wheal Coates, head back to the campsite.

Discover the best of everything Cornish – from spectacular coastline and countryside to the bustling village of **St Agnes**

KEY

▲ INFO

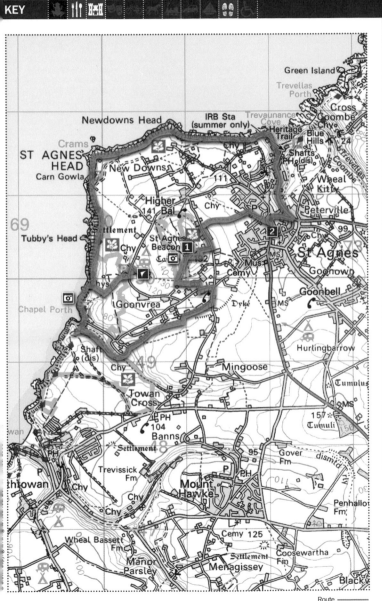

TERRAIN
Coast paths (steep in places), country footpaths with stiles and short sections on minor roads. Warm clothes recommended as the coastal path is exposed.

HOW TO GET THERE
BY CAR: Travelling westbound on the A30, drive to the Chiverton Cross roundabout and take the B3277 St Agnes turning. As you approach St Agnes, take the left-hand turning to Chapel Porth. From here follow the brown tourism signs until you reach Beacon Cottage Farm on your right.
BY PUBLIC TRANSPORT: Trains run to Truro, Newquay or Redruth. Take the bus T1 from Truro. Public Transport Information ☎ 01872 273453

MAP
Ordnance Survey Explorer Map 104.
Grid ref: SW 725 505

CAMPSITE
Beacon Cottage Farm Beacon Drive, St Agnes, Cornwall TR5 0NU ☎ 01872 552347 **beaconcottagefarmholidays. co.uk**
60 pitches and cottages to rent. Open April-Oct.

MORE INFO
St Agnes Tourist Information ☎ 01872 554150 **www.stagnes.com**

Route ——

27

Bodmin Moor Cornwall

Distance 5 miles (8 km) **Type** Moderate **Time** 2½ hours

> It's incredible to think that the seemingly infinite wilderness of Bodmin Moor is only 80 square miles

An old coaching house from 1750, the remote and rambling **Jamaica Inn** was a famous base for smugglers. Thought to be one of the most haunted pubs in the country, it supposedly harbours the spirits of a highwayman, a distraught young mother and child, and the ghost of a young murdered smuggler.

Daphne du Maurier was reputedly inspired to write her novel after getting lost in thick fog on the wild and treacherous moor. She sought refuge at the inn, where the landlord beguiled her with tales of ghosts and smugglers.

With the A30 cutting a straight line through the moors, the landscape may not immediately tally with the wild and lonesome descriptions penned by du Maurier, but venture a few

miles on to **Bodmin Moor** and you'll soon discover an untamed and inhospitable landscape that inspires intrigue with every step.

▶ START

From the Jamaica Inn, turn left on the road, then duck under the A30. Turn right down a lane, signed 'Bolventor Church', looking left for views of **Tolborough Tor**. Go through a gate, then turn right after 20m, following an old track.

Cross a narrow bridge over the **River Fowey**; go through a gate and head uphill on a steep rocky track. The path bears left through a field then downhill on rough terrain. Take a quick detour here to the top of the hill ahead for views of **⊙ Brown Willy**, a Bronze

Age field settlement and **Liskernick** farmhouse. Back on the path, turn left to a gate, then head for the fingerpost and bear right across the field and climb a stile.

1 | 2¼ MILES

Walk alongside the fence, then bear left uphill, following fingerposts, and turn left through gorse and rocks – all that remains of **Tresellyn** tin mine. Look out for a large entrance in the hillside (but for safety reasons do not enter) – this gaping hole would make quite a lair for the legendary Beast of Bodmin, a wild cat that allegedly prowls this area of moorland. Reports of mutilated slain livestock continue to stream in, but an official investigation in

1995 found "no verifiable evidence" of wild, non-indigenous cats in Britain.

Follow the fingerpost left and uphill to wooden gates, then join an old track that heads right and follows a wall above Trezelland farm. When the wall turns sharp right, continue across over rough ground to a gate.

Cross the track and continue down through the gorse to a stile. Don't cross the stile, follow the fingerpost sign to the left until you reach the top corner of a field on your right. Carry on uphill diagonally left, crossing an open area strewn with granite. Head in the direction of the phone mast to a waymarked gate. Now cross the next field to a farm track, then turn right.

2 | 3½ MILES

Head east to a tunnel under the A30, then double back. At the end of the road, turn left and then cross several fields in the direction of **Brown Gelly**.

After crossing a dry gully, continue through a field dotted with gorse bushes to a stone stile. Cross this and keep to the top edge of the field until signposts point you right to a bridge.

Climb up on a path that eventually takes you through a farmyard to a road, then turn right to **Bolventor** and back to the Jamaica Inn.

Step into the landscape that inspired Daphne du Maurier to write her tale of murder, deceit and smugglers on **Bodmin Moor**, *Jamaica Inn*

KEY

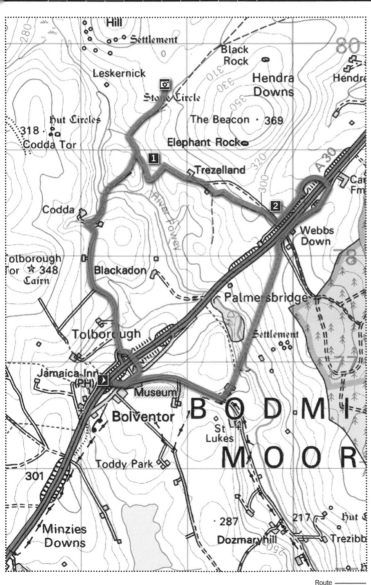

▶INFO

TERRAIN
Some short sections on road with no pavement. Lanes and moorland paths over farmland, which may be muddy in places.

HOW TO GET THERE
BY CAR: The Jamaica Inn lies just off the A30; it can be reached by driving up the Draynes Valley from Golitha Falls near St Cleer.
BY PUBLIC TRANSPORT: Bodmin Parkway station is on the London to Penzance train line.

MAP
Ordnance Survey Explorer Map 109.
Grid ref: SX 184 767

MORE INFO
Visit Cornwall
www.visitcornwall.com

Jamaica Inn
Bolventor, Launceston
PL15 7TS
☎ 01566 86250
www.jamaicainn.co.uk

Route ——————

29

Burrator Devon

Distance 5½ miles (9 km) **Type** Moderate **Time** 4 hours

> Sharpitor gives formidable views over the surrounding moorland

Dartmoor National Park

covers 368 square miles in **Devon**. It's mostly moorland, with patches of woodland providing some relief from the elements.

Dartmoor was populated from Neolithic times right through to the Bronze Age, as evidenced by the largest concentration of Bronze Age remains in the UK. Nowadays the national park is one of the country's leading tourist attractions, as well as an occasional military firing range.

▶ START

Looking south from the car park on the B3212, you can see **Sharpitor**. Climb the 500m or so to the top. It's a relatively easy climb, and the extensive views over 📷 **Burrator Reservoir**, with hills descending to **Plymouth** beyond, are well worth the climb.

1 | ½ MILE

Below you, you can see **Leather Tor** and beyond it the woods surrounding Burrator Reservoir. Head for Leather Tor and climb up. This one is slightly more difficult than Sharpitor, and it also requires more care. Tors are exposed granite hilltops, and they are so common on Dartmoor because the uplands are granite from the Carboniferous period. There are more than 160 tors on Dartmoor.

Bear slightly right, carefully descending from the tor until you reach **Cross Gate**. Go through, and follow the path, heading left, until it joins the road that runs around the reservoir. You can access the water from any one of many easy points, and it's well worth exploring. There are plenty of peaceful and picturesque picnic spots 📷 here too. Dartmoor's first reservoir, Burrator was built in 1898 and it was expanded in 1929. It washed over the leat that had been providing Plymouth with water for centuries – a leat that had been built by Sir Francis Drake.

2 | 1½ MILES

When you're finished with the reservoir, retrace your steps back up to Cross Gate, and turn right to follow the **Devonport Leat** up through the woods. The leat, which is fed by three rivers – the **Blackbrook**, the **Cowsic** and the **West Dart** – was built in 1790 to carry water from Dartmoor's high ground to the dockyards at **Devonport**.

The path leads up and out of the woods to some abandoned settlements. You can now see **Black Tor** directly ahead; it's one of three tors with the same name. It's too redolent a name to resists, it seems.

Dartmoor, of course, has always been food for fertile imaginations. Sir Arthur Conan Doyle and Dame Agatha Christie both set tales here, while legend has it that when the sun goes down you are likely to run into a headless horsemen, several pixies, at least one dragon, a pack of ghostly hounds, some disembodied hairy hands and the devil himself. So perhaps it's best you walk during the daytime, just in case.

3 | 3 MILES

Climb the tor, passing the aqueduct on your right, and the remains of the blowing house on the left. The blowing house, which contains a furnace and bellows with a water wheel nearby to generate power, was used for smelting tin on Dartmoor from the 14th to the 18th century. The ruins of more than 40 blowing houses are dotted around Dartmoor.

From Black Tor hop over to the road, and turn left. Follow the road for about 1½ miles, and you will return to the car park once again.

Rich in history and legend, **Dartmoor** offers an exhilarating challenge for walkers and some of the most dramatic views in England

KEY

▶INFO

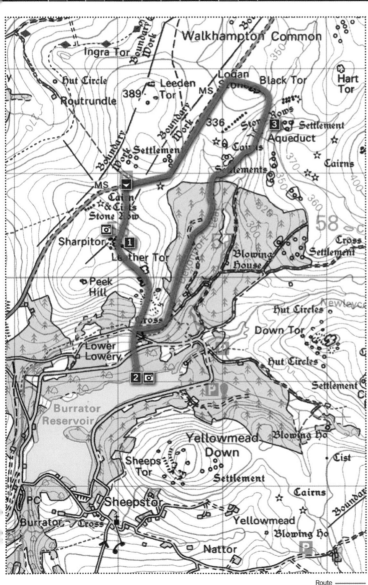

TERRAIN
Moorland and woodland; exposed in parts.

HOW TO GET TO THERE
BY CAR: The car park is on the B3212, halfway between Yelverton and Princetown.
BY PUBLIC TRANSPORT: From Plymouth connecting buses to Princetown run through Tavistock. A comprehensive bus timetable can be found at www.countrybusdevon.co.uk

The Dartmoor Sunday Rover bus service also provides access to Dartmoor on Sundays between May and September.
www.carfreedaysout.com

MAP
Ordnance Survey Explorer Map OL28.
Grid ref: SX 560 707

NEARBY EXCURSIONS
Princetown is just a couple of miles along the B3212, and it's the highest town on the moor. It's dominated by nearby Dartmoor prison, and there's a museum and visitor centre that's well worth a look. Open all year, Mon-Thu and Sat 9.30am-12.30pm and 1.30pm-4.30pm, Fri and Sun 9.30am-12.30pm and 1.30pm-4pm. No photography inside the museum.
www.dartmoor-prison.co.uk

MORE INFO
Dartmoor National Park Authority
☎ 01626 832093
www.dartmoor-npa.gov.uk

Route ———

Belstone Devon

Distance 7½ miles (12 km) **Type** Moderate **Time** 4 hours

> Between searching for letterboxes take time to enjoy the stunning views from the tops of each tor

Letterboxing involves searching for small weatherproof boxes dotted all over the tors of **Dartmoor**. Each letterbox contains a logbook and a rubber stamp, and you stamp your personal logbook with the public stamp inside the box, and use your personal stamp on the public logbook. It's a great hobby, especially for older children, and if you're successful enough you can join Dartmoor's 100 Club, for people who have found 100 or more letterboxes.

▶ START

While there is no official record of letterbox locations (it would defeat the point), on Dartmoor they are often on or around the tors – rocky outcrops on the summit of each hill. Start at **Belstone** and park by

the waterworks at the top end of the village. Walk back down, bearing right past the pub. Follow the track around the back of the Christian residential centre, through the edges of a farm, and follow the path alongside the roaring **River Taw**. This will lead you down into **Taw Marsh**.

The marsh is where the river stretches its legs and relaxes into a series of reed-lined pools that make for treacherous walking. Stay on the path – it is vague in places but will lead you to **Oke Tor**. This area is sometimes used as a military firing range, so check access times before setting off.

1 | 2½ MILES

The summit of Oke Tor offers extraordinary views of the expanse of

moorland and Taw Valley. Take time to scout around for letterboxes – they'll often be hidden in nooks and crannies

among the rocks.

Head north to **Steeperton**, a conical tor that dominates Taw Marsh and is certainly well named! Avoid the hill facing you unless you want to risk life and limb. Instead, bear right and you'll come across a path leading up the south side. Take the path left, and eventually you'll crest the summit of this magnificent tor. Spend some time searching for the elusive letterbox.

2 | 4 MILES

Retrace your steps to Oke Tor, then set your sights on **Higher Tor** and after that **Belstone Tor**. After descending the tor, cross **Belstone Common** and go through the gate to return to the waterworks.

▶ LETTERBOXING ON DARTMOOR

Letterboxing originated on Dartmoor. In 1854, moor guide James Perrott started leaving receptacles for visitor letters or postcards, perhaps as a way visitors could prove that they had visited this wild place. The first box was at Cranmere Pool, in the north of the moor. Initially other walkers would find the cards

and post them – hence letterboxing – though this has now been replaced by the logbook system. The number of boxes currently stands at 21,365 registered, with many more unofficial boxes also to be discovered. The box at Cranmere still exists, and is now maintained by the Western Morning News.

Go on a **Dartmoor** treasure hunt with our family introduction to letterboxing

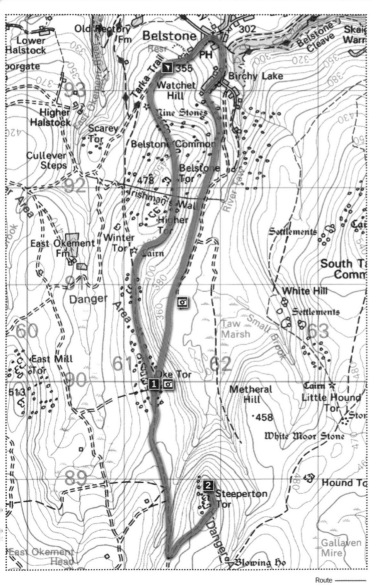

Route ———

TERRAIN
Moorland footpaths, boggy in places and with exposed areas – so wear sturdy walking boots and appropriate hiking gear. Make sure you take the correct detailed map and a compass with you, as Dartmoor can become difficult to navigate if the weather turns.

HOW TO GET THERE
BY CAR: Belstone is 22 miles east of Exeter on the A30, then turn left onto the B3260.
BY PUBLIC TRANSPORT: Regular buses run from Okehampton to Belstone and take around 25 minutes.

MAP
Ordnance Survey Explorer Map OL28.
Grid ref: SX 616 934

NEARBY EXCURSIONS
Museum of Dartmoor Life
Museum Courtyard
3 West Street, Okehampton
EX20 1HQ
☎ 01837 52295
www.museumofdartmoor life.eclipse.co.uk
Open Mon-Sat, 10.15am-4.30pm, last admission 4pm. Call ahead for Sunday and winter openings or group bookings.

MORE INFO
Dartmoor National
Park Authority
☎ 01626 832093
www.dartmoor-npa.gov.uk

Luccombe •
Timberscombe •
Exmoor
National
Park
WITHYPOOL ▷
Sandyway •   Brompton •
              Regis
        Highercombe •
Molland •   Bury •
East Anstey •
Knowstone •
        Bampton •

Withypool Somerset

Distance 4½ miles (7 km) **Type** Moderate **Time** 3 hours

▶ START

From the car park at **Withypool**, turn right and head a short way up the hill until you see a signpost on the right to Porchester Post. Follow this track. You'll now skirt **Withypool Hill**, and you might come across the herd of Exmoor ponies that makes its home in this area. Exmoor ponies are an ancient breed – or more accurately, landrace – that is believed to have crossed a land bridge from North America in prehistoric times.

They were hunted by cavemen, pulled Roman chariots, and there is a record of their presence on Exmoor as early as the *Domesday Book* of 1086. During World War Two, Exmoor was used as a training ground, and the ponies almost died out before locals managed to re-establish the herds. Nowadays the **Moorland Mousie Trust** supports the **Exmoor Pony Society**, which inspects and registers all foals.

1 1 MILE

The track now bends back towards the road, but don't follow it. Head for the hills, as it were, crossing two paths on the way. The second path leads you to an impressive stone circle, a diversion that is highly recommended.

When you reach a third major track, turn left on to it. The summit of Withypool Hill is now on

▶ The River Barle is a prominent feature on this picturesque walk on Exmoor

your left. You'll come to a road by a cattle grid.

2 2½ MILES

For a shorter walk, turn left here and follow the road to Withypool. If you're a hardier soul, turn right and follow it down the hill. Turn left on to a track, which is signposted Bridleway: No footbridge, and enter the farm, bearing left before the barns. Now cross two fields to reach the **River Barle**.

3 3 MILES

Cross the river, being very careful that the water level is not too high to do so. You should be OK to cross with caution in spring- and summertime, but the river will swell in winter.

Now turn left and follow the bank of the Barle right back into Withypool. If you're lucky you might even run across some ponies again! They are very hardy and strong, with a dense bone mass that allows them to carry heavy loads. But most of all, of course, they are gorgeous animals that grace the moorland.

They will move away if approached, but as long as you are quiet and considerate you should be able to view them from a reasonably close distance.

4 4½ MILES

In Withypool, the car park is on the left – though the **Royal Oak** on the right is a nice pub if you feel you've earned a pint.

▶ EXMOOR PONY PROTECTION

Exmoor ponies are vital for nature conservation efforts around the country. The Moorland Mousie Trust, a registered charity dedicated to the welfare of the pony, has helped export the breed as far north as Yorkshire, where their introduction – and grazing habits – has resulted in an increase in the diversity of local flora.

A walk on **Exmoor** offers incredible scenery and a chance to see
one of the world's oldest breed of pony

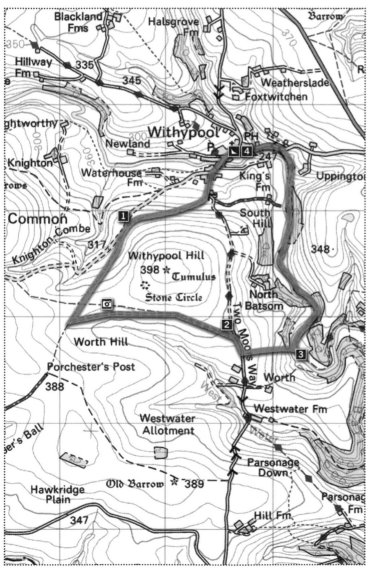

TERRAIN
Mostly gentle moorland and
good tracks, though there is
a river crossing which can
make this walk difficult in
winter.

HOW TO GET THERE
BY CAR: From the M5 exit
at J27 join the A361 to
Tiverton. Turn north on to the
A396 then take the B3222
to Dulverton. In Dulverton
take the B3223 to Lynton
and Exford. Follow this road,
climbing up on to Exmoor,
until you see a sign on the left
to Withypool.
BY PUBLIC TRANSPORT:
From May to October you can
catch the 285 North Exmoor
Circular bus from Minehead
to Withypool.
☎ 01823 356700

MAP
Ordnance Survey Explorer
Map OL9.
Grid ref: SS 844 356

NEARBY EXCURSIONS:
The Exmoor Pony Centre
Ashwick, Dulverton TA22 9QE
☎ 01398 323093
moorlandmousietrust.org.uk
Half-day pony experiences
including a two-hour ride are
available, as are 90 minute
taster sessions and an
adopt-a-pony scheme. Check
website for details.

MORE INFO
Visit Exmoor
www.visit-exmoor.co.uk
☎ 01984 635202

Exmoor National Park Authority
exmoor-nationalpark.gov.uk
☎ 01398 323665

Route ————

HORNER VALLEY · Minehead
· Wilton
EXMOOR NATIONAL PARK
· Winsford
· Brendon Hill
· Upton
· Dulverton

Horner Valley Somerset

Distance 4 miles (6½ km) **Type** Moderate **Time** 2 hours

> Horner Water winds through the ancient Horner Wood

The **Horner Valley** and its surrounds, including the **Vale of Porlock** and Exmoor's highest point **Dunkery Beacon**, lies within the National Trust's **Holnicote Estate**, once owned by the Acland family. **Burrowhayes Farm** nestles by **Horner Water**, ideally situated for excursions on foot or even horseback.

This route passes through 800-acre **Horner Wood**, one of our largest ancient oak woodlands, which is especially beautiful in spring and is a designated Special Site of Scientific Interest.

If you choose to ride, the route is suitable for intermediate riders; novices may prefer the short option. The farm also offers a leading rein route enabling parents to take children out to ride.

▶ START

Leave the campsite, looking out for the medieval packhorse bridge on your right. On meeting the lane turn left, then a few yards later turn left at the junction. Climb steadily to cross a cattle grid, then continue uphill on the woodland edge.

Turn left following signs to **Granny's Ride**, (many estate paths are named after the Acland family) a broad track that climbs up above **Halse Combe** with views to **Dunkery Hill**, once home to black grouse.

Patches of bracken have been cleared to encourage cow-wheat, the staple foodstuff of the rare heath fritillary butterfly. The track bears left around the head of the combe, climbing to a path junction.

1 ¾ MILE

Keep ahead on a narrow path; continue straight on at the next junction along the top of Horner Wood. Sheep and red deer shelter here in bad weather and you may spot butterflies and birds, including pied flycatcher and woodpecker.

The woodland also harbours over 200 species of lichen, more than 400 species of fungi and a wealth of wood ants, as well as 14 species of bat. Follow the path into woodland to cross another path, keeping ahead. Eventually the path curves right and narrows, passing into a tangle of small, twisted, low-growing oaks.

2 1½ MILES

Novices can take a sharp left on a path to **Horner**, signed 'Cat's Scramble'.

For a longer route, keep ahead on the narrow path to meet another junction. Bear left, and then bear right round the next spur. When you meet another junction keep ahead, eventually descending to a crossroads of tracks.

3 1¾ MILES

Turn left along **Lord Ebrington's Path**, dropping towards Horner Water, which flows through **Porlock Bay**'s 8000-year-old shingle ridge into the sea. Follow the track, keeping an eye out for dippers on the water, and pass through a gate and cross a bridge just before **Horner Green**. Meet the lane and keep ahead, before turning left just past the packhorse bridge for Burrowhayes Farm.

▶ THE CAMPSITE

Home to the Dascombes since back in the 1930s, **Burrowhayes Farm** in the Horner Valley is little more than a mile from the sea and provides the perfect venue for a family holiday. Three camping fields adjoin the pretty Horner Water and the farm buildings have been converted to stables, offering escorted rides across Exmoor.

This wonderful **bridle trail** explores Exmoor's ancient oak woodlands, renowned for its excellent wildlife-spotting opportunities

KEY

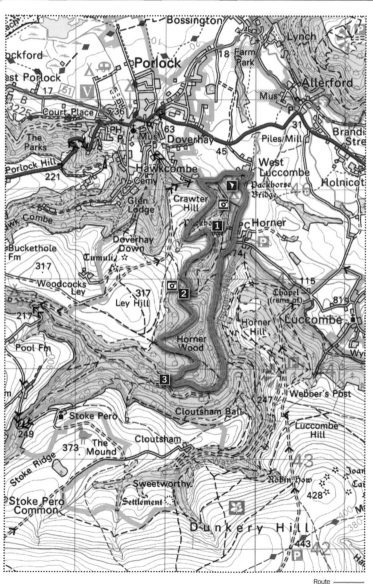

TERRAIN
Undulating woodland bridlepaths, some narrow and a little rocky.

HOW TO GET THERE
BY CAR: From the A39, 5 miles west of Minehead, pass Allerford then turn left signed West Luccombe and Horner. Burrowhayes is ¼ mile down the lane on the right.
BY PUBLIC TRANSPORT: The bus from Minehead to Lynmouth (along A39) stops ¼ mile away.

MAP
Ordnance Survey Explorer Map OL9.
Grid ref: SS 899 461

CAMPSITE
Burrowhayes Farm
West Luccombe, Porlock, nr Minehead, Somerset TA24 8HT
☎ 01643 862463
www.burrowhayes.co.uk
120 pitches for tents, caravans and campers, 19 statics; open Easter–end Oct; on-site riding stables.

MORE INFO
Holnicote Estate
www.nationaltrust.org.uk

Exmoor Tourist Information
www.visit-exmoor.co.uk
www.activeexmoor.com

Route

Yatton •
Weston-super-Mare •
Cheddar •
Highbridge •
Minehead •
• Exmoor
National Park
▸ QUANTOCK
HILLS
Bridgwater •
• Dulverton
Taunton •
Langport •
Wellington •

Quantock Hills Somerset

Distance 6¾ miles (10.8 km) **Type** Moderate **Time** 3½ hours

> ▸ Maritime heath, a mixture of bell heather, gorse and bilberry, paints the hills in a riot of colour

The **Quantock Hills** are a real hidden gem. Running from the **Vale of Taunton Deane** in the south to the **Bristol Channel** in the north, these small but perfectly formed hills offer truly sublime views, yet they're a world away from nearby Exmoor in terms of visitors. On a clear day you can see the Mendips to the east, the Gower Peninsula to the north, Exmoor to the west and Blackdown Hills to the south.

▸ START
Park in **Holford** and, with your back to the lane, follow the path that leads uphill and left from the back of the car park (ignoring the track that runs level past houses into Hodder's Coombe, as this is the return route).

Turn sharp right around the top of a garden, then keep on this path as it leads you up on to the Quantock Hills. Go through a gate and on to access land. Carry straight on the main path, ignoring any paths left or right. As you gain height, look back for view over the Severn Estuary. When you come to a crossroads, carry straight on along a path that curves left below **Lower Hare Knap**.

Bear right on the main path. Detour right to the summit of **Higher Hare Knap** for great views. Back on the path, bear left when the path splits at a Y, then head right, uphill on a rocky path.

Carry straight over at a crossing with a main path, and turn right after 200m to the summit of **Black Hill** and amazing views towards Exmoor. Carry on right and follow the path, via a gate, to the top of **Hurley Beacon**.

1 2½ MILES
Return to the main path, then turn left and follow the main track along the spine of the hills. The hilltops around you are covered in gorse, heather and bracken and, in late summer, will be ablaze with colour. The diverse range of habitats on these hills provide ideal conditions for a myriad of species: newts, frogs and toads find homes in the damper areas,

while grass snakes and common lizards live in the undergrowth and nightjars and ravens patrol the skies.

After 300m you'll come to **Halsway Post**. Carry straight on (the right path) and keep on the main path as a series of deep, stream-cut wooded coombes spread up the valley to your right. At the next junction take the right path and keep on to **Bicknoller Post**. From here you can enjoy superb views to the Exmoor coast.

2 4¾ MILES
Turn sharp right and take a path down **Sheppard's Coombe**. It's not immediately obvious, but you'll soon pick up the path of a stream. You then follow the course of the stream as it winds its way along **Lady's Edge** into the richly wooded **Hodder's Coombe**. This is real highlight of the walk, as the path follows the meandering stream through twisty, lichen-covered oak trees.

Cross the river and continue on the other side, bearing left. Pick up a track on your left, then cross the water a second time and pick up a path that runs to the right of the stream. Keep to the lower path and continue beside the stream, through a gate and back to the car park.

Discover a landscape shaped by man over thousands of years,
with awe-inspiring views over the **West Country**

KEY

INFO

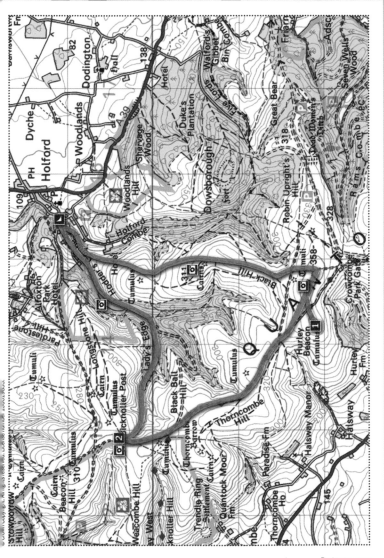

TERRAIN
Well-defined rocky paths,
with some steep climbs up
on to the hills. The hills are
crisscrossed with paths so
you can easily extend or
shorten your route.

HOW TO GET THERE
BY CAR: Holford is 14 miles
from Bridgwater on the A39.
BY PUBLIC TRANSPORT:
Trains run to Bridgwater, then
take a bus to Holford.

MAP
Ordnance Survey Explorer
Map 140.
Grid ref: ST 155 415

MORE INFO
Quantock Hills Area of
Outstanding Natural Beauty
www.quantockhills.com

Bridgwater Tourist
Information Centre,
Bridgwater House, King
Square, Bridgwater TA6 3AR
☎ 01278 436438

Visit Somerset
www.visitsomerset.co.uk

Route ————

Caldicot •
Bristol •
Clevedon •
Backwell •
Yatton •
Chew Magna •
Winscombe •
CHEDDAR ▸
Wedmore •
Wells •
Glastonbury •

Mendip Hills Somerset

Distance 3¼ miles (5 km) **Type** Challenging **Time** 2-3 hours

> After rain, Longwood is filled with the scent of wild garlic

Encompassing rugged open grassland and stunning ancient woodland, this trail is a true **Mendip** experience, and what's more – at dusk and dawn your walk will be accompanied by a symphony of birdsong. Many species frequent the scrub and woodland including willow warbler, yellowhammer, skylark and linnet, and at dawn you may even come across an adder or common lizard seeking out the first rays of sun.

▸ START
From the **Charterhouse Centre** car park turn left, passing St Hugh's Church. Walk down a steep hill, and then turn right through a kissing gate into **Velvet Bottom**.

Join the gravel track leading along the edge of a shallow valley; on your left is an open grassland habitat, which conceals the remnants of lead mining operations. Making the most of the quiet time between dusk and dawn are the hundreds of rabbits that have peppered the grassland with their burrows, and you will often see a fox skulking along the dry stonewalls eagerly watching for careless bunnies. You may also catch a glimpse of one of the barn owls that patrol this habitat, preying on voles.

The track passes an old Scout hut; on moonlit nights you may see bats hunting overhead and glow worms alongside the path.

1 | 1¼ MILES
📷 The track winds down to a kissing gate, where you join the main path, leading from **Cheddar**. Turn right to the entrance of **Longwood** (both Velvet Bottom and Longwood are nature reserves owned by Somerset Wildlife Trust). The smell of wild plants fill the air, and you are likely to hear one of the three pairs of tawny owl, busy feeding their noisy young. Tawny owlets leave the nest while still covered in fluffy down and completely unable to fly. Once they have branched they call repetitively so that their parents can locate them when returning with food – switch your torch off and listen! Climb the stile and follow the path through the wood. At night you will hear badgers and roe deer moving through the undergrowth, and the quiet rustling of mice. Soon you will reach a fast flowing stream that disappears into one of the area's many underground cavities. Past the stream, turn sharply right and head over a wooden bridge before climbing steeply. Stop here and enjoy the smells and sounds of the wood. The stream will help to mask your sounds and a seasonal carpet of bluebells and garlic will hide your scent in spring, making this a great spot to observe nocturnal wildlife at that time of year.

2 | 2 MILES
Follow the steep path up the side of the valley and over a stile. Turn left and follow the edge of the woodland over a ridge and down through a gate. Follow the track 100m to a road, and then turn right until you reach a junction. Turn right, follow the road to the crossroads, and then turn right again to reach the Charterhouse Centre car park.

▸ TAWNY OWLS

The tawny owl is the most common of all Europe's owls and is responsible for the more prominent myths about these birds of prey. Contrary to popular thought, no single owl has a call of 'twit-twoo'. It is in fact a duet between the male and female; the pigeon sized female calls out 'twit' and the male responds with a cry sounding like 'twoo'.

A **night hike** in the Mendips offers a rare opportunity to witness a host of nocturnal goings on as well as the magical dawn chorus

KEY

▶INFO

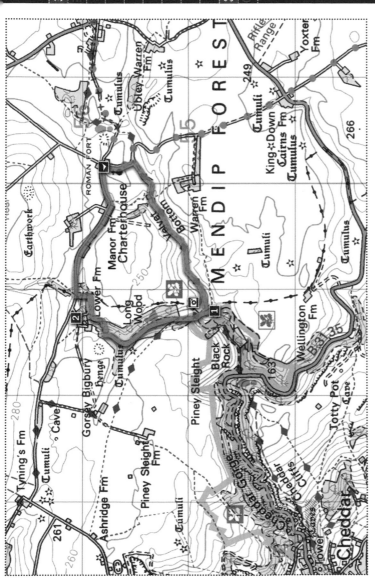

Route ————

TERRAIN
Most of the paths are in good order, but there are some rock steps to negotiate and the woodland path can get boggy and slippery after heavy rainfall. At night carry a torch and spare batteries, a mobile phone and wear suitable walking boots. Dogs must be under close control at all times to protect wildlife and livestock.

ACCESS
This walk is not suitable for wheelchair users, however there is an easy-going trail around Blackmoor Nature Reserve, situated behind the Charterhouse Centre, around which much of the same wildlife can be observed.

HOW TO GET THERE
BY CAR: Leave the A38 at the Churchill crossroads, signposted towards Bath on the A368. After 1¾ miles turn right on the B3134. Continue through Burrington Combe for around 3 miles until reaching a junction signposted Charterhouse. Continue for ¾ mile to the Charterhouse Centre.

MAP
Ordnance Survey Explorer Map 141.
Grid ref: ST 502 557

MORE INFO
Somerset Wildlife Trust
www.somersetwildlife.org
☎ 01823 652400

Charterhouse Centre
charterhousecentre.org.uk
☎ 01761 462267

For details of guided night hikes and owl prowls in the West Country visit
www.chrissperring.com

Chew Valley Somerset

Distance 8 miles (12.8 km) **Type** Moderate **Time** 4 hours

Portishead · Bristol · Nailsea · Keynsham · Dundry · Saltford · Corston · Chew Magna · Chew Valley Lake · **UBLEY** · Radstock

› The walk climbs from near-lake level on to the Mendip Hills escarpment for spectacular views

Somerset's answer to the lake district lies a mere 30 minutes drive from Bristol and Bath. With sublime views over **Blagdon Lake** and **Chew Valley**, and some thoroughly intriguing and wild landscapes around **Charterhouse**, this refreshing walk explores an interesting area of the county and feels a million miles away from the city.

▶ START

With your back to the church in **Ubley**, turn right then bear right at a roundabout. Turn left down **Tucker's Lane** then turn right at a public footpath. Bear right around the car park to the main road. Turn left then immediately right

on to a footpath. Carry on uphill, then continue on a footpath through woodland. Look back for views over Blagdon and Chew Valley lakes.

Go through a gate and follow the path through the edge of **Compton Wood**. Bear right through the woods, then left on a track. Go through a gate into a wildlife reserve. Cross two stiles, bear right towards **Limestone Link** then take a right at a road. Go through a series of gates and enter the **Hazel Manor Estate**. After ½ mile, turn right at a lane. Continue along the lane to a road then turn left then right down a lane, signed to Charterhouse.

1 3 MILES

Follow the track into **Blackmoor Nature Reserve** and **Ubley Warren**, an area of rough grassland and wetlands that has been mined for lead from Roman times through to the Victorian era. Lead from the area was used to line the Roman baths in nearby Bath Spa, as well as being distributed throughout the Empire. Spend time exploring this lunar landscape of mounds and spoil heaps, now being reclaimed by nature. Try to find the ruins of **Bleak House**, and picture the landscape in Victorian times, when chimneys spewed plumes of smoke

and black slag heaps marked the hillside. Nowadays Ubley Warren is home to rare mosses, liverworts and moths.

Continue past the car park and turn left on a permissive bridleway. At a lane, dogleg right then left on to a footpath and follow the path through a gate and into **Velvet Bottom Nature Reserve**.

Turn right when you reach what looks like a disused building and follow the path to the hamlet of Charterhouse.

2 4 MILES

Turn right at the road, then left at the next crossroads. After ¼ mile, turn left along a bridleway and follow this as far as a radio mast. Turn right and follow a path to the road.

Turn right on the main road (take care of traffic as the road can be busy) and take the next left. After ¼ mile, turn right down **Lease Lane**.

Take a right at a track to a gate, then turn left. Continue along this straight path as delightful views open up to your left over Blagdon Lake, and beyond, into Chew Valley. It's here that the lake district of the West Country tag begins to make sense.

Turn left when you reach **Ubley Grove**, then follow this track through **Ubley Wood**. Bear left and follow the path downhill and back into Ubley.

Explore the lake district of the West Country on this invigorating hike onto the **Mendip Hills** escarpment

KEY

▶INFO

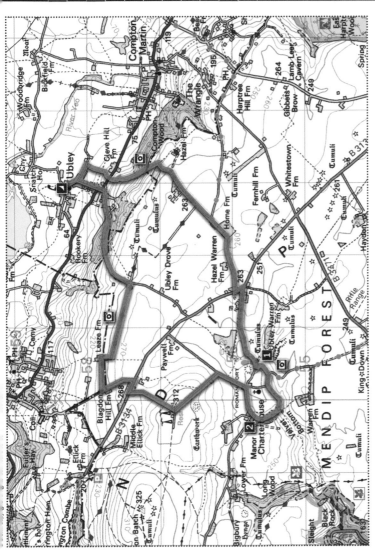

Route ————

TERRAIN
Mainly well-marked paths and quiet lanes. Can be muddy after rain.

HOW TO GET THERE
BY CAR: Ubley is 15 miles southwest of Bristol. Head south on the Wells Road (A37) before turning right at Belluton on the B3130 to Chew Magna then left on to the B3114 and right to Ubley.
BY PUBLIC TRANSPORT: Eurotaxis buses (numbers 672 and 674 to Cheddar) from Bristol to Ubley take just over an hour.
www.eurotaxis.com

MAP
Ordnance Survey Explorer Map 141.
Grid ref: ST 529 582

NEARBY EXCURSIONS
Charterhouse Centre
Charterhouse-on-Mendip, Blagdon, Bristol BS40 7XR
☎ 01761 462267
charterhousecentre.org.uk
This award-winning outdoor and environmental centre offers activities for youth and community groups as well as outdoor skills for adults.

MORE INFO
Visit Somerset
www.visitsomerset.co.uk

Mendip Hills AONB
Charterhouse Centre, Blagdon, Bristol BS40 7XR
☎ 01761 462338
www.mendiphillsaonb.org.uk

Somerset Wildlife Trust
www.somersetwildlife.org

Evershot Dorset

Distance 7 miles (11 km) **Type** Moderate **Time** 3 hours

West Coker
Haselbury•
Plucknett• •Holnest
EVERSHOT ▸ •Hollywell
•Beaminster
Piddlehinton•
Frampton•
•Bridport
Dorchester•

> Rebuilt in 1546 using ham stone from a local quarry, Melbury House is a snapshot of Dorset history

▸ START

Start at the **Acorn Inn**, Evershot, the village Hardy called Evershead in *Tess of the d'Urbervilles*. Follow the road uphill

▸ THE PUB

The Acorn Inn, Evershot, is a friendly and very atmospheric 16th century coaching inn renowned for its quality food and extensive selection of wine and ales. It appears in Thomas Hardy's *Tess of the d'Urbervilles* as The Sow and Acorn, and all of the rooms are named after characters or places in Hardy's books.

until you come to a right-hand turn with a signpost. Now follow this lane to Girt Farm Road. Follow the road down the hill. When you come to the fork, take the right-hand lane. Follow this lane to **Girt Farm**, walking between the two large outbuildings and skirting the deer park. At the open field bear right and head up the slope. You'll cross the field on a diagonal, leading to a gap in the fence. This leads to another field and then a gate directly ahead.

1 | 2 MILES

Go through the middle of the next field. Keep going until you reach a stile bearing a white arrow. Climb the stile and cross the stream, climbing the opposite bank and

clearing the next stile. There's a hill ahead, and at the top there are some tree stumps with a great view of the wood. It's the kind of view that makes you understand why Hardy felt such an attachment to the area. Now take the gate with the white arrow, cross the field and a stile on to the driveway of **Lewcombe Manor**.

2 | 3 MILES

Take a left, following the driveway out of the estate. When you come to the road take a right, then another right on to a bridle path. This section is muddy and overgrown. Go through the next gate, bear left and head down the hill, reaching a gate in the corner. Follow the bridle path to the

right and up the hill. Go through a gate, up the hill, and into the next field. Keeping the hedge close on the right, you'll come to a gate. Next you'll be presented with three paths. Take the middle one, straight ahead, passing from a gravel path on to a grassy lane.

3 | 4½ MILES

Continue straight on and you'll emerge in **Melbury Osmond**. Follow the road and take a left up the hill to see Melbury Osmond church. This is an ancient place, mentioned in the *Domesday Book*. In 1839 Thomas Hardy's parents were married here. Now turn and go back down the hill, following this road through the village until you reach the gates of Melbury Park, former seat of the Earl of Ilchester. Follow the path through the grounds, skirting **Melbury House** as you go. You'll pass through a deer park, which adjoins **Summer Lodge**, a hotel that the second Earl of Ilchester had built in 1798. The sixth earl added a second floor in 1893, designed by his friend Thomas Hardy, who was an architect by profession. Eventually you'll reach the gate that marks your exit from the estate. It's now a short stroll down the hill, following the road that bears right and takes you back up into Evershot, and to The Acorn Inn for a well-earned drink.

Open countryside, beautiful villages, breathtaking estates – the **Dorset** landscape that inspired Hardy's fictional Wessex is full of variety

KEY

▶**INFO**

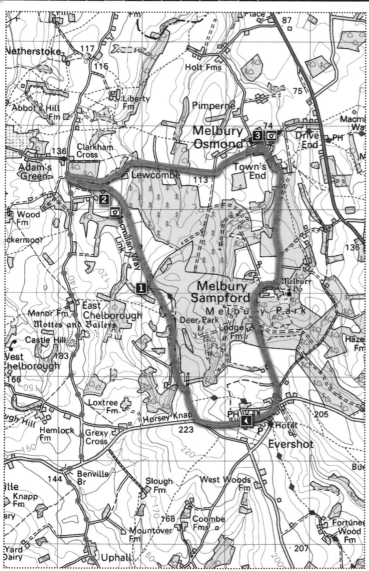

TERRAIN
Varied – tarmac roads, open fields, woods. Occasionally hilly or muddy.

HOW TO GET THERE
BY CAR: from the A37 near Dorchester, turn onto the B1353 at Holywell.
BY PUBLIC TRANSPORT: Take a train to Dorchester. The bus from Dorchester to Evershot runs regularly and takes 40 minutes.

MAP
Ordnance Survey Explorer Map 117.
Grid ref: ST 575 045

NEARBY EXCURSIONS
The Melbury Park estate is worth a visit in its own right. It's open all year to walkers. No vehicles are allowed into the grounds. Meanwhile the famous Cerne Abbas giant, featured as Abbot's Cernel in Hardy's *Far from the Madding Crowd*, is only eight miles from Evershot.

MORE INFO
www.south-coast-central.co.uk/hardy.htm
www.westdorset.com

The Acorn Inn
Evershot, Dorchester, Dorset DT2 0JW
☎ 01935 83228
www.acorn-inn.co.uk

Route ———

Chesil Beach Dorset

Distance 8 miles (12.8 km) **Type** Moderate **Time** 4 hours

> Set your sights on this world-famous natural phenomenon

In 2001 the **Jurassic Coast** was designated the UK's first natural World Heritage Site by UNESCO. One of the most stunning features along its 95-mile coastline is **Chesil Beach**, 100 million tonnes of pebbles protecting the **Fleet**, Britain's largest tidal lagoon, internationally important for birds and wildlife. The beach, which moves 5m (16ft) inland per century, is thought to

date back 6,000 years and is driven onshore during rising sea levels. Local salt-resistant plants include sea kale, yellow-horned poppy, and the rare sea pea.

▶ START

From Abbotsbury village car park, follow signs for Barn and Swannery to the top right-hand corner of the car park. Follow a gravel way

past **Abbey House**. Note a ruined gable end on the remains of the 11th-century Benedictine abbey, which fell to Henry VIII's dissolution of the monasteries in 1539.

The 15th-century **St Catherine's Chapel** on **Chapel Hill** ahead is dedicated to the patron saint of spinsters. Turn left for **Abbotsbury Swannery**; ahead stands the largest **tithe barn** in England (built circa 1400), originally 90m (295ft) long.

Pass the barn and join the lane; turn left. After 100m bear right down another. After 200m turn right over a stile, signed 'Chesil Beach'. Bear right and cross a concrete bridge, then sharp left to pass a footpath post. Walk through woodland then open ground around Chapel Hill; look left for views of the swannery and Chesil Beach. Follow the coast path signs to meet a track over a stile then turn left to reach the beach and car park.

1 | 1¾ MILES

Follow the rough track towards **West Bexington** (walking along the beach itself is not recommended). Pass **Lawrence's Cottage** after ¾ mile – not a reference to Dorset's famous residents D. H. and T. E. (Lawrence of Arabia), but to an old Dorset word that means 'the longest day in the sun'. Pass the **Old**

Coastguards, once home to 83 people. Look ahead across **Lyme Bay** to **Lyme Regis** and the 191m (626ft) flat-topped **Golden Cap**, the highest point on England's south coast. Reach the car park at **West Bexington**.

2 | 4 MILES

Turn right up Beach Road, passing The Manor Hotel. As the lane bends left keep up a track, signed 'Hardy Monument'. Climb steadily, eventually taking the right fork to the B3157. Turn right along an inland coast path. Cross a stile into open access land; the path runs along its right edge, ascending **Tulk's Hill**. Cross the road and enjoy views over Chesil Beach and the Fleet to the **Isle of Portland**. Follow the undulating ridge-top path across **Abbotsbury Castle** Iron Age hill fort then drop to a lane. Cross over and continue across **Wears Hill**, with views of the church below. Pass through a gate and reach a footpath post.

3 | 7¼ MILES

Bear right for the village of **Abbotsbury**. Descend via gates, following signs, to reach a downhill track. At Back Lane turn right. Turn left at Market Street; when the road turns sharp left keep ahead on Church Lane. Turn left through the St Nicholas' churchyard, then through a small gate into the car park.

Discover one of the world's finest barrier beaches, an extraordinary
geological feature running for more than 17 miles along the **Dorset coast**

KEY

▲INFO

TERRAIN
Field paths, rough tracks
and open down.

ACCESS
Generally not suitable for
wheelchairs or pushchairs.

HOW TO GET THERE
BY CAR: Abbotsbury village
car park signed off the B3157,
10 miles from Weymouth and
9½ miles from Bridport
BY PUBLIC TRANSPORT:
First bus X53 runs from
Exeter to Poole via Bridport
and Weymouth, while
First bus 253 runs from
Beaminster to Weymouth
via Abbotsbury.
www.firstgroup.com

The Jurassic Coast Bus
Service runs in the summer.
www.jurassiccoast.com

MAP
Ordnance Survey Explorer
Map 15.
Grid ref: SY 579 852

NEARBY EXCURSIONS
Abbotsbury
Subtropical Gardens
Bullers Way, Abbotsbury
DT3 4LA
☎ 01305 871387
abbotsbury-tourism.co.uk
Open daily (except during
the Christmas period)
10am–dusk.

MORE INFO
Weymouth Tourist
Information Centre
Kings Statue, The Esplanade,
Weymouth DT4 7AN
☎ 01305 785747
www.visitweymouth.co.uk

Route ⎯⎯⎯⎯

SOUTH EAST

Sitting in the middle of a London rush-hour it's easy to forget that within an hour you could be out of the city and driving through countryside so tranquil that it feels a million miles from the capital. What glories London has, right on its doorstep!

There's the chalk downland of the **South Downs**, recently crowned England's newest national park and often aptly described as the lungs of London. Certainly, an exhilarating walk along the South Downs will leave you buffeted by bracing winds and ruddy-cheeked, while further down the coast, sight of the towering pristine cliffs will strike you with awe. Constantly under threat from erosion, these Sentinels to the sea, the **Seven Sisters** and of course those famous **White Cliffs of Dover**, rightly deserve their iconic fame.

As you may have guessed, chalk features highly in this corner of England. Straddling four counties, the **Chiltern Hills** are an arc of greensand and chalk stretching from **Oxfordshire** to **Hertfordshire**, the perfect place to lose yourself as an escape from the daily grind. Smothered in ancient beech woodland, carpeted in spring by bluebells as far as the eye can see, the Chilterns are also one of the best places to see Britain's great conservation success of recent years, the outstanding red kite, returned to our skies after near extinction 20 years ago.

Another unmistakable feature of the South East is its miles of verdant farmland and, notably in Kent, orchards. Henry VIII first dubbed the county the 'Garden of England' after enjoying a satisfying bowl of **Kentish** cherries, but Charles Dickens best summed it up in *The Pickwick Papers*: 'Kent, sir – everyone knows Kent – apples, cherries, hops and women.' While we're not here to comment on the fairer sex of the region, the ale of these parts is still second to none, even though the traditional oast houses with their iconic conical roofs are now more likely to have been converted into B&Bs than contain delicious drying hops.

For that final retreat from the hubbub of modern life, there's no better place than the leafy glades of the **New Forest**. Thankfully for us, a combination of the Forest's Crown status, commons rights and the largely unsuitable nature of the soil for cultivation means that today we can enjoy a paradise populated by wild ponies and deer which is much the same today as it was in the time of William the Conqueror.

The Needles Isle of Wight

Distance 5½ miles (8.8 km) **Type** Moderate **Time** 2 hours

> Visit the remaining Needles before they fall beneath the waves

The Needles are a spine of 30m (98ft) tall sea stacks that stretch out into the sea off the western coast of the Isle of Wight. The same line of chalk runs under the Solent and connects with Lulworth Cove and Durdle Door in Dorset. Once part of the headland, these limestone outcrops have been shaped by coastal erosion – in 1764 a fourth pinnacle, named Lot's Wife, collapsed and the crash was heard in Portsmouth harbour.

▶ START

From The Needles Park car park, look for the National Trust sign for the **Needles Old Battery**, situated just past the coach park. After 45m, just past **Gnome Cottage**, turn left, signposted path T25. Go up some steps and over a stile, proceeding in an easterly direction below **West High Down**. In places, there is no obvious path and it can be muddy, so wear a good pair of boots. Stop every now and then to take in the expansive views of the **Solent** and the mainland beyond. Adders are plentiful when not hibernating through the winter months.

The large white square building jutting out along the coast is **Fort Albert**, sister to Fort Victoria further up along the coast and part of the old coastal defence system. In front of you, high up on the down, you can see the imposing granite cross of **Tennyson's Monument**. The path rises gently to a junction; bear left, descending to an old chalk pit, then take the right-hand path, which is steeply stepped in places, through low woods up on to **Tennyson's Down**, 147m (482ft) above the frothy sea below. The views down the coast to **St Catherine's Point** are amazing.

1 2½ MILES

Follow the coastal path westwards, gently down to the fingertip of the westerly point of the island. A stunning display of pink thrift emerges through the downland grass during springtime.

At the **Old Nodes Beacon**, cross a stile and continue along the path, which bends right past a row of coastguard cottages. On the left is a fence stile; cross over this and take the right-hand path, which joins a road that bears left, leading to the **Needles New Battery**, where an exhibition about the part the site played in the space race can be seen. To your left are the remains of the old rocket-testing site, while down some steps is a fenced viewpoint overlooking the sheer cliffs of **Scratchell's Bay**, where many ships have floundered in the treacherous waters.

2 4¾ MILES

Include a visit to the Needles Old Battery and incorporate the 61m (200ft) long tunnel carved through chalk cliffs to the spectacular 19th century searchlight perch overlooking the Needles. Keep a lookout for cormorants nesting in the stacks plus rock pipits and stonechats nesting along the cliff-tops.

3 5 MILES

Leave by the tarmac road, where sweetly fragrant heliotrope grows by the roadside. Listen to the song of the salty wind as it blows through the grass. In front of you are the coloured cliffs of **Alum Bay**, complete with a chairlift down to the beach, where you can see what remains of the small pier from which pleasure craft used to ply their trade.

Proceed down this road until you reach Gnome Cottage with the car park in front of you.

Take a stroll around the **Isle of Wight** coastline to explore one of britain's most impressive natural wonders

KEY

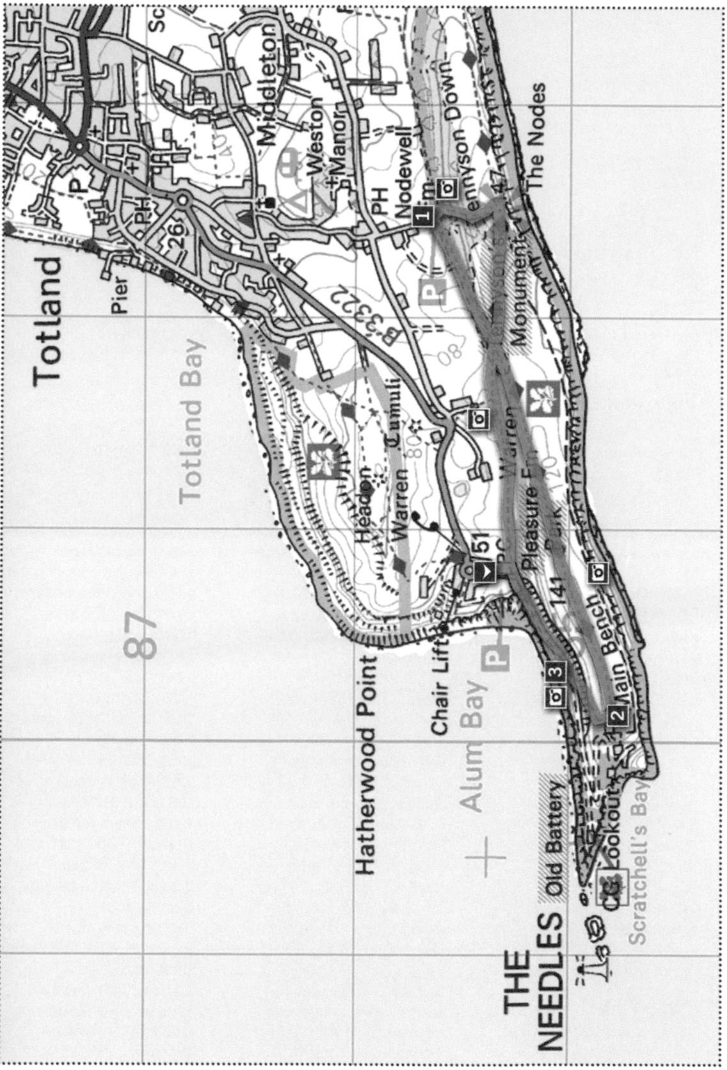

TERRAIN
Some steep ascents and descents. Be very careful during high winds.

HOW TO GET THERE
BY PUBLIC TRANSPORT:
Bus Southern Vectis number 7 runs regularly to the Needles Pleasure Park.
☎ 0871 200 2233
www.islandbuses.info

The Needles Tour open top bus operates between Yarmouth and Alum Bay. (Mar–Oct).

Island Coaster, run by Southern Vectis, serves the Needles Park every day in summer. It leaves Ryde at 9.30am and 10am, and leaves Needles Park at 4.30pm and 5pm.

The Wightlink, Lymington to Yarmouth ferry route takes 30 minutes.
☎ 0871 376 1000
www.wightlink.co.uk

Red Funnel runs a Southampton to East Cowes Route, taking 55 minutes.
☎ 0844 844 9988
www.redfunnel.co.uk

MAP
Ordnance Survey Explorer Map OL29.
Grid Ref: SZ 307 853

MORE INFO
Isle of Wight Tourism
☎ 01983 813813
www.islandbreaks.co.uk

Route ———

Solent Way Hampshire

Distance 10 miles (16 km) **Type** Moderate **Time** 3-4 hours

The coastline of the **New Forest National Park** is often overlooked but holds many delights from salt marshes, mudflats and lagoons to the history of our seafaring nation. The **Solent Way** is a 60-mile coast path, which starts in **Milford-on-Sea** and ends in **Emsworth Harbour**, and a large part of the route goes through the national park.

▷ The picturesque Bucklers Hard, on the banks of the Beaulieu River, has a rich naval history

▶ START

From **Lymington** cross the river on Bridge Road and head south. Turn left where the road becomes wider and continue up the path through the woods, passing a monument and taking a right at Monument Lane. Follow the path along the edge of the golf course and on to Snooks Farm, where you are treated to striking views over to the **Isle of Wight** and the **Solent** (the thin stretch of sea between the mainland and the Isle of Wight). Head south on Shotts Lane and pick up the footpath east towards **Pylewell Park**. Continue through the park, past the grand house and the old mill.

1 2½ MILES

Continue on this easterly line through **Sowley Woods** and on to **Sowley Pond**, which played an important part in two large iron works in the 17th century. This is also where the monks from Beaulieu Abbey kept fish. Today the pond is protected as a Special Site of Scientific Interest and is a good spot for wildfowl, including the great crested grebe, which is known to nest here. Continue along the land and take a right at the T-junction. After passing **Bergerie Farm** you walk on through the site of **Needs Oar Point** airfield, built in World War Two and home to more than 100 Hawker Typhoons, fighter-bombers that supported the Allies' progression in Normandy.

2 6 MILES

Follow the road round to the left past the old barn at St Leonard's Farm and continue onwards along the wooded lane. Turn right at the crossroads and then take the next left up to **Bucklers Hard**. This picturesque 18th century village was once a hive of activity for shipbuilding and some of Nelson's fleet that took part in the Battle of Trafalgar were launched from here, including the 64-gun HMS *Agamemnon*. The ship saw action in three major battles. The village also saw preparation for war in 1944 as landing craft for the Normandy landings were constructed there.

Walk down towards the river and left round by the pier, where river cruises set out, and head northwesterly. This area is internationally recognised as a Special Area of Conservation and the whole **Beaulieu River** complex is important for many rare species as the salt marsh and mudflat habitat supplies rich feeding grounds. Look out for teal, ringed plover, tern, curlew, redshank and oystercatcher.

The path now continues through attractive woodland, following the river and into beautiful **Beaulieu**, where buses can be caught for the return journey to Lymington.

Stroll down the Solent Way and discover another side to the
New Forest National Park

TERRAIN
All of the walk is level and is either on rights of way or quiet lanes. Note that after heavy rain the path next to the river can get muddy.

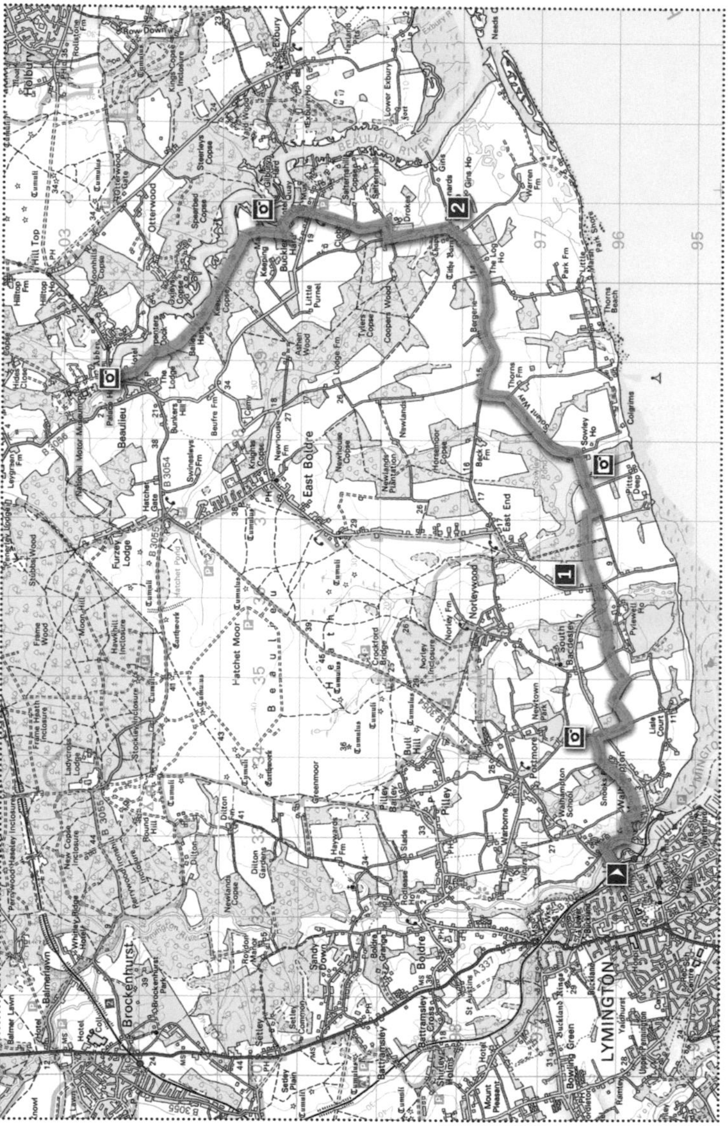

HOW TO GET THERE
BY CAR: Drive to Lymington on the A337, which is connected to the M27 and A31.
BY PUBLIC TRANSPORT: Lymington Town station is the nearest station to the path, with trains from Brockenhurst connecting to the mainline. There are also frequent bus services to Lymington, run by the Wilts and Dorset Bus Company and then in the summer there is the New Forest open-top bus service, operated by Solent Blue Line.

MAP
Ordnance Survey Explorer Map OL22.
Grid ref: SZ 327 960

NEARBY EXCURSIONS
The Maritime Museum Bucklers Hard, Beaulieu, Brockenhurst SO42 7XB
☎ 01590 614645
www.bucklershard.co.uk
Open every day except Christmas Day.

MORE INFO
Lymington Visitor Information New Street, Lymington SO41 9BH
☎ 01590 689000
www.thenewforest.co.uk

New Forest National Park
www.newforestnpa.gov.uk
☎ 01590 646600

Route ———

Meon Valley Hampshire

Distance 12¾ miles (20 km) **Type** Moderate **Time** 5-6 hours

> This walk offers a perfect blend of impressive natural wonders and interesting historical sites

▶ START

From the **Sustainability Centre**, follow the **South Downs Way** north towards **Salt Hill**. On your right you will pass a redundant Royal Naval base, designed for officer training in the height of the Cold War. As you continue past the radio masts, expansive views will open up around you and on a good day you can see the **Isle of Wight** on the horizon.

Take the footpath heading east on the brow of Salt Hill and follow the path towards the ridge of **Small Down**. From the top you will be treated to a view of the picturesque village of **East Meon** and the upper **Meon Valley**, with the impressive **Butser Hill** standing tall to the east.

1 2 MILES

Continue on the footpath and enter the woods, heading northwest.

Once you reach the lane head north and pick up the next footpath to the west. Proceed and rejoin the South Downs Way, heading southwest.

Head north along the lane and take the next left, following the national trail, towards **Whitewool Farm**.

2 5 MILES

Pass over a crystal clear chalk stream, one of the tributaries of the **River Meon**. These waters are famed for trout fishing and producing watercress – the underlying chalk rock filters the water.

Follow the South Downs Way up the hill, along the trackway and cross the lane to the **National Nature Reserve** of **Old Winchester Hill**. This rare habitat has been shaped by nibbling livestock and man for hundreds of years, and needs continual management by grazing to maintain its rich wildlife.

You may be lucky to see the array of orchids here or plants such as devil's-bit scabious, cowslips or ox-eye daisies.

3 7½ MILES

A prominent **Iron Age hill fort**, once home to a Celtic chieftain, illustrates the long relationship between man and the downs, and was apparently constructed some 2,500 years ago. Take the bridleway to the fort on the gravel track and take time to walk round the earthworks and enjoy the spectacular scenery of the Meon Valley. You will also see **Bronze Age burial mounds**, between 4,500 and 3,500 years old, within the forts ramparts.

Return on the gravel track and head south along the lane, keeping an eye out for traffic, then take the footpath eastwards by a planted copse of trees, following the path over the next lane, under the down slope and on to the quiet road. Keep an eye out for buzzards soaring on warm air thermals.

Continue over the road and take the path in a southeast direction until you reach a large block of woodland on your left, here take the path leading northwest back to the Sustainability Centre.

▶ THE CAMPSITE

The Sustainability Centre is perched by the South Downs Way in rural Hampshire, within 55 acres of woodland and chalk grassland. Set up by the charity Earthworks Trust, its aim is to "demonstrate, develop and promote knowledge, skills, technologies and lifestyles that improve peoples quality of life without damaging the local and global environment." The centre offers a learning experience for all ages, from bushcraft to renewable energy. The campsite is in a peaceful location and also hires tipis and yurt tents.

Discover a landscape shaped by man and nature over 6,000 years on a walk that enters the heart of the **South Downs** in Hampshire

KEY

▲INFO

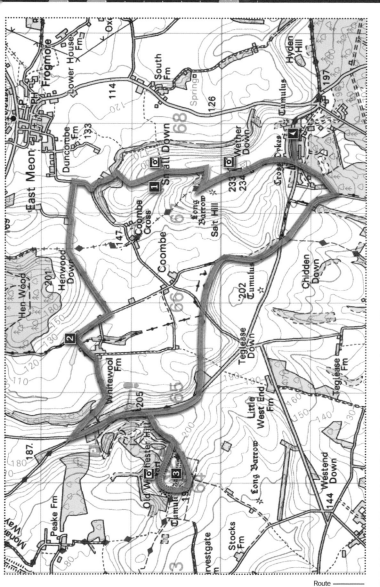

TERRAIN
Chalk and grass pathways. Some sections pass along roads, so watch for traffic.

HOW TO GET THERE
BY CAR: Old Winchester Hill is signposted and accessed from the A32 at Warnford. The Sustainability Centre is signposted from the A3(M) by brown and white signs.
BY PUBLIC TRANSPORT: Guests at the centre can book a lift from Petersfield station, which is on the London Waterloo to Portsmouth line.

MAP
Ordnance Survey Explorer Map 119.
Grid ref: SU 678 192

CAMPSITE
The Sustainability Centre Droxford Road, East Meon, Petersfield GU32 1HR
☎ 01730 823 166
www.sutainability-centre.org
The camping field is in a peaceful open space, ideal for individuals, families and groups. You can hire a tipi and yurt. Campfires and barbecues by arrangement.

MORE INFO
Petersfield Tourist Information Office
☎ 01730 268829

Old Winchester Hill
www.naturalengland.org.uk

South Downs
www.southdownsonline.org

Route ————

Liphook •
Fernhurst •
• Petersfield   Petworth •
▶ NORTH MARDEN
• Waterlooville
Chichester
Littlehampton •
• Portsmouth Bognor Regis •
Selsey •

North Marden West Sussex

Distance 7¼ miles (11½ km) **Type** Moderate **Time** 4-5 hours

After a lengthy campaign, the South Downs was granted National Park status in 2009

take the footpath north on the edge of Inholmes Wood, which heads back to East Marden through the farm and past some cottages on a bank on your right. Follow the footpath heading northeast opposite the red phone box hidden in the hedge. At the B2141 take care crossing and head north back to Hooksway.

Enjoy views the 📷 towards the **Trundle Hill** and **Goodwood** racecourse before returning for a well-earned rest.

▶ START

Start from the car park of the Royal Oak at **Hooksway** and head up the hill along a lane. Take the first right and follow the old track way, then take a left at the footpath that runs through the hedge. These thick wooded hedges are called shaws or rews locally and resemble old woodlands with many plants such as wild garlic, bluebells and yellow archangel. When you reach the B2141 continue west for a few yards and cross opposite the lane for **North Marden**.

1 1 MILE

St Mary's of North 📷 Marden is a stunning downland church with a rounded chancel built in the 12th century. Follow the footpath to the side

of the church down into the valley and up on to the ridge, then turn south towards Long Lane. Cross the lane and pick up the footpath opposite and head down the hill. Stay on the same line to the village of **East Marden**; on your right is the next footpath, but East Marden is well worth a quick detour. The church was built in the 13th century and sits on a little green on its own.

2 2¾ MILES

Return to the footpath over the stile, across the pasture and head up and into the hanger woodland. Woods on steep sided hills in the South Downs are known as hangers; many are ancient and have been around for more than 400 years and have particular species

of orchids and rare molluscs living in them. At a crossroads of paths, take a right through the wood and up on to the lane. Head south into the 📷 hamlet of **Up Marden** and follow signs to the church. St Michael's is a 13th century structure and again reflects the simple nature of architecture in these rural downs, a place where shepherds could worship. Flint is the stone from this land and is put to good use on most buildings in the area.

3 4 MILES

From the church door take the footpath through the yew trees, across the field and past the old well house. Walk over the lane to the next field and wood and on to a bridleway.

Now head east and

▶ SOUTH DOWNS

The South Downs was one of the original national parks proposed in the 1930s and although designated as an Area of Outstanding Natural Beauty, it wasn't until the late 1990s that the government declared the intention to see the South Downs designated as the 15th national park in Britain. Following two public inquiries the final decision came in 2009. England's newest national park will secure the long-term protection of this iconic landscape for the 21st century and beyond.

Enter a tranquil landscape of ancient field patterns, Norman churches and wooded hills on the **South Downs**

KEY

▲INFO

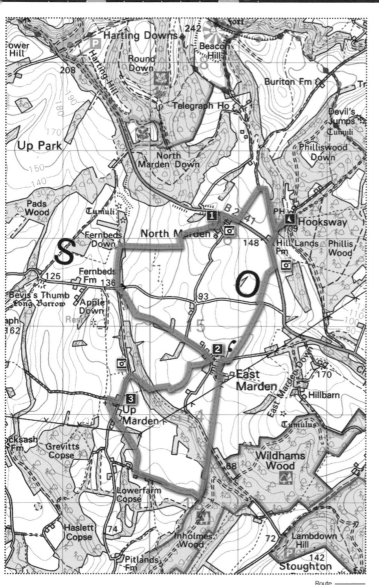

TERRAIN
The majority of the walk is on public rights footpaths and bridleways with the odd muddy section. There are short stretches on country lanes, so keep an eye out for traffic.

HOW TO GET THERE
BY CAR: The car park at the Royal Oak Hooksways is signposted off the B2141 between South Harting (3¼ miles) and Chichester (8½ miles).

MAP
Ordnance Survey Explorer Map 120.
Grid ref: SU 815 163

NEARBY EXCURSIONS
Weald and Downland Open Air Museum
Singleton, Chichester
PO18 0EU
☎ 01243 811363
www.wealddown.co.uk
Open daily 10.30am-6pm, last admission 5pm.

Uppark House and Garden
South Harting, Petersfield
GU31 5QR
☎ 01730 825857
www.nationaltrust.org.uk/uppark
Open Mar–Dec, Sun-Thur.

MORE INFO
South Downs
www.visitsouthdowns.com

Route ———

Burgess Hill •
Uckfield •
STREAT ▶
Offham •
Lewes •
Hove •
• Brighton
Newhaven •

Ditchling East Sussex

Distance 10 miles (16 km) **Type** Moderate **Time** 4-5 hours

▶ START

Set off from **Blackberry Wood**, head south down Streat Lane and take the bridleway by **Brocks Wood**, heading in a southwesterly direction. At the next rights of way junction, turn south toward the scarp of the downs until you come to the road.

Take care crossing and head up the track, or bostall as they are known locally. These ancient routes have been used by shepherds for thousands of years.

As you climb the bostall, keep an ear out for the song of the skylark as you approach **Streat**
📷 **Hill** and enjoy the view from the top of the ridge.

▷ Ditchling Beacon is the third highest point on the South Downs and offers some cracking views

1 3 MILES

From the top, head west on the **South Downs Way National Trail**, which runs from **Eastbourne** to **Winchester**. Along the way you will see numerous humps and bumps, some of which are **Bronze Age burial mounds** positioned here on the high ridge. On your left towards the road is a dewpond. These ponds were made mainly in the 19th century, when sheep numbers increased in the downs.

2 4¾ MILES

Take care crossing the road and continue on the bridleway through the gate. Take the footpath off to the right after a

few hundred metres. Follow the path down the slope, entering **Ditchling Beacon Nature Reserve**. This rare area of chalk grassland is home to many different herbs and flowers, which in turn create habitats
📷 for butterflies and other insects. This is thanks to the countless years of sheep grazing, and also man's hand.

Continue on the footpath and past the old pits, dug for making lime for building and agriculture over 200 hundred years ago, until you reach the small car park. Here, head west and take the path to **Ditchling**.

3 7½ MILES

Ditchling is a renowned home for those inspired by the surrounding landscape, including sculptor Eric Gill.

Take the path heading east past the Bull pub on the B2116 and pick up the footpath. Continue on this course out of the village and over a footbridge, crossing a

lane on to a bridle path along the Wealden ridge and on to the 11th century church at **Streat**.

From this spot you can understand why Rudyard Kipling described these hills as blunt and whale-like in his poem *Sussex*. Once on the lane, head back to Blackberry Wood, where your campfire awaits.

▶ THE CAMPSITE

Blackberry Wood offers a truly tranquil setting and prides itself in offering cosy camping in private woodland clearings, with open fires giving guests an intimate experience with nature. Campfire grills are provided, there are mountain bikes for hire and recycling is encouraged, ensuring a green experience.

Follow in the footsteps of ancient shepherds, as you stroll the South
Downs and ramble through the **Low Weald**

KEY

▲**INFO**

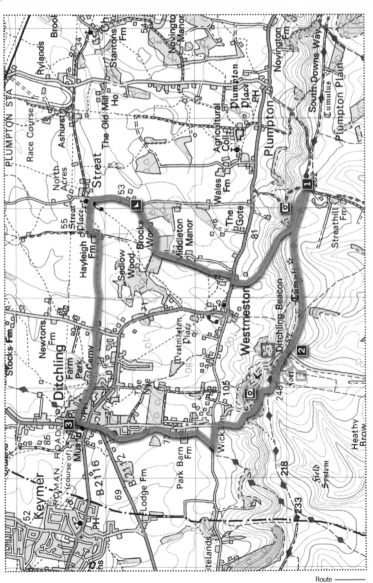

TERRAIN
Short sections of the walk are
on quiet lanes, so keep an
eye out for traffic. Take care
on exposed chalk, which can
be slippery.

HOW TO GET THERE
BY CAR: From the M23,
heading south, continue on
to the A23, turn left on to
the A273 for 1 mile and then
head right on to the B2112
for 2 miles. Turn right on to
the B2116 Lewes Road for
2 miles then turn left on to
Streat Lane.
BY PUBLIC TRANSPORT:
The nearest train station is in
Plumpton, a 30 minute walk
to the campsite along rights
of way.

MAP
Ordnance Survey Explorer
Map 122.
Grid ref: TQ 352 148

CAMPSITE
Blackberry Wood
Streat Lane, Streat,
East Sussex BN6 8RS
☎ 01273 890035
www.blackberrywood.com
Minimum two nights April–
Oct weekends, minimum
three nights on bank holidays.
Online booking only.

MORE INFO
South Downs
www.southdownsonline.org

Cool Camping
www.coolcamping.co.uk

Route ⎯⎯⎯

White Cliffs of Dover Kent

Distance 4 miles (6.4 km) **Type** Moderate **Time** 2 hours

The **White Cliffs of Dover** were formed 65-80 million years ago at the bottom of a tropical sea and are arguably Britain's most famous natural landmark. Their vast size and location at Dover port made them the last feature of Britain visible to those leaving the country and the first sight for those returning, inspiring great affection, particularly during the war years.

▶ START

To really feel this iconic history beneath your boots, start at **The Gateway to the White Cliffs** visitor centre and take the path that leads from the far end of the car parks.

At the viewpoint, use the telescope to identify points on the French coast, 21 miles away, and watch cross-channel ferries squeeze through the gap in the harbour wall below you. Then take the stony path round the coast, go through the kissing gate and head down the steps to the cliff terrace. Take the path towards the sea, following signs for the **Saxon Shore Way**.

1 1 MILE

Pass through the gate and take the coastal path down into the hollow of **Langdon Hole**, staying on the seaward side of the fence. As you climb up to the rim, you pass the top of **Langdon Stairs**, where a scramble and rough zigzag path

▷ The White Cliffs of Dover are up to 106m (348ft) in places

offer a fair-weather detour 📷 down to the small beach of **Langdon Bay**. The twisted metal showing at low tide is the remains of cargo-ship MV *Summity*, beached by its crew after German bombing in the Second World War.

After winter storms you may also see huge piles of chalk, washed from the cliffs. Wave erosion helps to keep the cliffs sparkling white – but is also widening the Channel by around an inch each year.

2 1¼ MILES

Continue along Langdon Cliffs, keeping an eye out for the fulmars and kittiwakes that nest here. If you're lucky you may even spot a peregrine falcon, although sightings of Dame Vera Lynn's bluebird remain unconfirmed. Rare wildflowers such as orchids also thrive.

Lift your eyes back to the sea and you have a 180° view of one of the world's busiest shipping lanes, with tankers and

container vessels slowly moving through the water and nippy car ferries heading to and from the continent.

3 1½ MILES

The path now heads inland round the hollow of **Fan Hole** and through yellow-flowered gorse. After about ½ mile it turns sharp left to the **South Foreland Lighthouse**, built to warn mariners of the treacherous **Goodwin Sands**, known locally as the Great Ship Swallower. The present structure was built in 1843 and in 1898 it hosted the world's first international radio transmission by Italian Gugliemo Marconi. It is open to visitors in season.

4 2 MILES

For a different route back, turn left out of the lighthouse and walk directly behind the building, parallel to the sea. This brings you on to a surfaced track. Follow this track along the top of the cliffs, keeping left when the path forks. After another mile or so, turn left on to a cinder path that takes you back down to the cliff terrace. Climb the wooden steps up towards the lifeguard station then retrace your steps back round to the visitor centre, stopping just before the viewpoint to admire majestic **Dover** 📷 **Castle**, directly in front of you across the valley.

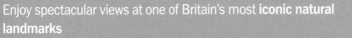

Enjoy spectacular views at one of Britain's most **iconic natural landmarks**

KEY 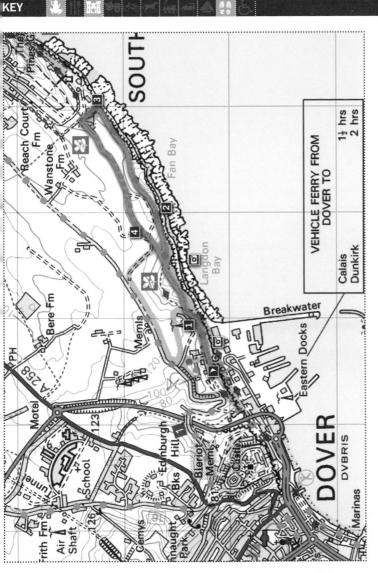 INFO

TERRAIN
Rough chalk paths, which can be slippery when wet. Stay at least 5m from cliff edges. The route can be confusing as paths often diverge – but they later rejoin.

HOW TO GET THERE
BY CAR: From A2/A258 Duke of York roundabout, take the A258 towards Dover town centre. In 1 mile turn left into Upper Road, and after ¾ mile turn right into the entrance.
BY PUBLIC TRANSPORT:
Take the P&O Ferries bus PO from Dover Priory Railway Station to Eastern Docks, or the Stagecoach bus service 15A from town centre to Eastern Docks. It is then a 10 minute walk away.

MAP
Ordnance Survey Explorer Map 138.
Grid ref: TR 336 422

MORE INFO
South Foreland Lighthouse The Front, St Margaret's Bay, Dover CT15 6HP
☎ 01304 852463
www.nationaltrust.org.uk
Closed end Oct-Mar. Call for opening times.

Visit Kent
www.visitkent.co.uk

Dover Tourist Information Centre, Old Town Gaol, Biggin Street, Dover CT16 1DL
☎ 01304 205108
whitecliffscountry.org.uk

Route ———

61

Bigbury Hill Fort Kent

Distance 4½ miles (7 km) **Type** Easy **Time** 2½ hours

Southend-on-sea
Chatham   Ramsgate
Maidstone   ▶ CHARTHAM
Ashford   Dover
Folkestone
Dymchurch

▸ The Kent Downs AONB is a landscape of chalk escarpments, dry valleys and ancient hedgerows

▶ START

Start at **Chartham** station. Walk south along the lane into the village, passing the church on your right. Turn left along the **Stour Valley Walk** as it runs alongside the 📷 **Great Stour River**. Pause where a farm track comes from the left to cross the river to your right. Until the 19th century this was the site of a ford.

Caesar was advancing north from the coast and intended to use this ford to cross the Stour and head inland. The warriors of the Cantii tribe of Celts massed here to block his march. The river was then much wider and lined by marshy banks and damp meadows. The battle began with a showy demonstration of chariot driving by the Celtic nobles on the wide meadows to your left. Caesar then sent his X Legion, backed by auxiliary infantry to cross the river. This was the hardest fought part of the battle, lasting about two hours and involving heavy casualties on both sides. When the Romans got over the river the Celts broke and a rout ensued.

Continue along the riverbank until the path meets the A28. Turn left to follow the signs for the Stour Valley Walk. Take the first lane on the right, then follow signs for the Stour Valley Walk through a small industrial estate

then through orchards 📷 to **Tonford Manor**. Turn left up the lane and under a railway bridge. Follow the lane as it bends right, then take the first lane on the right. Just before the lane crosses the motorway, go left along the **North Downs Way**.

1 1¾ MILES

As you follow the North Downs Way through the woods you will see the banks and ditches 📷 of the **Bigbury Hill Fort**.

The Celtic warriors rallied here, trusting in the defences to hold off the Romans until nightfall. The defences are now overgrown and tumbled, but can be clearly traced. Caesar assaulted the hill fort at once and drove the Celts fleeing further north, to be pursued and cut down by his cavalry. You can see the route followed by the fugitives by looking north across the valley. The following year Caesar extracted

tribute from the tribes of southern Britain, but retreated to Gaul. It would be another 90 years before the Romans returned to Britain.

Follow the North Downs Way to **Chartham Hatch**, leaving the village along a lane with a pub on the right-hand side. At a T-junction, abandon the trail and turn left down the hill to return to Chartham railway station.

Follow the course of Caesar's great battle, fought in 55BC, while exploring the **Stour Valley Walk**

KEY

▲**INFO**

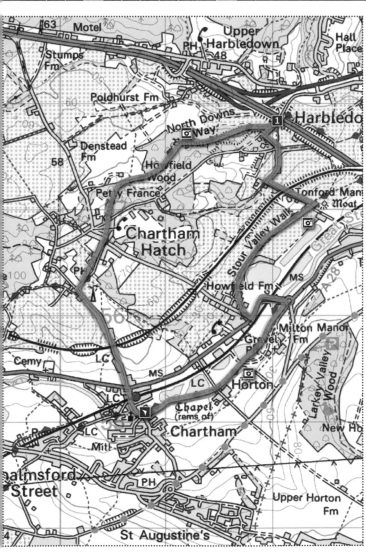

Route ————

TERRAIN
Footpaths and lanes with generally good surfaces, though the riverside stretches can be muddy after rain. There is a steep hill up to the hill fort and another down out of Chatham Hatch.

HOW TO GET THERE
BY CAR: Chartham is just off the A28 west of Canterbury.
BY PUBLIC TRANSPORT: Trains run to Chartham station from Canterbury West and London Victoria via Ashford International.

MAP
Ordnance Survey Landranger Map 179.
Grid ref: TR 105 545

NEARBY EXCURSIONS
Canterbury Cathedral
11 The Precincts,
Canterbury CT1 2EH
☎ 01227 762862
canterbury-cathedral.org
Open all year 9am-5pm.

Canterbury Roman Museum
Longmarket, Butchery Lane,
Canterbury CT1 2JR
☎ 01227 785575
Open Mon-Sat, 10am-5pm.

MORE INFO
Canterbury Visitor
Information Centre
The Butter Market,
12-13 Sun St, Canterbury
CT1 2HX
☎ 01227 378100

Kent Tourist Board
www.visitkent.co.uk

Kent Downs AONB
www.kentdowns.org.uk

Canterbury •
Chilham •
CHARING ›
Ashford •
Kingsnorth •   Lyminge •
Folkestone •

The Pilgrims' Way Kent

Distance 9 miles (14½ km) **Type** Easy **Time** 4 hours

> This walk is peppered with beautiful wild poppies in the summer

It was now more than 600 years ago that Chaucer imagined a band of pilgrims telling stories as they rode from **London** to **Canterbury** to visit the tomb of Thomas Becket, who was murdered in **Canterbury Cathedral** in 1170. The shrine was Britain's most important place of pilgrimage.

Many treated the journey seriously, while others, like Chaucer's characters, treated it more like a holiday. The exact route of the pilgrims is unknown and there are now both an alleged **Pilgrims' Way** and a modern **North Downs Way National Trail**. Sometimes they overlap and this stretch uses both.

> Take the Pilgrims' Way to Wye

▶ START

Charing was ages old in Chaucer's day and its rail station lies half a mile from the original village. Exiting left from the station, cross the A20 and follow **High Street**

uphill until you reach a narrow road on the right leading to St Peter and St Paul's church, and the remains of an archbishop's palace.

1 ½ MILE

The huge church tower and flint-walled barns show this was once a splendid place. Tradition says Henry VII and Henry VIII feasted here and Chaucer may well have stayed in the archbishop's guesthouse.

Carry on up the High Street, turn right on to the A252 and right again on to the **Pilgrims' Way**, leaving Charing Hill and the windmill behind. The mill is relatively modern but it's a reminder of the Reeve's smutty story about two lads who take revenge on a greedy miller by bedding his wife and daughter.

For half a mile the lane dips round the hills before skirting an open quarry, which gleams brilliant white in the chalk hillside, and running along the edge of Westwell beech woods. This is part of the **Kent Downs Area of Outstanding Natural Beauty** and a Site of Scientific Interest; the woodland flora includes common rock roses and lady's bedstraw, proving this was open grazing land before the Weald and Downs became thickly wooded. Despite the sheltering trees, the path can be wet and slippery here.

2 3½ MILES

After **Dunn Street Farm**, the **North Downs Way** crosses a stile on to **Eastwell Park** farm and twists round fields and woods to a lake and ruined church. This is a good spot to picnic and recall more *Canterbury Tales*. The Clerk's romantic story suits the setting, but the Miller's bawdy tale of a student who gets branded on the bum, while mooning out of his lover's window, is more fun.

Continue over **Eastwell** estate and drop down across a hotel drive to the A251 and **Boughton Lees**. At the village green take a right to Boughton Aluph, rejoining the Pilgrims' Way. After half a mile the path turns off left then passes through woods to **Boughton Aluph** church.

3 7 MILES

All Saints Church is another medieval gem, admired by countless pilgrims before they set off on their final stretch to Chilham and Canterbury. To reach **Wye** turn down the lane and (ignoring the sign to Wye) walk a few yards towards Boughton Lees. Soon a footpath leads left to the A28, the Roman road to Canterbury, and through **Perry Court Farm** to the pretty market town of Wye.

Follow in the footsteps of medieval pilgrims who journeyed along the
North Downs and inspired Chaucer's classic, *The Canterbury Tales*

KEY

▶INFO

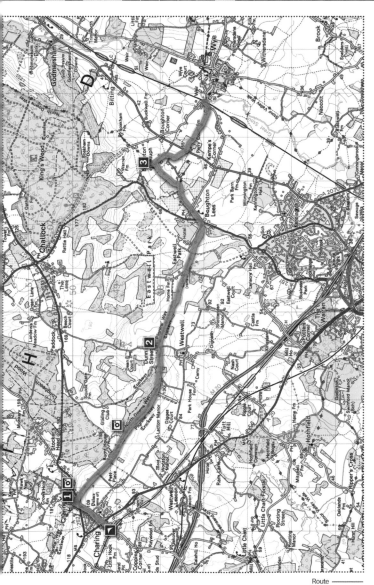

TERRAIN
Some lanes but mostly farm
and woodland tracks.

HOW TO GET THERE
BY CAR: Charing is 6 miles
northwest of Ashford on A20,
and 12 miles southeast of
Maidstone on A20. Wye is
3 miles northeast of Ashford
and 9 miles southwest of
Canterbury off A28.
BY PUBLIC TRANSPORT:
Regular trains run to Charing
on the Maidstone East to
Ashford line, and to Wye on
the Ashford to Canterbury
West line. Charing is on
Stagecoach bus route
510 between Ashford
and Maidstone; Wye is
on Stagecoach bus route
652 between Ashford
and Canterbury.

MAP
Ordnance Survey Landranger
Map 189.
Grid ref: TQ 949 493

MORE INFO
Explore Kent
☎ 08458 247 600
kent.gov.uk/explorekent

North Downs National Trail
**www.nationaltrail.co.uk/
Northdowns**

Route ———

High Wycombe •   Watford •
Marlow •   London •
Slough •
• Reading   Richmond •
Egham •
SANDHURST ▶   • Camberley   Epsom •
• Basingstoke   Guildford •   Dorking •

Blackwater Valley Berkshire

Distance 6 miles (9½ km) **Type** Easy **Time** 3 hours

▸ Thanks to careful environmental management, wildlife is thriving once again in Blackwater Valley

The **Blackwater Valley** is an 18-mile green corridor, containing two Sites of Special Scientific Interest (SSSIs), three nature reserves and another 31 designated wildlife sites. It's a landscape frequented by kingfishers, damselflies, water voles, lapwings, roe deer and otters – but what makes this an unlikely spot for wildlife, and an unusual conservation success story, is that the valley is a working gravel extraction site.

▶ START

Park at the **Horseshoe Lake Activity Centre**, on **Mill Lane**. Walk right, past the activity centre and through a gate. Continue on the path, through a kissing gate, then cross a lane and pick up the path. Cross several stiles and continue to a lane.

Turn left then, after 100m, right through a metal gate into woodland. This patch of woodland,

which is carpeted in bluebells in spring, has been untouched since 1750 and harbours woodpeckers, nuthatches and roe deer.

Where the path splits, turn right then keep straight ahead, bearing left at a junction, and following the track past houses. Ignore a National Trust sign on the right and continue downhill until you reach **Lower Sandhurst Road**.

1 1¾ MILES

Turn right, and after 500m turn right up **Dell Road**. As the slope gets steeper, look back for views over the **Blackwater Valley**, with the **North Downs Way** running along the ridge. Turn left at the road and keep left at the next junction. Opposite the white **Court Cottage**, turn left and walk along a new permissive footpath through farmland,

which is currently being managed to create new habitats for wildlife.

Turn right at the lane, then left at the corner of **Cricket Hill**, before bearing left through a kissing gate. Cross the road and continue along a track. Turn left at **Field House**; on your right is a plaque marking the spot where, in 1501, Henry VII and his sons Arthur and Henry, out in hunting in the woods, heard news of the arrival of Prince Arthur's bride, the Infanta Katherine of Aragon.

2 3¾ MILES

Join the **Blackwater Valley Path**, then cross a stream, go through a kissing gate and follow the path around the edge of the field to a road. Cross the road and pick up a path between the river and gravel pits. Gravel extraction has sculpted this landscape for the last 60 years, and

today the valley presents a perfect example of how we can manage our environmental impact to create new habitats for wildlife. The lake on your left is a relatively new creation, but already water birds and waders have moved in.

Follow the path between gravel pits and the river, which is named after the black, peaty soil that makes up its bed.

3 5 MILES

Cross a conveyor belt and leave the gravel pits behind, entering **Moor Green Lakes Nature Reserve**, a series of lakes lined with reeds and teaming with wildlife.

The Blackwater Valley Countryside Partnership have turned these excavated gravel pits into lakes, wet meadows, reed beds and woodlands, encouraging wildlife and wild flowers to flourish. In summer wild flowers cover the banks, 30 species of dragonflies and 32 species of butterflies live here, and you may be lucky enough to spot an adder or common lizard sunning itself on the path. Recently a number of otter spraints have been found, a sure sign that water quality is improving.

Carry straight on a junction of paths, and later take the lower path beside the river. Just before you reach Mill Lane, take a left along a boardwalk to return to the car park.

An active gravel extraction site and thriving nature reserve, the
Blackwater Valley offers an unlikely haven for wildlife

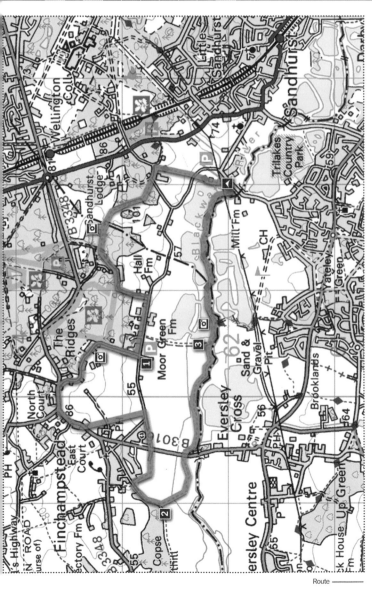

TERRAIN
Broadwalks, lanes and footpaths. Can be muddy in places.

HOW TO GET THERE
BY CAR: Horseshoe Lake car park is 1 mile west from Sandhurst, which is 12 miles east from Reading on the A329 (M), then A321.
BY PUBLIC TRANSPORT: The start point is ½ mile from Sandhurst station, which is accessible by train from Reading.

MAP
Ordnance Survey Landranger Map 175.
Grid ref: SU 820 620

NEARBY EXCURSIONS
Horseshoe Lake
Activity Centre
Mill Lane, Sandhurst
GU47 8JW
☎ 01252 871808
www.watersport.freeuk.com

MORE INFO
Blackwater Valley
Countryside Partnership
Ash Lock Cottage,
Government Road, Aldershot
GU11 2PS
☎ 01252 331353
www.blackwater-valley.org.uk

Route ⎯⎯⎯

Chess Valley Buckinghamshire

Distance 10 miles (16 km) **Type** Easy **Time** 4 hours

Welwyn •
Garden City
Cheshunt •
▶ CHESHAM
Slough •
Windsor •
Staines •
Weybridge •
London •
• Richmond
Park

At the far reaches of the Metropolitan line lays a bucolic valley, hugging the **River Chess**. It's one of the Chilterns' chalk streams, rivers fed by mineral-packed springs, filtered clear by the surrounding rock. This warm, shallow water breeds a unique ecosystem, where wildlife, such as trout, water voles and kingfishers, flourishes. But it's not all about wildlife. With its history of paper mills, medieval agriculture techniques and grand residences, the **Chess Valley** is an interesting ramble from the capital.

▶ START

From **Chesham** tube station, follow **Station Road**, turning left at the roundabout to walk through **Lowndes Park** and **Meades Water Gardens**, a wildlife haven in the town centre. Emerge at a roundabout, crossing to **Moor Lane**. Continue south along the stream, past the swimming pool and on to the grassy **Moor**, once a river island.

1 1 MILE

At the far end of the Moor, dip down a path on the left and walk through the woods to a weir. This was once the site of **Canon's Mill**, one of many that used to dot the river to make flour, then pulp – this region was the hub of the 18th-century papermaking boom.

Carry straight on, past a bottling plant, into

▶ The River Chess begins its journey deep in the Chilterns

a field. Turn left, cross a stile, walk down the road and turn left at the junction, turning right opposite the sewage works. Hop over the stile and head across the fields, out on to a road and right down a track. Here the countryside opens up – watch out for hawks circling above.

2 3½ MILES

After crossing three fields and entering woodland a sign prohibits walkers veering left; instead keep right, leaving the wood

to cross **Latimer Park** (of Capability Brown design), walking around the boundary of imposing **Latimer House** until you reach a road. Take the path opposite to another road (with a quick detour north to Latimer's cute cottages), then turn left across a field with wide valley views – a copse conceals where the 13th century **Flaunden Church** once stood.

3 5 MILES

Carry on through **Mill Farm**. Turn right to

divert to **Chenies**, with its 13th century manor, before backtracking to **Frogmore Meadows**. This rare ecosystem is rich in wildlife – look out for meadowsweet, marsh marigold and herons. Walk alongside the meadows, past the watercress beds through **Sarratt Bottom**, then straight on through a kissing gate; to the left you'll see strip lynchets – field furrows thought to be the remains of ninth century vineyards.

You're now in **Chorleywood Park**; the house is private, but the grounds are open and great for picnics. Follow the path, past the information board and right along a wide track.

4 8 MILES

Breaking up this idyll is the M25, so cross the footbridge, turning immediately right to walk down a narrow path, with traffic thundering to your right.

Cross a stile into a field, keeping left to emerge among tidy houses. Continue straight on down an alley, before eventually emerging on to a road. Turn right down the footpath opposite, which bends round a field, the river to your left, before walking to the right of a playing field. Emerging at a church, head right down the road to **Rickmansworth** train station.

Explore this beautiful chalk stream in the **Chilterns**, an Area of
Outstanding Natural Beauty at the end of the Tube

KEY

►**INFO**

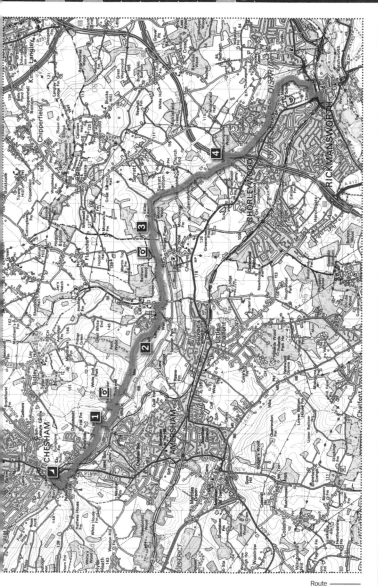

TERRAIN
Footpaths run across fields
and through woodland, so
it may get muddy after rain,
but walking boots are not
essential in dry weather.
Some stretches follow
quiet roads.

**HOW TO GET THERE
BY PUBLIC TRANSPORT:**
Take the Metropolitan
line from central London
to Chesham (changing at
Chalfont & Latimer).
Return via the Metropolitan
line from Rickmansworth.
☎ 020 7222 1234
www.tfl.gov.uk

MAP
Ordnance Survey Explorer
Map 172 and 181.
Grid ref: SP 960 015

NEARBY EXCURSIONS
Chenies Manor
Chenies WD3 6ER
☎ 01494 762888
cheniesmanorhouse.co.uk
Open Apr-Oct, Weds, Thurs
and Bank Holiday Mon
2-5pm.

MORE INFO
Chilterns Conservation Board
The Lodge, Station Road,
Chinnor OX39 4HA
☎ 01844 355500
www.chilternsaonb.org

Route ———

Ashridge Woods Hertfordshire

Distance 8 miles (13 km) **Type** Moderate **Time** 4-5 hours

Leighton Buzzard
Luton
Aylesbury ▶ ASHRIDGE WOODS
Wendover Hemel Hempstead
Chesham
Watford

▶ Explore Ashridge on a spring dawn and have bluebells to yourself

No one would call the bluebell woods of the **Ashridge Estate** a best kept secret – they are known and loved by walkers all over the Chiltern Hills and far beyond. But it's an entirely different kettle of fish when you walk there before dawn on a beautiful morning in spring. Songbirds chorus the sunrise with a vigour and tunefulness that will astound you. Muntjac and roe deer bound off under the trees, startled to see an intruder at this hour. The great column raised to the memory of the 3rd Duke of Bridgewater stands pale

and ghost-like in the early sun. And up on **Ivinghoe Beacon** at the apex of the ancient Ridgeway track, you can stare over 30 miles of country in a sea of mist.

▶ START

Leaving the **Greyhound Inn** in **Aldbury**, turn right along the road. In 150m, turn right opposite Applegarth up a gravelled track into the trees. Climb to turn left on a sunken trackway, and follow this for ¼ mile to reach the **Bridgewater Monument**. Francis Egerton, 3rd Duke of

Bridgewater owned Ashridge House and 6,000 acres of surrounding countryside. He was dubbed the Father of Inland Navigation because of his success as a pioneer of canal building. Together with engineer James Brindley, he built Britain's first canal (opened in 1761) to carry coals from his mines at Worsley in Lancashire. In a deep cutting at Tring you can see the Grand Junction Canal, built by the Duke to link London and Birmingham. The fluted 100-foot column of the Bridgewater Monument is open at weekends.

1 ⅔ MILE
Just past the monument, the path forks; keep ahead on a clear track for 2 miles through woods carpeted with bluebells and wood 📷 anemones in spring. They are also a favourite location for songbirds. In the early morning you will certainly hear the chittering of wrens, the mellifluous warble of blackbirds and wood warblers, and the soft, throaty cooing of wood pigeons. You may also be lucky enough to catch the bubble-and-squeak of a blackcap, and – if very fortunate – the rich, operatic performance of a nightingale. Look out for the tiny shapes of muntjac deer.

The path runs north by way of **Moneybury**

Hill, **Hanging Isley**, Duncombe Terrace and **Clipper Down** to meet Beacon Road.

2 2¾ MILES
Bear left and follow footpath signs downhill for 300m to turn right along the **Ridgeway National Trail**. Follow this trackway, well waymarked with white acorn symbols, for ¾ mile to Ivinghoe Beacon viewpoint. The Ridgeway is one of the oldest roads in Britain, a system of ancient tracks across the chalk uplands of southern Britain that has been in continuous use for at least 6,000 years. The National Trail starts at Avebury in Wiltshire and runs for 87 miles to 249m (817ft) Ivinghoe Beacon, a high chalk promontory with Iron Age hill fort ramparts that offer superb views across 30 miles of country.

3 3⅔ MILES
Return along the waymarked Ridgeway, through the woods on **Steps Hill** and then **Pitstone Hill** with 📷 its wonderful views, following the National Trail south for 3 miles to a crossing of tracks by **Westland Farm**.

Turn left along a clear track to return to Aldbury, taking time to look around the village's pretty houses, duck pond, welcoming pubs, manor house and village stocks on the green.

Enjoy a dawn walk through **bluebell woods** to an ancient viewpoint

KEY

▶INFO

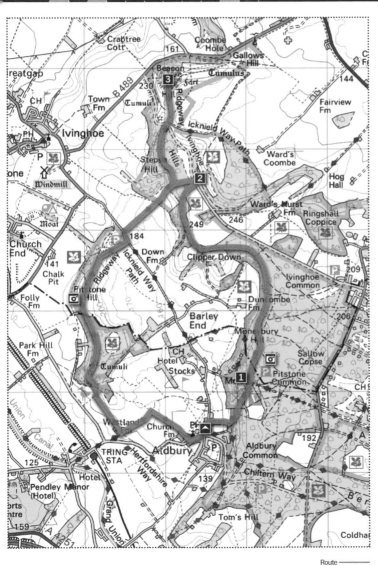

TERRAIN
Woodland paths and the
well-marked Ridgeway
National Trail. Some short,
steep ascents. Can be sticky
underfoot after rain – wear
boots or good walking shoes.

HOW TO GET THERE
BY CAR: Take the M25 to
J20, the A41 to Tring and a
minor road to Aldbury.
BY PUBLIC TRANSPORT:
Trains run from London
Euston to Tring station,
which is 1 mile by footpaths
to Aldbury.

MAP
Ordnance Survey Explorer
Map 181.
Grid ref: SP 965 125

MORE INFO
Tring Tourist
Information Centre
99 Akeman Street, Tring
HP23 6AA
☎ 01442 823347
www.tring.gov.uk

Ashridge Estate Visitor Centre
Moneybury Hill
Berkhamsted
HP4 1LX
☎ 01494 755557
www.nationaltrust.org.uk

Route ────────

EAST

'Very flat, Norfolk,' sneers Amanda in Noel Coward's *Private Lives*, but let's get one thing straight: when it comes to the East of England flat does not mean boring. True, **Cambridgeshire**, **Norfolk**, **Suffolk** and **Essex** aren't known for challenging climbs, but what they lack in rising peaks they more than make up in sheer, vast glory. Gazing over the landscape endlessly stretching out under immense skies cannot fail to quicken the pulse. Most of all, it urges you to step out and explore.

There is so much to see. The exalted **Stour Valley**, winding between Suffolk and Essex, for instance, is arguably the most celebrated patch of waterway in England (save, perhaps, the Thames). Pictures of its banks hang in galleries, are delivered on postcards and printed on tea-towels the world over. It inspired John Constable, who was born in the valley, to paint his series of rural river tableaus. His art records the relationship between man and his environment. In reaction to the trend of using the countryside as a mere set, Constable's rivers are bustling with activity, places of hard graft as well as relaxation, beneath swirling and often heavy weather systems.

It is over 180 years since Constable finished *The Hay Wain* and the scene has hardly changed. Granted, the industrial nature of the **Stour** has diminished, but the relationship with water is as vital as ever. The battle to control the sea in Norfolk has never been so greatly felt, with environmentalists clashing with farmers over whether the **Broads** should be left to flood or stay reclaimed farmland. What is indisputable is that the wetlands are some of the most important wildlife habitats in the United Kingdom and, some would argue, the world. Even the most reluctant of bird-watchers, will find something to marvel at all year round, from grey plovers in spring, stopping off on their way back from Africa, breeding terns in summer and the unmissable sight of 400,000 birds that make the **Norfolk** coast their home over winter. Watching pink-footed geese erupting in huge, noisy numbers and swooping low overhead is a truly unforgettable experience.

•Welwyn Garden City   •Kelvedon
  Chelmsford•

Brentwood•
      ▶ LANGDON NATURE
        RESERVE
•London

  Chatham•   •Gillingham

Langdon Nature Reserve Essex

Distance 1 mile (1½ km) **Type** Easy **Time** 2 hours

Langdon Nature Reserve is a unique area of **Essex** landscape with a historic settlement dating back to Neolithic times. The Saxons gave the area the name **Long Hill** and after the agricultural depression in the late 1800s, enterprising Londoners gradually settled the land. During the interwar years, the **Dunton** community grew to more than 200 plotland bungalows, but the advent of **Basildon**, a new town, triggered another decline. Nature has now reclaimed the area, which is managed by Essex Wildlife Trust.

The habitat is a special blend of former garden shrubs, wild fruit trees and hedgerow species all mingling together to form shady paths, quiet glades and dense undergrowth, crawling and teeming with wildlife. And on the top of the eastern ridge at 117m (385ft) is a wonderful panorama that includes many London landmarks. The **Duck Walk** offers a delightful insight into the reserve and gives children a chance to hunt for bugs and identify different species.

▶ Take a walk on the wild side around this reserve that's packed full of interesting flora and fauna

▶ START

Follow the finger signposts opposite the **Visitor Centre** and stick to the path as it leaves by the car park, past the picnic area and through mixed woodland where blue tits fly among the branches and speckled wood butterflies flit just above the ground. Duck waymark signs show the way, and at the squeeze the path runs straight ahead. Large gateposts are visible among the undergrowth, marking the old entrance to one of the houses, and today they offer a bug hunt haven! Challenge the kids to find woodlice and millipedes under logs, ground beetles under stones, cardinal beetles on the foliage, and spiders in bushes and trees.

1 ½ MILE

At the next squeeze the walk joins what used to be **First Avenue**; a short distance further a left turn heads towards the lake. At the T-junction turn right and follow the path on the eastern lakeshore, where mute swans glide gracefully on the surface, tufted duck and mallard dabble about and Canada geese wander in and out of the water.

The grassy meadows rise uphill to an excellent butterfly and insect hunting area. The meadows are home to around 30 species such as yellow brimstones, peacock butterflies and meadow browns. Pay particular attention to the edge of the fields, where brambles creep forth, as these are prime areas to spot gatekeeper butterflies – look out for their orange and brown wings and prominent eye spots. Also keep an eye out for the Essex skipper, while if you're lucky you may also see a rare grizzled skipper.

Follow the path as it circles the lake then turn right on to a bridleway and left to the start of the lake.

2 ¾ MILE

Retrace the route to a waymark and turn left uphill. The Duck Walk then turns right over a crossroads and continues for ½ mile to the main track, which returns to the Visitor Centre. At the centre, keen detectives can join in the pond dipping (led by Wildlife Trust staff due to the presence of great crested newts). Spotting great diving beetles, grass snakes, water scorpions, and smooth newts is a great way to finish an adventurous day with nature.

Become a nature detective – go bug hunting and identify dabbling ducks at **Langdon Nature Reserve**

KEY **▶INFO**

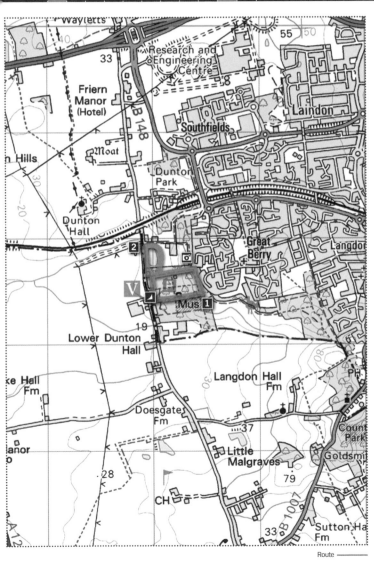

TERRAIN
Well-marked footpaths.

HOW TO GET THERE
BY CAR: From J29 on the M25 take the A127 east towards Basildon. Turn right onto the B148 and follow reserve signs. Car parking on site, but barriers close at 5pm.
BY PUBLIC TRANSPORT: Bus services operate from Basildon town centre to Langdon Railway Station (on the Fenchurch to Southend Lane) less than ½ mile away from the Langdon Hills.

MAP
Ordnance Survey Landranger Map 177.
Grid ref: TQ 659 875

MORE INFO
Langdon Visitor Centre 3rd Avenue, Lower Dunton Road, Basildon SS16 6EB
☎ 01268 419103
www.essexwt.org.uk
Open Tues–Sun, 9am–5pm and bank holiday Mondays. A Wildlife Explorer Kit containing binoculars, bug box and brush, bird and insect identification cards, activity ideas and paper and crayon for bark rubbing can be hired.

Route ——

Cambridge •

Cherry •
Hinton
▶ GRANTCHESTER
Trumpington •

Hauxton •   Great •
Shelford

Newton •   Sawston •

EAST

Grantchester Cambridgeshire

Distance 5 miles (8 km) **Type** Easy **Time** 3-4 hours

▷ **Amble through Grantchester Meadows as many literary figures have done before you**

Southwest of Cambridge lies a retreat that has played host to some of Britain's finest literary minds.

The walk begins in **Cambridge** then follows the River Cam out to **Grantchester** along a route taken by numerous artistic, scientific and literary figures before you.

▶ START

From the car park on **Corn Exchange Street**, turn left on to **Downing Street**, taking a right at the crossroads. Cross over and walk along **Mill Lane** to the river.

Follow the path to your left along the river and through one of many water meadows. Head left of Bella Italia, crossing the road to a park and bearing diagonally right. At the end of the park, follow the sign marked 'Grantchester' until you reach the edge of urban Cambridge.

1 1¼ MILES

On your left you'll see an iron lamppost in the middle of Skaters' Meadow, evidence of when the field was flooded in the 19th century for ice skating. Now the meadow provides ideal conditions for marsh marigold and southern marsh orchid.

Just after this the path splits; take the left turn. From here on follow the river as it carelessly winds along, edged by creaking willows. The river has been a source of enjoyment for centuries. The Grantchester Group, which included Rupert Brooke, E.M Forster and Virginia Woolf, spent long days punting on the water, picnicking and swimming naked by moonlight. Woolf later dubbed the group the neo-pagans due to their bohemian lifestyle. They were young, creative, intelligent and, during their times in Grantchester Meadows, free from the rigours of academic life. As Gwen Darwin later said: "If one of those afternoons could be written down, just as it exactly was, it would be a poem." It was while wandering through these meadows that Alan Turing first considered the idea of artificial intelligence, where Keats, Byron and Coleridge would leave the city and where Sylvia Plath recited Chaucer.

Follow the path over the stile to **The Orchard**, surely Britain's most intellectual tea gardens. In a bid to escape his chaotic social life in the city, Rupert Brooke moved here in 1909, but where Brooke led, many followed. From A.A Milne to Emma Thompson, Stephen Hawking to J.B Priestley, an impressive array of notable people have taken tea in the deckchairs beneath the blooming apples. There's a small **Brooke Museum** in The Orchard car park, which is worth a look.

2 2½ MILES

Leaving the car park, turn left to the **Old Vicarage** where Brooke once lived, and the setting for his poem *The Old Vicarage, Grantchester*: "But Grantchester! Ah Grantchester! There's peace and holy quiet there, great clouds along pacific skies, and men and women with straight eyes..."

Turn back on yourself and follow the road up to the church, immortalised by the same poem: "Yet stands the church clock at ten to three? And is there honey still for tea?"

From here take the footpath just downhill from the entrance to the church, back to the tarmac path running through the meadows and back past Skaters' Meadow to the city of Cambridge.

Follow in the footsteps of countless fine literary minds
on a stroll along the River Cam in **Cambridgeshire**

KEY

▶INFO

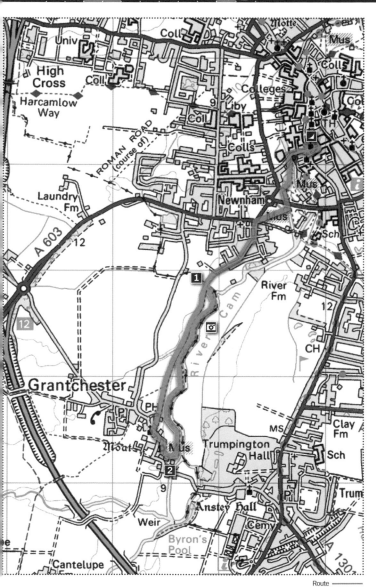

TERRAIN
A flat, river path, which may
be muddy and can be quite
exposed on a windy day.
Walking boots, waterproofs
and warm layers are
recommended.

ACCESS
There is easy access for
bikes, wheelchair users and
buggies on an alternative
tarmac path running across
Grantchester meadows to The
Orchard through the village.

HOW TO GET THERE
BY CAR: Access Cambridge
from the south via the M11,
coming off at J11 for the
A1309 into the city centre,
follow directions for the
city centre and park at
the NCP car park on Corn
Exchange Street.
BY PUBLIC TRANSPORT:
Direct trains from London
Kings Cross, National Express
coaches from London
Victoria.

MAP
Ordnance Survey Explorer
Map 209.
Grid ref: TL 448 585

NEARBY EXCURSIONS
Rupert Brooke Museum
Orchard House
☎ 01223 551118

Wicken Fen nature reserve
Lode Lane, Wicken, Ely,
Cambridgeshire CB7 5XP
☎ 01353 720274
www.wicken.org.uk

MORE INFO
Cambridge Visitor Centre,
The Old Library,
Wheeler Street,
Cambridge CB2 3QB
☎ 0871 226 8006
www.visitcambridge.org

Route ——————

The Devil's Dyke Cambridgeshire

Distance 5½ miles (8.9 km) **Type** Easy **Time** 4 hours

Spalding · King's Lynn · Norwich · Peterborough · Thetford · DEVIL'S DYKE · Southwold · Cambridge · Bedford · Ipswich · Stevenage · Colchester

Standing on the hinterland between Fenland and upland wood, the ancient defensive earthwork of **Devil's Dyke** embraces Cambridgeshire's wide-open skies and landscape, seemingly far removed from the bustle and buildings of the city.

The start of this huge earthwork seems insignificant in this modern age, but during Anglo-Saxon times the ancient port of **Reach** stood on a small promontory jutting out into the watery lands of the East Angles. Linking the impenetrable fens with heavily wooded upland 7 miles to the south, the defensive structure of Devil's Dyke protected land of the Wuffing Kingdom.

▷ The Devil's Dyke in Cambridgeshire is the finest Anglo-Saxon earthwork of its kind in the country

▶ START

From the car park, pass beside the small playground and walk up the eastern flank of Devil's Dyke on to its crest, leaving Reach behind. The early section of this walk runs along the man-made ridge away from the village, dropping down to the track bed of a disused railway line before regaining the top, each step of the trail dominated by the prominent ditch on the western flank.

The path stretches ahead, interrupted by the Burwell to Swaffham Prior road. After crossing this, the earthwork reaches the highest point on **Gallows Hill**, 10m (34ft) from the ditch bottom to ridge top. Testament to

its construction must be reserved for the builders, who achieved such a near perfect profile that the dyke has sustained minimal damage despite around 1,500 years of seasonal weather.

1 2 MILES

Beyond Gallows Hill, walk down a set of steps on the western flank that drop down to a hedge where a stile marks the start of a permissive farmland footpath, leaving the straight line of Devils Dyke. Crossing agricultural land, head towards **Swaffham Prior**, noted for its two churches and two windmills; walk across the fields in the direction

of the stiles, these will lead into the village centre.

The chalky grassland ecology on and around the dyke is good habitat for chalk hill blue and common blue butterflies, as well as brown hares and skylarks.

Nearing the village, follow the path past the windmills. Just before you reach the first houses, you come to a road. Turn right to a crossroads, then carry straight over and walk down **Cage Hill**. At the bottom of the hill, turn right and continue to the edge of the village.

2 4 MILES

Follow the Devil's Dyke pathway sign on the left, along a track and past a

modern barn. Follow this track where it runs beside a drainage dyke until you meet **Little Fen Drove**. The low-lying land here is a reminder of a time when this was swamp and marsh. Head to the bridleway on the right and follow the track for about 100m, then turn left, alongside a meadow on a slight gradient as the land rises above former watery fen. The path now joins a recently planted wood, and gradually drops down, so carry straight on at the junction of paths. The bridleway then emerges opposite Reach Green with the starting point off to the right.

Stroll along one of the finest **Anglo-Saxon earthworks** in Britain and enjoy expansive vistas along this defensive monument

KEY ▶INFO

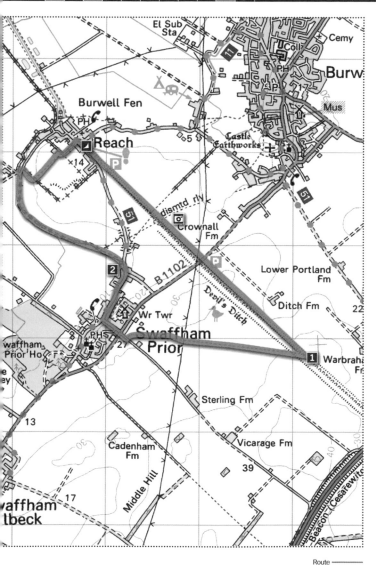

TERRAIN
Footpaths and grassy area. Can be muddy in places.

HOW TO GET THERE
BY CAR: From the A14 J35, turn northeast on to the B1102. Follow the Road through Stow-cum-Quy, Swaffham Bulbeck and Swaffham Prior. Reach is signposted from Swaffham Prior. With the Dykes End Public house in front of you, there is a small car park to your right, on the bend.
BY PUBLIC TRANSPORT: Cambus operate a bus service from either Cambridge or Newmarket which goes to Swaffham Prior, enabling you to start the route in Swaffham rather than Reach.

MAP
Ordnance Survey Explorer Map 226.
Grid ref: TL 568 661

MORE INFO
www.visitcambridge.org

Route ——————

Cavenham Heath Suffolk

Distance 5 miles (8 km) **Type** Easy **Time** 3 hours

Breckland, straddling **Norfolk** and **Suffolk**, is one of the driest places in Britain. During the Neolithic period the mixed oak forest underwent a striking change to more open vegetation of grasses, bracken and heather, coinciding with the beginnings of Neolithic culture in the region. The open nature of the landscape endured to the **Cavenham Heath** landscape of today, where sheep and rabbits continue to crop the heathland grass.

▶ START

From the car park turn left and walk down the road on the **Heathland Trail**. Woodland runs parallel on the left for a short distance with heathland on the right. Attractive views soon open up across the **Lark Valley**, where the extensive heath area becomes apparent further down the sandy track. Rabbits can be seen nibbling the grass here. Following their introduction to Britain by the Romans, evidence exists of farmed rabbit warrens here as early as 1300. During the late 18th century, eight farmed warrens covered several thousand acres of heathland.

1 1 MILE

The heath on the southeast of the track is attractive grass and heather, backed by trees including the Scots pine, a landmark species in the Brecks planted to create

> The River Lart provides a respite from the dry Breckland habitat

shelter belts. To the north of the sandy track is an area of ideal stone curlew habitat. This rare bird nests on bare, sparsely vegetated ground with good visibility, a result of the symbiotic relationship with the rabbit. During the late summer, when the birds gather prior to their migration south, several may be seen together on this heath.

The track now reaches the **River Lark**; from here follow the Wetland Trail, which runs close to the river, into an area of reed,

birch and willow where a loop in the path links back along the riverside. Sedge warblers, grey wagtails and kingfishers frequent the reeds and clear, fast-running waters, as do dragonflies and damselflies. On the opposite bank you may see cattle grazing the flood meadows.

2 2 MILES

At the junction with the sandy track, rejoin the Heathland Trail by going left over the heath among the heather, lichen and

long grasses, which are an ideal habitat for numerous butterflies in summer. In the warmer months expect to see small coppers, small heath, grayling and brown argus butterflies here. This area is also ideal for spotting linnets, yellowhammers, stonechats and tree pipits; at dusk you can hear the churring of nightjars, which catch insects in mid flight during the twilight hours.

The path then enters an attractive area of open birch wood before joining the sandy track back to the car park.

3 5 MILES

From the car park enter the **Woodland Trail** and follow this through the mixed wood with views over the grassy meadows. Oak, beech, birch and chestnut stand alongside the Scots pine, and fallen boughs provide habitat for beetles, fungi and mosses. You may hear or see woodlarks here, and as the track reaches the walker's extension, roe deer wander through the fallen trunks and branches. The trail ends at a thoughtfully placed seat among an open reed area, deep beyond the wooded part of the nature reserve.

Retrace the walker's extension, and then join the main track as it runs on the western boundary of the reserve back to the car park.

Discover the untamed **Breckland** landscape, on a walk through the heather-clad wilderness of Cavenham Heath

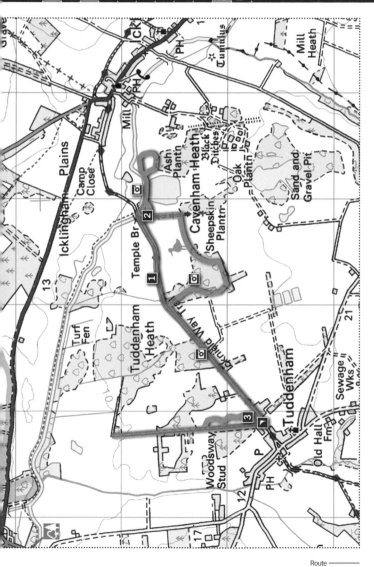

TERRAIN
Well-marked footpaths.

HOW TO GET THERE
BY CAR: Take the turning, marked Tuddenham, off the A11 near Barton Mills. Continue east on this road until you reach Tuddenham St Mary and turn left on to The Green. Carry on past the signs for the closed bridge and continue to the parking area on your left.
BY PUBLIC TRANSPORT: Bus services 355 and 356 operate between Mildenhall and Bury St Edmunds, stopping at the Red Lion in Icklingham, which is the village just north of Cavenham Heath.

MAP
Ordnance Survey Landranger Map 155.
Grid ref: TL 755 724

MORE INFO
Natural England
☎ 01284 762218
www.naturalengland.org.uk

Cavenham Heath is a National Nature Reserve and Site of Special Scientific Interest, open all year. It is a breeding location for the stone curlew. The Heathland is an Open Access area but from 1 Mar-1 Nov access is restricted in areas where the stone curlew is nesting. But this does not detract from the enjoyment of walking in the nature reserve and you can spot stone curlews with binoculars.

The Brecks
www.brecks.org.uk

Route ———

Dedham Vale Essex/Suffolk

Distance 7 miles (11 km) **Type** Easy **Time** 3 hours

Ipswich •

• East Bergholt

DEDHAM ▶ • Manningtree

• Colchester

▶ START

Start at Manningtree station on the Essex-Suffolk border, where the **River Stour** spreads out to meet the sea. Leave the car park by a ramp on the right leading down to a track, signed '**Flatford**'. At the end turn right under the railway arch and follow the path across the meadows to the edge of the Stour.

1 ¾ MILE

This is the valley where **Constable** grew up in the late 18th century and painted his most famous pictures. Years later he explained: "I associate my careless boyhood with all that lies on the banks of the Stour; these scenes made me a painter." Still wonderfully unspoilt, **Dedham Vale** is now an Area of Outstanding Natural Beauty. Turn left and follow the riverside embankment to an old flood barrier. Walk behind it, not across, and keep to the path. Don't wander down on to the marshes: they are criss-crossed with gullies and the wildlife hiding in the dense reeds is better left undisturbed. Bring binoculars if you want some close-up encounters with shy waterfowl and herons.

2 1¾ MILES

As the path nears Flatford lock you can see the large redbrick watermill that Constable's father owned. He also had a

▶ Willy Lott's house looks as it did when Constable painted it

windmill at nearby **East** 📷 **Bergholt,** where John was born in 1776. It was not till 1799 that young Constable was allowed to abandon milling to become an artist in London, returning each summer to paint the scenery he loved. Nowadays the National Trust keeps his viewpoints free of overgrown trees and shrubs and in winter, when skies are overcast,

trees are bare and few visitors come, you get the clearest views of all.

Pass the lock and cross **Flatford Bridge** to reach the thatched **Bridge Cottage.** Inside is a Constable exhibition and next door a tearoom and shop, with books and leaflets that pinpoint the artist's favourite locations. Carry on past the tiny dry dock he painted in *Boatbuilding near Flatford Mill* and *The*

Valley Farm to *Flatford Mill* and finally *Willy Lott's House*, reflected in the mill pond, just as it is in *The Hay Wain*.

3 2 MILES

Return to the bridge, go right up the lane past the information centre and turn left at the T-junction. Follow the lane up hill, with wide sweeping views 📷 of **Dedham Vale** on your left, to the track at the top, marked 'Private Road, public footpath to Dedham and Stratford'.

This was Constable's regular footpath to the grammar school in Dedham. Follow the path down hill, over **Fen Bridge,** and along the narrow woodland path that forks right to the river meadows.

Cross the flat grassy field diagonally left to the riverbank and carry on to **Dedham Bridge.** Walk left over the bridge and you come to Dedham village, a picture-book place with pastel-coloured houses, teashops and the handsome house that was Constable's school.

4 4½ MILES

From Dedham, it's a mile back to Flatford across the water meadows. The path starts on **Dedham Hall** drive and bears left at the sign to Dedham Hall Farm. At Flatford mill, retrace the path to **Manningtree** for 1¾ miles to return to the station.

Walk through the unspoilt valley where artist **John Constable** painted some of his most famous works

KEY

▶INFO

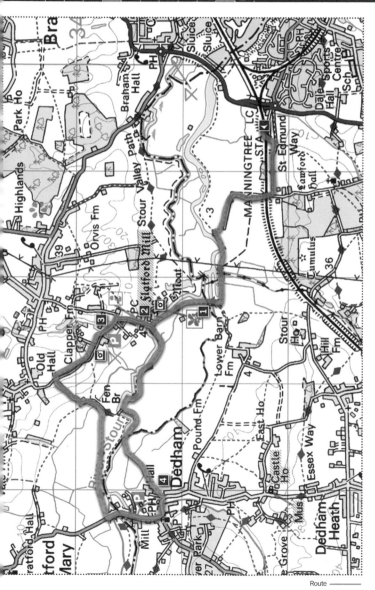

TERRAIN
Mostly gravel or grass footpaths (no stiles) with some woodland tracks and tarmac lanes. Take care on the riverside paths and bridges in wet weather and never wander off the path on to the marshes.

HOW TO GET THERE
BY CAR: Manningtree is northeast of Colchester on the A137
BY PUBLIC TRANSPORT: Trains run regularly to Manningtree on the London Liverpool Street to Norwich and Harwich lines.

MAP
Ordnance Survey Explorer Active Map 196.
Grid ref: TM 093 322

MORE INFO
National Trust property Flatford Bridge Cottage has a Constable exhibition, excavated dry dock, and guided rambles, which last between two and three hours. Jan-Feb open weekends only. Nov-Dec and Mar-April open Wed-Sun. May-Oct open daily.
Flatford Bridge Cottage East Bergholt, Suffolk CO7 6UL
☎ 01206 298260
www.nationaltrust.org.uk

Flatford Visitor Information Flatford Lane, East Bergholt, Suffolk CO7 6UL
☎ 01206 299460
www.visit-suffolk.org.uk

Route ⎯⎯⎯

Orford Ness Suffolk

Distance 4½ miles (7 km) **Type** Easy **Time** 2-3 hours

Stowmarket •
Aldeburgh •
Ipswich • **ORFORD** ▶
• Sudbury **NESS**
Colchester • Felixstowe •

Clacton-on-sea •

From the quay at **Orford**, you cross the **River Ore** in the National Trust's ferry – and in those couple of minutes you pass out of the everyday, and into another world. **Orford Ness** is a shingle spit off the Suffolk coast that stretches like a crooked arm from **Aldeburgh** down to **Shingle Street**. The wide elbow of the Ness lies opposite Orford, and this was where the MoD conducted secret trials between 1913 and 1993, trials that included testing the casings and innards of nuclear weapons.

▶ START
Walk the **Red Trail** by following red arrow waymarks. From the landing stage head left along the road past the old airfield, then bear right to a T-junction. The Information Building here contains an excellent display on Orford Ness.

1 ¾ MILE
Bear left in front of the Information Building and follow the roadway past buildings in various states of repair – the **Barracks**, the **Warden's Office** and a pair of battery charging shops now used by the Orford Ness bird ringing group – until you reach the Bailey bridge across **Stony Ditch**, with a stretch of marshes in front and the large grey box of the **Cobra Mist** building beyond. This once housed the top secret Cobra Mist radar system, designed

▶ Composer Benjamin Britten wove the Orford Ness backdrop into *Curlew River* and *Peter Grimes*

to discern potentially threatening missile movements behind the Iron Curtain. Plagued by a mysterious hum, it never worked properly.

2 1 MILE
Turn right across the Bailey bridge and follow arrows towards the lighthouse, pausing to climb to the roof of the **Bomb Ballistics Building**, which monitored the performance of bombs during flight. Admire the view over the vegetated ridges of the shingle spit, a rare habitat sheltering white sea campion and purple sea pea. Descend and continue to the lighthouse, built in 1792.

3 1½ MILES
From the lighthouse bear right along pebbly **Orford Beach**, where the waves drag and hiss among the stones – a hypnotic sound that inspired local composer Benjamin Britten. In 450m you reach the **Police Tower**, an observation post for the Atomic Weapons Research Establishment's (AWRE) security; turn inland to reach the **Black Beacon** building. Hares, rabbits and marauding feral cats inhabit the acid grassland here. Turn left along the track to reach **Lab 1**.

4 2½ MILES
Lab 1 was the first of six experimental laboratories where atomic bombs were spun, dropped, shaken and subjected to extremes of heat, cold and air pressure – all complete except for their fissile material, we are told. It saw Orford Ness AWRE's first test on an atomic bomb in 1956; other test were carried out in the strange pagoda buildings seen beyond, with their heavy roofs that were designed to soak up the force of any accidental explosion.

Return along the track to the Black Beacon and bear left to return to the Bailey bridge. From here, retrace your steps to the Information Building and back to the landing stage.

Immerse yourself in one of the truly **wild places** on the British coast,
a vast shingle spit with rare wildlife and a secret Cold War past

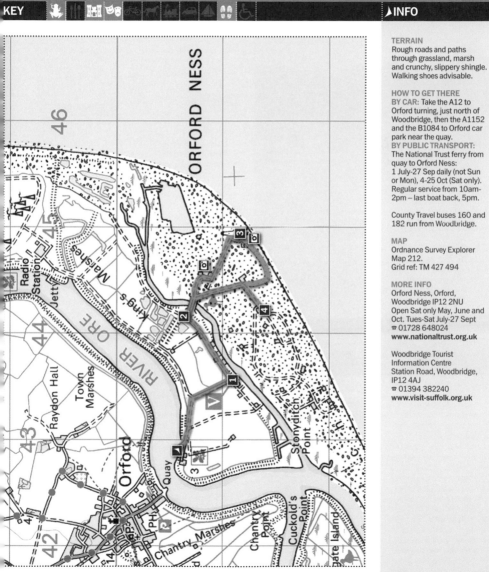

TERRAIN
Rough roads and paths
through grassland, marsh
and crunchy, slippery shingle.
Walking shoes advisable.

HOW TO GET THERE
BY CAR: Take the A12 to
Orford turning, just north of
Woodbridge, then the A1152
and the B1084 to Orford car
park near the quay.
BY PUBLIC TRANSPORT:
The National Trust ferry from
quay to Orford Ness:
1 July-27 Sep daily (not Sun
or Mon), 4-25 Oct (Sat only).
Regular service from 10am-
2pm – last boat back, 5pm.

County Travel buses 160 and
182 run from Woodbridge.

MAP
Ordnance Survey Explorer
Map 212.
Grid ref: TM 427 494

MORE INFO
Orford Ness, Orford,
Woodbridge IP12 2NU
Open Sat only May, June and
Oct. Tues-Sat July-27 Sept
☎ 01728 648024
www.nationaltrust.org.uk

Woodbridge Tourist
Information Centre
Station Road, Woodbridge,
IP12 4AJ
☎ 01394 382240
www.visit-suffolk.org.uk

Route ⎯⎯⎯

Dunwich Heath Suffolk

Distance 2¼ miles (3½ km) **Type** Easy **Time** 2 hours

Aylsham •
Norwich •
Bradwell •
Lowestoft •
Southwold •
DUNWICH HEATH ›
Stowmarket •
Woodbridge •
Ipswich •

> The National Trust's Dunwich Heath is home to a variety of wildlife

The **East Suffolk Sandlings** are unique areas of low heathland, characterised by light, sandy and acidic soils. Once upon a time the Sandlings stretched in a continuous line between Ipswich and Lowestoft, but nowadays only fragments remain.

One such fragment is **Dunwich Heath**, managed by the National Trust and located in the **Suffolk Coast and Heaths Area of Outstanding Natural Beauty**.

> **Look and keep a listen out for nightjar on this walk**

Here the grassland, wet woodland, coconut-scented gorse and bell heather harbour rare birds such as the nightjar and Dartford warbler, and if you follow this route at dusk, especially

on a warm, still summer evening, you may have a rare opportunity to listen the hypnotic churring song of the nightjar.

▶ START
With the old coastguard cottages on the right, walk forward a few paces and turn left to pass the **Field Studies Barn**. Don't miss the sculptured bronze head of a nightjar set in an oak plank.

Turn right by a picnic area and look for a purple-banded post. Continue on a narrow path that gently rises with tracts of heather and gorse either side.

Listen out for the churring song made by the nightjar as it hunts for insects between dusk and dawn. A migrant from Africa, the nightjar arrives in the middle of May to spend summer on the Sandlings. It's an elusive bird and its grey-brown, mottled feathers provide the perfect camouflage when nesting on the ground or perched in a tree. With its silent flight and haunting song, the bird has an almost supernatural reputation and is sometimes referred to as the goatsucker, owing to its mythical ability to steal milk from goats.

Keep a look out for tawny owls, plus noctule and pipistrelle bats that may be active in the late evening. There may be red and munjac around deer, along with

a hobby hawking for dragonflies. Earlier in the day, Dartford warblers and stonechats are often seen, singing from nearby gorse bushes.

1 | ¾ MILE
Stay on the path as it descends to the bottom of a shallow valley with acidic grassland on the right. The first of two fenced-off areas contain soft sand and the nest holes of antlions, small insects that grab their prey with a pair of long, spiny, pointed jaws.

Continue ahead and bear right downhill. Swing left and follow yellow and green-banded posts, continuing along the path with a sloping bank on the left and wet woodland on the right.

2 | 1¼ MILES
Continue to **Nightjar Corner**, a good spot to listen out for these shy creatures. Keep forward to reach **Docwra's Ditch**, a lovely reeded area of water. Pass a further antlion enclosure and shortly arrive at **Centenary Pond**, where water voles may be present.

Carry straight on for 300m and afterwards swing left by a marker post to climb up a bank. Pause a on a nearby seat for spectacular views over **Minsmere** and beyond, then retrace your steps back to your departure point.

Walk at dusk over the **Suffolk Sandlings Heath** to listen out for the churring nightjar and encounter other nocturnal wildlife

KEY   ▲INFO

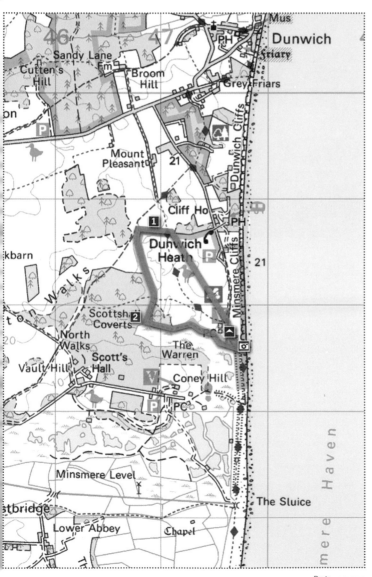

TERRAIN
Waymarked paths across heathland.

HOW TO GET THERE
BY CAR: Leave the A12 north of Yoxford and a take road signposted to Westleton and Dunwich. Follow signposts to Dunwich Heath.
BY PUBLIC TRANSPORT: Coastlink buses from Darsham and Saxmundham train stations, book only on ☎ 01728 833526

MAP
Ordnance Survey Explorer Map 212 and 231.
Grid ref: TM 477 678

NEARBY EXCURSIONS
Orford Castle
☎ 01394 450472
www.english-heritage.org.uk
Open all year round.

MORE INFO
Southwold Tourist Information Centre
69 High Street, Southwold
Suffolk IP18 6DS
☎ 01502 724729

Dunwich Heath
Dunwich, Saxmundham, Suffolk IP17 3DJ
☎ 01728 648501
www.nationaltrust.org.uk
Open daily, Mar- Sept dawn-dusk, check website for other times.

East of England Tourism
visiteastofengland.com
☎ 01284 727470

Route ———

Cromer
Aylsham
Taverham
Norwich
The Broads
Attleborough
Lowestoft
BERNEY MARSHES

Berney Marshes Norfolk

Distance 7 miles (11 km) **Type** Moderate **Time** 3 hours

This route takes you through rustling reed-bordered marsh tracks and along the flood banks of **Breydon Water** where wigeon, shelducks and Bewick's swans winter.

▶ START

From Stone Road in **Halvergate**, take the track that leads to the right, straight into the marsh landscape passing **Mutton's Drainage Mill** to the south. During the Roman period this area was an estuarine environment; the linear dykes and channels are evidence to centuries of drainage work and the importance of wind power to control the ever-changing water levels.

The path heads towards **Marshman's Cottage**, with the redundant **Stones' Drainage Mill** beyond, and continues to **Berney** 📷 **Arms Mill**, a long-standing focal point in this flat landscape. A track from Wickhampton meets the path from the right and, about 365m further on, crosses a footbridge with a gate on either side of the dyke. The route then enters cattle-grazed marsh to the railway line crossing at **Berney Arms Station**.

▶ Mutton's Mill overlooks an estuarine environment populated by water deer, wigeon and barn owls

1 3 MILES

The mill marks a transition from marsh to riverbank; originally the wind-powered mill ground a constituent of cement, before conversion to a drainage mill, assisting the reduction of marsh water levels. Heading towards **Berney Arms Pub**, follow the path along the flood-protecting bank in a typical Norfolk Broads landscape – the realm of the sedge cutters. Sedge and reed cutting remains a centuries-old harvesting industry, the winter-cut reeds being used for roofing material on thatched cottages, churches and agricultural buildings. The more flexible sedge, harvested during the summer months, is used for roof ridge and capping locations. New and old drainage pumps dot the marsh landscape to the north as the tidal section of the River Yare to the south opens into

Breydon Water.

The extensive mudflats are home to wintering wigeon, shelducks, Bewick's swans and many other birds that enjoy this inter-tidal habitat. The culvert at **Breydon Pump** marks the end of the flood-bank trail, and the track drops down below sea level again and on to the marsh route.

2 4½ MILES

As the path follows the **Weavers Way** west through **Beighton Marshes**, the wide track is bordered by reed and sedge-lined dykes. The adjoining flood meadows are rich feeding grounds for flocks of curlew and open hunting land for short-eared owls. The Fleet channel forms a

southern water boundary as the trail passes **Howard's** and **High's Drainage Mills**. The route is obvious as it curves through the heart of **Halvergate Marshes**. In this secluded length of trail, the shy, secretive water deer can be seen emerging from reeds to graze. The walk reaches its conclusion soon 📷 after passing **Manor Farm**. Berney Arms Mill, the country's tallest wind pump, remains a constant sentinel. In a fading sunset it's a magnificent backdrop that may be accompanied by the silent flickering of the wings of the barn owls as they hunt. As the walk reaches the west end of Halvergate Marshes, rejoin Stone Lane and the car parking area.

Explore the history of sedge cutting industry in the **Norfolk Broads**, a watery world of marsh, Broad and river that sparkles beneath wide-open skies

KEY

▶INFO

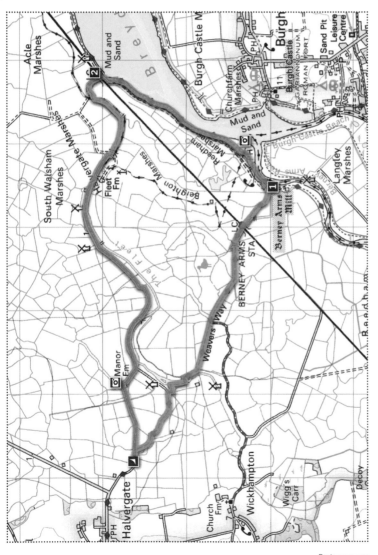

Route ————

TERRAIN
The walk is on grassy tracks and paths, which can be muddy. Cattle and sheep graze the marsh grassland, so keep dogs on leads and securely close farm gates. The path goes into the RSPB Halvergate Reserve; there are no visitor facilities.

HOW TO GET THERE
BY CAR: From Norwich follow the A47 towards Acle, turn right after Tunstall onto Branch Road, towards Halvergate, then left into Stone Road. Stone Lane is the main public access point for the reserve.
BY PUBLIC TRANSPORT: Wherry Lines operate a regular train.
www.wherrylines.org.uk
Berney Railway Station is in the centre of the walk but does not have any vehicular access.
Bus Routes are limited.
www.carlberry.co.uk

MAP
Ordnance Survey Explorer Map OL40.
Grid ref: TG 433 067

NEARBY EXCURSIONS
Berney Arms Windmill has recently been refurbished and is once again open to the public, albeit on a limited basis.
english-heritage.org.uk

MORE INFO
Norfolk Tourism
www.visitnorfolk.co.uk

Berney Marshes and Breydon Water Nature Reserves
☎ 01493 700645
www.rspb.org.uk

EAST

HOLKHAM ▶
Docking•
Cromer•
Fakenham•
Holt•
Aylsham•
•Gayton
Swaffham•
Norwich•
Attleborough•

Holkham Beach Norfolk

Distance 5 miles (8 km) **Type** Easy **Time** 3 hours

▶ START

Starting from the **Victoria Hotel** walk along **Lady Ann's Drive** for half a mile, accompanied perhaps by horses on their way to canter in the sea. The Holkham area is a haven for migrating birds arriving from colder climates – take a 📷 look across the grazing marshes for large flocks of wigeon ducks, the males conspicuous with their buff cream and chestnut heads. Start early and you may even witness one of nature's greatest spectacles – hundreds of pink-footed geese taking flight at dawn, making their way to inland fields for feeding before returning at late afternoon to roost. The high-domed sky, filled

▶ THE PUB

Relax in these cosy surroundings after a bracing beach walk. Owned by the Coke family since 1837, the **Victoria Hotel** prides itself in sourcing seafood from the Norfolk coast and game shot on the local Holkham estate. There is a comprehensive wine list to choose from and a wide selection of delicious real ales. Spacious rooms reflect Victorian and Colonial periods with furniture imported from India.

with skeins of geese circling and calling, is simply breathtaking and a sight not to be missed.

1 2½ MILES

Pass through a gate to enter **Holkham Nature Reserve**. The beach is one of the most unspoilt and beautiful stretches of sand in the country, and if it looks familiar, you may remember Gwyneth Paltrow walking across the sand at low tide during the closing scenes of the film *Shakespeare In Love*. Carry straight on along a boardwalk to Holkham Bay. Behind the shoreline lies a semi-circular basin, which, at very high tides, rapidly fills to form a spectacular shallow lagoon.

2 2½ MILES

Turn right and continue along the beach in an easterly direction, skirting pinewoods on the right. 📷 Make a brief detour if you wish to view any small wading birds on the tideline, which is another half-mile away to your left. Breathe in the bracing sea air and maintain direction along a wind-swept beach, which is far too expansive to be overcrowded. Tread carefully among the white-gold sand and you may discover seashells of every shape and hue. Keep a look out around the dunes for visitors such as shorelarks and snow buntings in winter. The larks are easily

recognised by their dull black and sandy facial patterns, while the snow buntings are also easy to spot, with their white wing patches and a loud, clear call.

3 2½ MILES

At the far end of some beach huts, cross a wooden bridge and swing right beside the coastal lookout building. In front of you are grand views 📷 looking towards **Wells Harbour**, with the lifeboat station on your left. Turn right to walk through a car

park and exit by a kissing gate. Pass a boating lake and, in 70m, turn left to join the **Peddar's Way** and **Norfolk Coast Path**. Follow the stony path beside the relative silence of the pinewoods. Hereabouts you may be fortunate enough to see birds of prey such as harriers or kestrels quartering the marshes. Finally emerge into Lady Ann's Drive and return to the Victoria Hotel to relax and unwind in pleasant surroundings with some fine locally-sourced food.

▶ Holkham beach offers an uncrowded haven for walkers in winter

▶ A canter in the dunes is an exciting, fun-filled alternative to a walk

Take an invigorating walk along an unspoilt beach and witness one of **nature's greatest spectacles** – fantastic in winter months

KEY

▶INFO

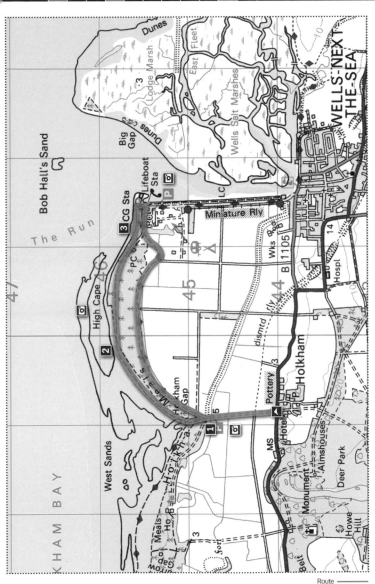

TERRAIN
Mostly sandy beach and stony earth paths.

HOW TO GET THERE
BY CAR: Holkham is 2 miles west of Wells-next-the-Sea on the main A149 coast road.
BY PUBLIC TRANSPORT: The Coast Hopper bus runs in either direction from Kings Lynn and Sheringham.

MAP
Ordnance Survey Explorer Map 251.
Grid ref: TF 890 439

NEARBY EXCURSIONS
Holkham Hall is closed during winter months, but the park is open every day of the year except Christmas Day.
☎ 01328 710227
www.holkham.co.uk

MORE INFO
Wells-next-the-Sea Tourist Information Office is open Easter-Oct
☎ 01328 710885
www.visitnorthnorfolk.com
www.wellsnorfolk.com

Victoria Hotel
Holkham, Wells-next-the-Sea, Norfolk NR23 1RG
☎ 01328 711008
www.holkham.co.uk/victoria

Route ——

BURNHAM
OVERY STAITHE

King's
Lynn

Norwich•

Lowestoft•

Ely•   Thetford•

Burnham Overy Staithe Norfolk

Distance 5 miles (8 km) **Type** Easy **Time** 4 hours

This invigorating ramble over farmland tracks and marsh is set under an ever-changing sky where harriers rake the wind and thousands of pink-footed geese fly home to their roosts. Finish with a well-earned drink by a log fire in one of the coast's many old pubs.

▶ START

From the **Staithe Head** along **East Harbour Lane**, cross **Tower Road** into **Gong Lane**, where the road becomes a lane and peters out to a farm track protected from the often biting winds. The slight incline is deceptive for the views that open up around all points of the compass. **Burnham Overy Towermill** is a constant landmark throughout the walk providing an interesting and historic focal point.

The flourmill was built in 1816 and worked in conjunction with **Burnham Overy Watermill**, constructed in 1790, which nestles over the **River Burn** a short distance away.

After a mile the track turns right along a former drove road. The embankments and high hedges, abundant with berries, form an ideal larder in winter for redwings, fieldfares and waxwings. At the road turn left on a path that runs through the churchyard of St Clement in Burnham Overy, then head across the road and on to a tarmac footpath opposite.

> Catch the phenomenal sight of tens of thousands of pink-footed geese in flight over north Norfolk

1 1¾ MILES

Beyond the river bridge turn right up **Friars Lane**. Opposite the footpath beside the playing fields you'll find the ruins of **Burnham Priory**, the first Carmelite Foundation in the country, founded in 1241 by friars who fled the loss of Mount Carmel during the crusades.

Walk along the narrow path to **Herrings Lane,** and then follow this to the church and **Cross Lane**, which is actually a track. Much of the walk follows old routes that have slowly become redundant save for walkers; they afford a delightful perspective of the surrounding landscape and beyond to the coastal area. The

expansive skies give you the opportunity to scan the skies for marsh and hen harriers, frequently seen as dark outlines gliding over the marshes, searching for prey.

2 2½ MILES

At the end of Cross Lane turn right, then take a slight right-hand bend to enter farmland on the left with a descent towards **Burnham Norton**. At the bottom of the field cross the road and head through the hamlet; as the lane turns sharp left enter the coastal marshes on the right.

3 3½ MILES

Follow the path beside cattle grazed marsh, which in winter is home

to teal, widgeon, lapwing and geese, then climb to the top of the sea bank for expansive views over salt marshes on one side and grazed marsh on the other.

As dusk clothes the landscape this can be a wonderful spot to watch skeins of pink-footed geese flying in to roost.

The path now loops along the bank then heads back inland to a junction over the River Burn. Walk diagonally left across a field past Burnham Overy Towermill into Burnham Overy Staithe. Then turn left into **West Harbour Way** and return to the start of the walk.

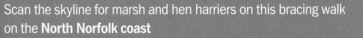

Scan the skyline for marsh and hen harriers on this bracing walk
on the **North Norfolk coast**

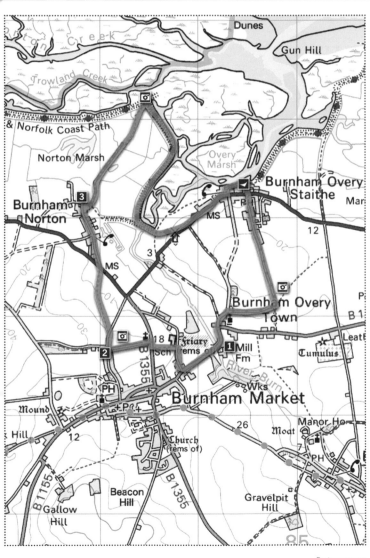

TERRAIN
The tracks and lanes will be muddy during wet weather. Short sections of footpath.

HOW TO GET THERE
BY CAR: Follow the A149 coast road from Kings Lynn to Burnham Overy Staithe. Free parking can be found just off East Harbour Way.
BY PUBLIC TRANSPORT: There is a regular Coast Hopper service which can be caught from Kings Lynn Bus Station and also from Norwich. This drops you off opposite The Hero in Burnham Overy Staithe.

MAP
Ordnance Survey Landranger Map 132.
Grid ref: TF 845 443

CAMPSITE
Deepdale Camping
Deepdale Farm, Burnham Deepdale, Kings Lynn
PE31 8DD
☎ 01485 210256
www.deepdalefarm.co.uk

MORE INFO
Norfolk Tourism
www.visitnorfolk.co.uk

Wells-Next-The-Sea Tourist Information Centre
Staithe Street,
Wells-Next-The-Sea
NR23 1AN
www.visitnorthnorfolk.com

Route ───────

The Wash Norfolk

Distance 7¼ miles (11.6 km) **Type** Easy **Time** 4½ hours

Skegness
THE WASH
Kings Lynn
Wisbech
Norwich
Lowestoft
Cambridge · Newmarket
Ipswich
Colchester
Harlow · Chelmsford
· Basildon

▷ Watch as the tide comes in and hundreds of thousands of waders are pushed towards the land

As the largest estuarine system in the UK, **The Wash** makes a significant contribution to global biodiversity in its role as a stopping-off point on the major migratory routes of wildfowl and waders, which use these coastal wetlands and estuaries as habitats for feeding, roosting and breeding. Sea level rises and climate change are major threats to this coast and fenland environment. Storm surges sufficient to overwhelm the coastal defences are becoming ever more likely. Yet managing the tide height will create its own problems, with a major impact on marginal habitats such as salt marsh, mudflats and sandbanks.

In 1863 Edward VII, the then Prince of Wales, alighted with his bride Princess Alexandra at Wolferton on their way to nearby Sandringham. The village was the location for the Royal Family's Railway Station before it closed in the 1960s.

▶ START

Park at **Dersingham Bog National Nature Reserve**. Walk down the hill, passing the railway crossing gates. Go to the side of **Marsh Farm** and follow the track beyond the farm buildings. After 600m, at a convergence of tracks, walk over the bank, turn right, and head towards a line of trees. Carry straight on to **Wolferton Pumping Station** to your left.

1 1¾ MILES

Head up the steps left of the gates and turn right along the grass bank. After 200m, as the track swings right, carry straight on.

Birdwatchers converge hereabouts, witnessing the thousands of wading birds that are pushed in to the roost banks and islands in front of the RSPB hides on big tides. When the tide comes in, clouds-like masses of hundreds of thousands of knots shimmer over the mudflats as they are pushed further towards the land. Around two million birds use this embayment of the North Sea for feeding and roosting during their annual migrations. Aim for the four wooden benches to enjoy some splendid views.

Continue onwards to **Shepherd's Port**. At the pebbled shoreline, walk in front of the RYA Training Centre and two white buildings, before heading up to a grey gate. Turn right along the road.

2 3¾ MILES

Head uphill, pass a telephone box and turn right at the entrance, signed 'KLAA Lakes' and 'Snettisham Nature Reserve'. At the far side of the RSPB car park, follow the path signed 'Rotary Hide 1.5km'. Pass several lagoons (old gravel pits); these are an important roost for waders. The pits stretch for more than 1½ miles. At **Rotary Hide**, turn left at the 'Circular Walk' sign. Follow the path past another lagoon, then **Roost Hide** and **Sanctuary Hide**.

3 5½ MILES

Keep left and pick up the fence line, which leads you back to the grass bank and Wolferton Pumping Station. Walk past the farm buildings. Note the solitary English oak, planted in memory of an RAF pilot who died when his Tornado crashed near here in 1983. Head into Wolferton, turn left at the T-junction and retrace your steps to the car park. Wander into Dersingham Bog National Nature Reserve, which represents one of the few remaining wilderness areas left in this part of Norfolk's landscape.

Immerse yourself in **The Wash**, renowned for its striking natural beauty and its magnificent birdlife

▶INFO

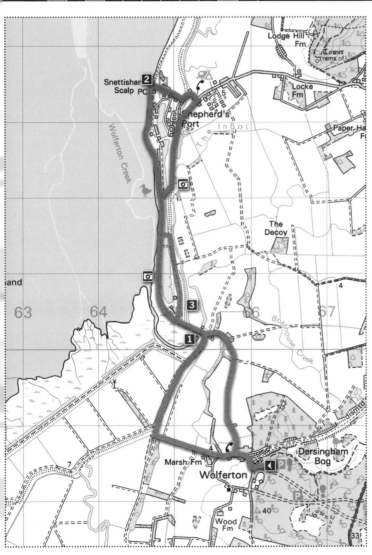

TERRAIN
In the main, the route is easy to follow on wide farm tracks, open land, concrete roads and gravel paths, some of which can be boggy underfoot after rain. Don't forget your binoculars.

ACCESS
For wheelchair users, leave the car at the large car park close to the beach at Shepherd's Port, and head southwards along the road towards the mudflats and hides.

HOW TO GET THERE
BY CAR: Take the A419 north from King's Lynn and, after 5 miles, turn left to Wolferton. As you head through the trees you will come to a crossroads. Go straight over and into the car park down the hill on the right. There is only room for about 10 cars.
BY PUBLIC TRANSPORT: Norfolk Green runs the popular Coasthopper service along the north Norfolk coast all-year round, including daily runs from King's Lynn to Cromer. You will need to alight at Castle Rising and hike the rest of the way to Wolferton, mostly along the main A149.
www.coasthopper.co.uk

MAP
Ordnance Survey Landranger Map 132.
Grid ref: TF 664 274

MORE INFO
King's Lynn Tourist Information Centre
The Custom House, Purfleet Quay, King's Lynn PE30 1HP
☎ 01553 763044
www.west-norfolk.gov.uk

Snettisham RSPB Reserve
☎ 01485 542689
www.rspb.org.uk

Route ———

HEART OF ENGLAND

Welcome to the quintessential English countryside. The Heart of England is also the heart of the rural dream, the idyll so beloved of manufacturers of boxes of fudge and jigsaw puzzles. Sweeping hills, tiny cottages, majestic church spires, all connected by dry stone walls, painstakingly built mile upon mile.

Nowhere better sums up this picture-perfect scene than the **Cotswolds**. Like much of the central region of England, the Cotswolds were built on the fortunes of the golden fleece. Wool was king, and the area even took its name from the industry ('cot' means a sheep's enclosure and 'wold' is a rolling hillside). The many grand houses and achingly charming churches were all bankrolled by the wool merchants and though the industry has all but died, the legacy lives on.

Away from the tourist traps and retaining the allure of a slower pace of life, the wider reaches of **Gloucestershire** abound with seemingly slumbering villages, and on the border with Wales is the lush calm of the **Royal Forest of Dean**. Further north, the marches – once fierce battleground between England and Wales – provides a beguiling mixture of farmland, moor, wooded valleys and half-timbered buildings. You're never far from the ruins of a castle, a reminder of the bloody history of the land, but today, the tranquillity of **Herefordshire** and **Worcestershire** is almost tangible.

Traditional British food abounds in the Heart of England. **Ludlow**, nestled in the **Shropshire Hills**, has crowned itself capital of the modern slow food movement and hosts an annual food festival. But there are many culinary delights to be had here: think of Shropshire Blue, Double Gloucester, Red Leicester, Sage Derby and Stilton – made only in **Derbyshire**, **Nottinghamshire** and **Leicestershire**. Melton Mowbray pork pies also put Leicestershire firmly on the food map, alongside Lincolnshire sausages, while the whole region is famed for its waters: **Malvern**, **Buxton** and **Ashbourne** – enough to quench the thirst of an army of walkers.

But of course, for walkers, there's a far more compelling reason to visit – the **Peak District**. It's not for nothing that the Peak District is the second most visited National Park in the world (pipped to the post only by Japan's Mount Fuji). Crossed with a veritable honeycomb of trails and paths, the Peaks offer exhilarating hikes over moorland and gentler strolls on limestone hills, and here too the lengthy **Pennine Way**, starts on its thrilling meander up to Scotland.

Clipsham Rutland

Distance 3 miles (5 km) **Type** Easy **Time** 2 hours

›Take in the scenery on this satisfying stroll through Rutland

› THE PUB

Church pews arranged around log-burning fires, menus on chalkboards, and an intimate atmosphere that's full of character – it's no wonder **The Olive Branch** was awarded the title of Michelin Pub of the Year in 2008. Expect proper British hospitality, with complimentary roasted chestnuts on the bar and mulled wine on sale throughout Christmas, ready for walkers coming in from the cold.

› START

Cross the road from the pub and take the first left along a public footpath. Go through a gate and walk diagonally left through the field, then follow the path alongside a cornfield towards an evergreen wood ahead.
Pass over a bridge and along the path to the left of the trees. Watch out for the brown and white mottled fallow deer and the much smaller, muntjac – listen out for their barking call along the wooded sections of the walk. Carry straight on after the wood finishes, past a pond.

At the next field boundary turn left and walk along the edge of the quarry – a landscape of exposed white limestone cliffs. Clipsham stone has been well known since Roman times, when it was used to build villas on the road from London to Lincoln.

Turn right and walk down into the quarry. Watch your step, the limestone spoil can get slippery after rain. Cross the quarry road and walk up the ridge ahead, following the bridleway sign up the hill. In an old quarry on your left you can see the vegetation start to reclaim this man-made landscape. Take the path along the edge of the field as the track veers into the wood. To your right you can see expansive views over cornfields and to your left lies the ancient **Pickworth Great Wood**.

1 1 MILE

At the corner of the field, take the bridge into the woods, rather than the path in the far corner. Follow the path through the woods and to a gate, then cut diagonally through the crop field towards a line of trees. Go through a gate and bear left along the edge of the field until you reach a road. Turn left and enter **Pickworth**. In a clearing on your left is a restored lime kiln where John Clare, known as the Peasant Poet, worked as a limeburner back in the early 1800s. Clare's

work celebrates nature and the cycle of rural life, and many of his verses contain his distinctive local dialect: he uses the word pooty to describe a snail, crizzle means to crisp and throstle means song thrush.

2 1½ MILES

Take the first left at the public bridleway sign past farm buildings. Through the gate, follow the path left around the field. Follow the yellow signposted path through **Pickworth Great Wood**. Keep your eyes and ears peeled for muntjac deer, which can easily camouflage in the thick undergrowth. When you reach a junction of five paths, keep straight ahead.

3 2¾ MILES

As you leave the wood there are great views over Rutland to your left. Follow the path downhill past a farmhouse. At the road, turn left then, after 5m, right along a public footpath. Turn left and follow the path as it bears right past a paddock. After a gate bear left, following the field boundary and hedge. There's a pheasant farm on your right, so watch out for the birds scrabbling in the hedgerow. Carry on ahead, through a cropfield until you reach **Clipsham**, where it's straight ahead and left to the Olive Branch.

Walk in Britain's smallest county and enjoy an **ancient woodland**, a peasant poet and an award-winning pub

KEY

▶INFO

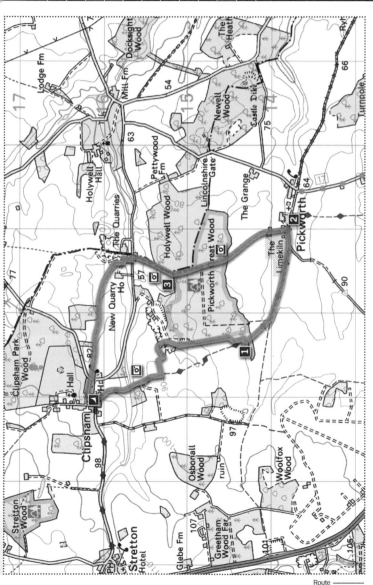

TERRAIN
Well-marked public footpaths and woodland tracks. These can be muddy after rain, so bring wellies or walking boots.

HOW TO GET THERE
BY CAR: Clipsham is 37 miles east of Leicester, just off the A1.
BY PUBLIC TRANSPORT: The nearest train station is Oakham, which is found on a main line between Cambridge and Birmingham.

MAP
Ordnance Survey Landranger Map 130.
Grid ref: SK 965 165

MORE INFO
www.discover-rutland.co.uk
www.rutnet.co.uk

The Olive Branch Pub
Main Street, Clipsham,
Rutland LE15 7SH
☎ 01780 410355
www.theolivebranchpub.com

Route ——

Normamby •
Le Wold
          Stainton •
          Le Vale
Walesby •

TEALBY ▶
• Market Rasen

The Wolds Lincolnshire

Distance 9 miles (14½ km) **Type** Moderate **Time** 4½ hours

▶ Picnic spots and views abound on this picturesque ramble through countryside rich in tradition

▶ START

At **Tealby** walk up the steps to **All Saints church.** The church dates back to the 12th century and is made from locally quarried ironstone. Inside you'll find a memorial to **George Tennyson,** grandfather to poet laureate Alfred Lord Tennyson. Walk left through the churchyard to the road, then along **Rasen Road** for 100m before turning right at the public footpath sign to Walesby. Pass through a gate and follow **The Viking Way** through the field, watching out for buzzards and kestrels circling the sky. Follow the yellow markers as they direct you through a kissing gate then along the edge of the next field. Cross over a bridge and walk through a gateway, continuing uphill. At the next yellow marker, bear right, skirting around the

base of the hill towards farm buildings. At the gate in the corner turn right and follow the footpath alongside the woods. Now pass through a gate and follow the field boundary to your right, keeping an eye out for yellow markers. Look to your left for outstanding views towards the **River Trent**. In the fields on your right you may notice a flock of **Lincoln Longwools**, a native rare breed of sheep with a long dreadlocked coat. Cross the farm track and follow the line of the fence. Cross a bridleway, and after a kissing gate, continue diagonally uphill. Continue along the path as it veers steeply downhill into the valley and then up the other side. The path can be a little slippery here so watch your step. The bumps on your left are yellow meadow anthills,

▶ All three of the churches visited on this walk have open doors and welcome visitors

which attract green woodpeckers from the nearby woodland. At the top bear left towards the Rambler's Church.

1 | 2 MILES

The atmospheric **Rambler's Church** is a great place to shelter from the weather and enjoy a picnic. Unusually for such a small village, **Walesby** has two churches, the original **All Saints'** on the hill top and **St Mary's** in the centre of the village, which was built in 1913 when it was assumed parishioners were unwilling to walk

up to the church on the hill. Inside you'll find a stunning stained glass **Rambler's Window.** Walk left around the church and through a gate, then down the hill. Take a right at the road, before turning left after 15m down **Moor Road.** Turn right at the bridleway sign and follow the trail to the end of the field, before bearing left across the next field to a cattle grid. Pass through the gate and walk uphill. As the path forks bear right around the hill, looking back for amazing views over the Wolds. Pass through a gate and follow the footpath alongside a dry stone wall. Follow the path as it zigzags along the edge of the field, before passing through a gate and walking along the right of the field. Climb over a stile and on to **Normanby Le Wold.**

2 | 4 MILES

Walk past the church, then take a left-hand footpath leading downhill along the edge of Claxby wood into the village. Turn left at the road along **Normanby Rise**, and follow it as it turns sharp left. When the road bends right, continue ahead down a minor road. Turn left up a track just before a farm. After half a mile this brings you back to the fork where the path split just north of Walesby. Here you rejoin the Viking Way and retrace your steps back to Tealby.

This wonderfully scenic walk in the Wolds proves that the
Lincolnshire countryside is anything but flat

INFO

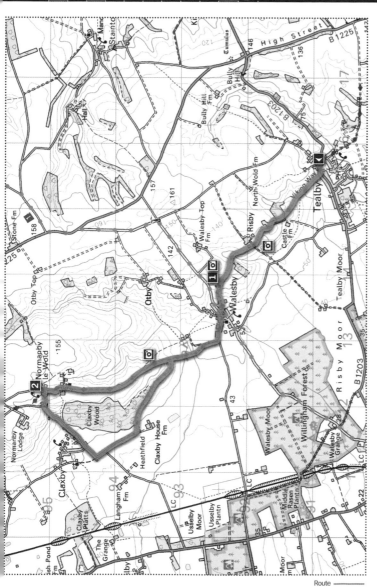

TERRAIN
Waymarked footpaths, minor roads and bridleways. Some steep sections, which may be slippery after wet weather. Some sections may be muddy.

HOW TO GET THERE
BY CAR: Tealby is northeast from Lincoln on the A46 to Market Rasen, then the B1203. Roadside parking is available in the village, but please park with consideration.
BY PUBLIC TRANSPORT: A flexible call and connect bus service is available from Market Rasen. Bookings can be made by calling the MATRIX booking line on 0845 234 3344 at least two hours before you wish to travel. Bookings are dependent on the availability of seats and are allocated on a first come first served basis.

MAP
Ordnance Survey Explorer Map 282.
Grid ref: TF 155 905

MORE INFO
www.visitlincolnshire.com
www.lincswolds.org.uk

Route ———

· Bradford
Pontefract ·
        Scunthorpe ·
Doncaster ·
The Peak ·   · Sheffield
District
Chesterfield ·   ▶ CRESWELL
      Mansfield ·   CRAGS
            Balderton ·
Nottingham ·
Derby ·
Loughborough ·

Creswell Crags Derbyshire

Distance 6½ miles (10.4 km) **Type** Easy/Moderate **Time** 3-4 hours

The caves and fissures that line this dramatic limestone gorge on the Derbyshire/Nottinghamshire border have unearthed a treasure trove of prehistoric finds, including primitive tools and Britain's only Ice Age rock art. Early hunters, sheltering in the caves, engraved figures of birds, bison, deer and horse on the rock walls, and you can learn more about what life must have been like for our ancestors between 10,000 and 50,000 years ago at the new **Museum and Archaeology Park**. However, the **Creswell Crags Heritage Area** also contains a number of other important natural sites, and this walk visits **Markland Grips**, a wildlife-rich limestone valley whose caves have yielded Neolithic human remains.

▶ Step back up to 50,000 years and explore a limestone gorge that was once home to prehistoric man

▶ START

From the car park, walk down past the visitor centre and through **Crags Meadows** to reach the lake. Follow the waterside path (on either bank – you can return on the other) all the way to the western end, where the two paths meet up. There are information panels along both routes and steps to the most prominent caves, but for a closer inspection, book your place one of the popular guided cave tours that run every weekend.

1 | ½ MILE

Continue along a wide track out of the valley that eventually becomes a lane. At the end go left, then right on to the A616. Turn left on Elmton Road and walk through the centre of **Creswell**. On the left is the Model Village, built in the late 1890s for the workforce of the newly-opened **Creswell Colliery** and whose 286 houses are built around a huge octagonal green.

2 | 1½ MILES

Continue out of Creswell until the road swings left at a junction. Go straight ahead for a public footpath to the right of the hedge that crosses fields to reach the small village of **Elmton**.

3 | 2½ MILES

Turn right and walk along the peaceful Markland Lane, all the way to the junction at the very far end. Turn sharp right over a stile for a signposted field path to the left of Markland Farm, after which you join a wide, hedged track downhill. At the bottom turn right on to a disused railway line and then, when you reach a former viaduct, follow the path down into Markland Grips and swing left (a 'grip' is a local term for a narrow, steep-sided gorge). The lower part of Markland Grips is owned by Derbyshire Wildlife Trust, which manages it as a nature reserve – bluebell, wood anemone and dog's mercury are among the woodland flowers that can be found here.

4 | 4¼ MILES

Follow the clear path along the bottom of the valley, close to the foot of the cliffs. At the far end go right on to a surfaced drive, past an education centre, and where this comes out at a road go left. Turn right on to Skinner Street and walk the pavement back into the centre of Creswell. At the end turn left to rejoin the outward route back to Creswell Crags.

Travel back in time on this archaeological adventure and unearth
the secrets of **Derbyshire's impressive limestone gorges**

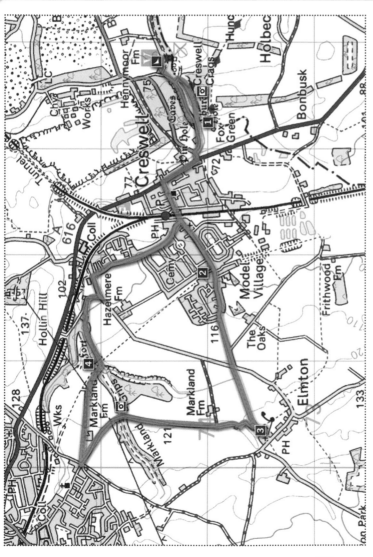

TERRAIN
Mostly firm paths and field
tracks, but can be slippery in
Markland Grips.

ACCESS
All paths around the Creswell
Crags site are accessible
by wheelchair.

HOW TO GET THERE
BY CAR: Located off A60/
A616 south of Worksop,
or north from Mansfield.
Creswell Crags is 1 mile east
of Creswell village.
BY PUBLIC TRANSPORT:
Creswell Station, on the Robin
Hood Line from Nottingham,
is 15 minutes walk away from
the Crags.

MAP
Ordnance Survey Explorer
Map 270.
Grid ref: SK 537 745

NEARBY EXCURSIONS
Poulter Country Park is two
miles south of Creswell
between Langwith and
Whaley Thorns. The
wildflower meadows boast
large numbers of cowslips,
and from the viewpoint you
can see across Welbeck Park
to Lincoln Cathedral on a
clear day.

MORE INFO
Creswell Crags Visitor Centre
Crags Road, Welbeck,
Worksop S80 3LH
☎ 01909 720378
www.creswell-crags.org.uk

Route

Sherwood Forest Nottinghamshire

Distance 4½ miles (7 km) **Type** Easy **Time** 2½ hours

Worksop • • Retford
• Chesterfield
Mansfield • ▶ EDWINSTOWE

Nottingham •
Derby • Grantham •

Like the medieval rogue himself, the forests of olde England have largely faded into the mists of time. **Sherwood Forest** offers tantalising glimpses into this lost world, an enticing mix of woodland, heath and glades, scattered with oaks that started growing when Robin was a lad. The forest is a **National Nature Reserve**, protecting Western Europe's greatest concentration of ancient trees.

▶ START

Facing the **Visitor Centre** from the car park, turn sharp left along the waymarked **Greenwood Walk** and walk to a major junction of tracks. Keep straight ahead past the barrier on to a track that runs just within the forest's edge, with fields to your left. This particular woodland is named **Birklands**: here the old gentlemen of the woods stand gaunt and decaying. Contorted guardians of the forest, these gnarled and twisted old oaks loom from the shadows as they have for well over 600 years. There are nearly 1,000 such trees in Sherwood. After a mile you reach a T-junction and a wide, grassy forest ride.

1 1¼ MILES

Turn right, shortly reaching the **Centre Tree**, a modest oak said to mark the centre of the medieval Sherwood. At this junction of paths and cycle route 6, continue

> Even without the legendary tales of Robin Hood in mind, the Major Oak is a superb sight to behold

ahead along the avenue of majestic birch trees.

Sherwood Forest is the traditional home of Robin Hood, a shadowy figure of legend and folklore. His connection to Sherwood is based largely on a medieval poem held at Lincoln Cathedral – hence his clothes of Lincoln green. Other 14th century documents record that, after the Battle of Boroughbridge in 1322, Robert Hode, an outlaw, took refuge in Barnsdale Forest in nearby Yorkshire, in those days part of Sherwood Forest.

In a further ½ mile you reach another major waymarked crossroad. Turn right, pass the barrier and keep ahead at the nearby junction, leaving the signed bridlepath, and walking through airy birch, fir woods. Recently longhorn cattle, a breed common in medieval times but rare today, are being used to graze the undergrowth and help restore the medieval heathland. Remain on the main path; in a mile you reach a crossway at the corner of an expanse of heathland, **Budby South Forest**.

2 3½ MILES

Turn right beside the barrier and walk to a major junction. Turn right towards the **Major Oak**, keeping the fence to your left, to reach this behemoth of Sherwood. For more than 200 years its huge limbs have been supported by props. Up to 1,000 years old, it is the biggest, heaviest oak in Britain, estimated to weigh 23 tonnes. Little wonder that legends tell of Robin Hood and his Merry Men hiding within its trunk! From here follow signs back to the nearby Visitor Centre.

Explore ancient **Sherwood Forest**, where Robin hood romanced
Maid Marion and taunted the sherrif of Nottingham

KEY

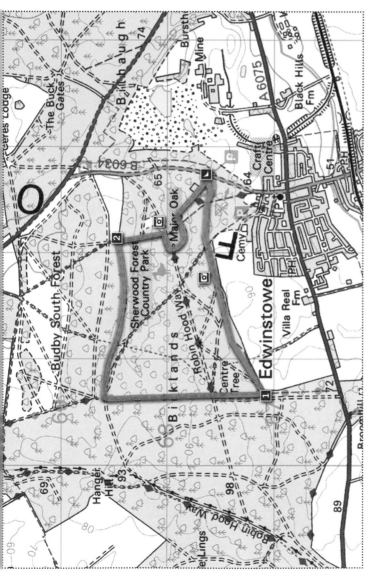

Route ——————

▶INFO

TERRAIN
Compacted tracks and
woodland paths.

HOW TO GET THERE
BY CAR: Edwinstowe is
5 miles northeast of
Mansfield on the A6075.
The Sherwood Forest
National Nature Reserve
and Visitor Centre is well
signposted to the north of
the village. Free parking
on weekdays; charged at
weekends and bank holidays.
BY PUBLIC TRANSPORT:
Buses to Edwinstowe from
Mansfield and Nottingham
☎ 0871 200 2233
travelineeastmidlands.org.uk

MAP
Ordnance Survey Explorer
Map 270.
Grid ref: SK 626 676

NEARBY EXCURSIONS
Sherwood Forest Farm Park
Lambs Pen Farm,
Edwinstowe NG21 9HL
☎ 01623 823558
**www.sherwoodforest
farmpark.co.uk**

MORE INFO
Sherwood Forest National
Nature Reserve
Edwinstowe, Mansfield
NG21 9HN
☎ 0844 9808080.

Ollerton Tourist
Information Centre
Ollerton Roundabout,
Sherwood Heath NG22 9DR
☎ 01623 824545

Nottinghamshire Tourism
☎ 08444 775678
www.visitnottingham.com

105

Deepdale Derbyshire

Distance 6 miles (10 km) **Type** Moderate **Time** 4½ hours

Oldham • · Barnsley•
·Manchester
Ecclesfield•
·Stockport
Sheffield•
Bradwell•
Tideswell•
Chesterfield•
The Peak District ▶ **DEEPDALE**
National Park •
Matlock •

Behind **Topley Pike Quarry** lies the secluded valley of Deepdale, a Site of Special Scientific Interest (SSSI), bursting with wildflowers and tattooed with crags and caves. It's a real haven of peace at the heart of the **White Peak**, where **Chelmorton** stands amid medieval fields on the limestone plateau. **Chee Dale**'s twisting gorge is unsurpassed.

▶ START

Check the **River Wye** beside the car park. If it is running high or coloured, follow the alternative return route from Point 3, as Chee Dale's stepping-stones will be impassable.

Take the fenced path for Chelmorton, immediately left of the quarry's entrance. At a fork bear right up steps. Industry soon fades and Deepdale reveals its tranquil heart. Jackdaw-haunted crags tower above the limestone chasm, designated a SSSI because of its rich flora. From late April, floral tableaux dapple the dale – drifts of bloody cranesbill, banks of bellflowers, carpets of orchids, stands of yellow globeflowers and tangles of rock rose attract a wealth of butterflies.

Rounding a bend, the maw of **Thirst House Cave** looms to your left. Legend has it that a hobgoblin lived here, and that if you drink from the cave's spring on

▶ Chee Dale's twisting gorge offers a memorable end to this tranquil walk in the Peak District's Deepdale

Good Friday then all your ailments will be cured!

At a fork beyond the reserve fence, bear left into **Horseshoe Dale** along the **Priest's Path**, named after priests who used it as a sheltered link between local church and chapels. Continue to the main road beyond barns.

1 2 MILES

Turn left and follow the main road around bends to a waterworks; fork right along a walled track opposite this. At the end, walk half-left to the corner, climb a stile and turn right on another track. Turn right along the tarred lane through Chelmorton's remarkable strip fields. These tiny walled hay-meadows preserve the medieval open-field plots that villagers tilled before

Georgian enclosure destroyed the system over nearly all of England. Walk to the church. Claimed (at 369m, 1,209ft) as the highest parish church in England, it has some remarkable stone carvings in the porch. The village well – part of the old village water supply, fed by the worryingly-named **Illy Willy Water** – has a well-dressing ceremony in June.

2 3¼ MILES

Beyond the church fork right, climbing the wide track to a lane. Go left on the **Pennine Bridleway**; shortly a concessionary path to the right leads to and from the **Five Wells Burial Chamber**. Follow the Pennine Bridleway across the main road into a lane for **Blackwell**,

reaching a sharp bend.

3 5 MILES

If the Wye is high, follow the Pennine Bridleway left into Chee Dale and then upstream to the car park. Otherwise, turn right into Blackwell; at a fingerpost take the path left at Cottage Farm. The well-waymarked path reaches a farm complex. Pass beside this and follow waymarks along field-edges and down to a footbridge over the River Wye. Cross it and turn upstream. Enjoy a memorable walk up the Wye's twisting gorge, at several points using stepping stones beneath overhanging crags. The path eventually reaches **Blackwell Mill** cottages; cross the bridge and walk the track back to the car park at Topley Pike.

Delve into **Deepdale** before discovering Chelmorton's ancient field systems and the Wye's gorgeous Chee Dale

▶INFO

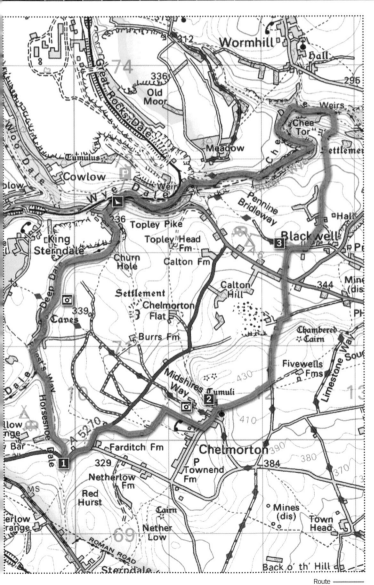

TERRAIN
Paths, field roads and lanes. It is rough underfoot in Deepdale and Chee Dale, and there are stepping stones in Chee Dale.

ACCESS
The riverside track between the car park and Blackwell Mill cottages is suitable for wheelchair users. Chee Dale's stepping-stones are challenging for younger children.

HOW TO GET THERE
BY CAR: Peak National Park Wyedale car park (pay and display) at Topley Pike, beside the A6 between Buxton and Bakewell.
BY PUBLIC TRANSPORT: Buses run to Topley Pike from Buxton and Bakewell.
☎ 0871 200 2233
travelineeastmidlands.org.uk

MAP
Ordnance Survey Explorer Map OL24.
Grid ref: SK 104 725

NEARBY EXCURSIONS
Poole's Cavern, at Buxton Country Park in Buxton, lets you see the limestone dales from beneath.
☎ 01298 26978
www.poolescavern.co.uk

MORE INFO
Buxton Tourist Information
The Crescent, Buxton
☎ 01298 25106
www.visitpeakdistrict.com

Peak District National Park
www.peakdistrict.org
☎ 01629 816200

Route

Sheffield •
• Buxton   Chesterfield •
    Bakewell •
STANTON MOOR ▶
The Peak District •   • Matlock
National Park
    Ashbourne •   Kilburn •

Stanton Moor Derbyshire

Distance 7½ miles (12 km) **Type** Moderate **Time** 4 hours

› Are these the remains of a troupe of ladies, turned to stone due to their wickedness?

A Bronze Age necropolis litters **Stanton Moor**, with barrows and the Nine Ladies Stone Circle creating an enigmatic landscape above picturesque villages at the heart of the **White Peak**.

▶ START

From **Youlgrave** church descend Bradford Road. Some 100m beyond the bridge, turn left on the waymarked **Limestone Way** and trace the well-walked path to a gate below **Castle Ring** hill fort, built beside the prehistoric Portway track. Keep ahead, steeply uphill for Stride, shortly following a farm drive to a lane. Rejoin the Limestone Way ahead.

To your left is the superb
📷 **Nine Rings** (or Grey Ladies) **Stone Circle** – four stones remain standing, although the site has no public access. The Grey Ladies are said to dance at midnight.

The walk continues into the crags and rocks just ahead. Here is **Robin Hood's Stride** (right) with its Iron Age rock shelters, cup marks and history of Roman finds, and **Cratcliff Rocks** (left) with its hill fort and evocative **Hermit's Cave**, complete with medieval carving. This area of **Harthill Moor** is access land, so explore with care. Robin Hood is said to have leaped from

one rock pillar to the other, hence the name. Rejoin the Limestone Way to reach the nearby main road.

1 | 2 MILES

Turn left; in 150m take the **Birchover** path right, up sloping pasture to a wider track, along which turn left. This skirts the edge of another wooded, rocky outcrop (keep left at a fork) before reaching Birchover. On your left
📷 are **Rowtor Rocks**, another fantastical array of tors, boulders and caves where druids are said to have performed rituals. Look across the main road at the bend for a path up through

woodland screening the village, rising to a lane.

2 | 3¼ MILES

Turn left; in 250m go right on a wide path on to **Stanton Moor**. Pass by the curious **Cork Stone** and continue to a major cross-path; go left here.

This strikes across the heathery moor, eventually entering woods and the
📷 **Nine Ladies Stone Circle**. Legend has it that the Nine Ladies and the nearby King Stone were dancing maidens and a fiddle player, turned to stone for dancing on the Sabbath.

Remain on the path through a gate and continue to a lane. Turn left to pretty **Stanton in Peak** and walk downhill through the village all the way to the main road.

3 | 5½ MILES

Cross straight over and cut the field corner on a grassy path (left of the barn). Turn left along a lane to reach a caravan site road. Walk up this to the fork then turn left as signed for Alport, across pasture then beside a wall to reach a lane. Walk uphill, then take the path right, down to cross a packhorse bridge. Turn left to a junction, then left and left again on to a farm lane. This winds into pretty **Bradford Dale**; use another packhorse bridge and climb back to Bradford Road.

Walk amid the stone circles and tors that pepper the ancient landscape of **Stanton** and **Harthill Moors**

KEY

▶INFO

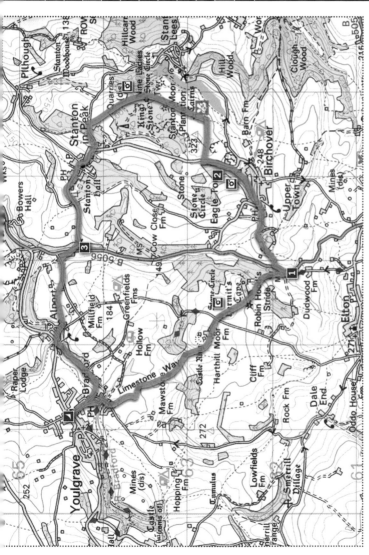

TERRAIN
Mainly field paths and tracks that may be muddy. Some road walking on largely quiet lanes.

HOW TO GET THERE
BY CAR: The walk starts from Youlgrave, 3 miles south of Bakewell, along minor roads. Park with consideration on village streets or use the small car park beside the road to Middleton.
BY PUBLIC TRANSPORT:
Take the 171 bus to Youlgrave from Bakewell.
☎ 0871 200 2233
travelineeastmidlands.org.uk

MAP
Ordnance Survey Explorer Map OL24.
Grid ref: SK 215 644

NEARBY EXCURSIONS
Haddon Hall
Bakewell DE45 1LA
☎ 01629 812855
www.haddonhall.co.uk
This medieval manor house, featured in countless films and TV series, is 2 miles from Youlgrave. Open from Apr-Oct, noon-5pm; only open Sat-Mon during Apr and Oct.

MORE INFO
Bakewell Visitor Centre
Old Market Hall,
Bakewell DE45 1DS
☎ 01629 816558
www.visitpeakdistrict.com

Route ——

The Roaches Staffordshire

Distance 6 miles (10 km) **Type** Moderate **Time** 3½ hours

Macclesfield
Cat and Fiddle
Sutton
Wildboarclough
Brandside
Wincle
THE ROACHES
Upper Hulme

> The region's varied terrain shelters a wealth of fascinating, and often surprising, wildlife

▶ START

Start at The Roaches Tea Rooms (or park in a lay-by nearby) and walk north along the lane. The outcrops of the **Five Clouds** and **The Roaches** to your right have long been a favourite climbing location; the renowned mountaineer Don Williams was one of many climbers who trained here.

The crags and moorland are home to a great range of wild birds; listen for red grouse chuckling in the heather and watch out for birds of prey such as **buzzards** and **sparrowhawks**. More elusive residents are **Bennett's Wallabies**. During WW2 a local private zoo released its exhibits into the wild,

> The Roaches Tea Rooms

among which were these Tasmanian marsupials, the descendents of which are still occasionally seen. Keep ahead for Royal Cottage.

1 1½ MILES

Some 100m past a gate across the road, fork left along a grassy track for **Clough Head**.

At the next lane, turn left, then right in 100m at the cattle-grid along a signed footpath. Drift right beneath telephone

wires to rejoin a lane and bear left. At a left bend, fork ahead-right to a stile in a wall. Keep ahead on a path for **The Ridge** and pass through a gate. Carry on for **Lud's Church** then down the path into woods. Within the trees, turn left for Lud's Church and follow a path into this dramatic gritstone chasm.

2 3 MILES

Lud's Church is allegedly named after Walter de Ludauk, leader of the local Lollards (15th-century religious dissenters who secretly worshiped here). The fern and moss-covered gorgc is more prosaically said to be the Green Chapel where Sir Gawain slew the Green Knight. From the mouth of the gorge turn right

along a woodland path. Fingerposts guide you to a lane at Roach End.

3 4 MILES

Cross to the main path as it rises to the crest of The Roaches ridge. The views of the uplands, dappled with renovated and derelict farmsteads, are stunning. For centuries, this area has been used to graze sheep – the remote farms were self-sufficient, and the major crop was oats, which grew well in the damp climate. Rolled, mixed with milk and cooked on a bakestone, the oats were transformed into a staple foodstuff, the **Staffordshire oatcake**.

Written records mention them in the 17th century and they were a common, nourishing meal enjoyed by pottery workers until the 1960s. Filled with cheese, they remain a tasty treat – try one at **The Roaches Tea Rooms**.

Continue along the ridge, passing **Doxey Pool**, apparently haunted by a terrifying 10m tall water sprite. Shortly after this, turn right down a wide gully, then left along a path through the woods below the crags, eventually reaching **Rockhall**, a crenulated cottage-cum-cave built into the cliff.

Turn right to the road. The Roaches Tea Room is situated at Paddock Farm, on the way back to **Upper Hulme**.

Look out for wallabies while enjoying folklore and oatcakes amid striking **Staffordshire** gritstone outcrops

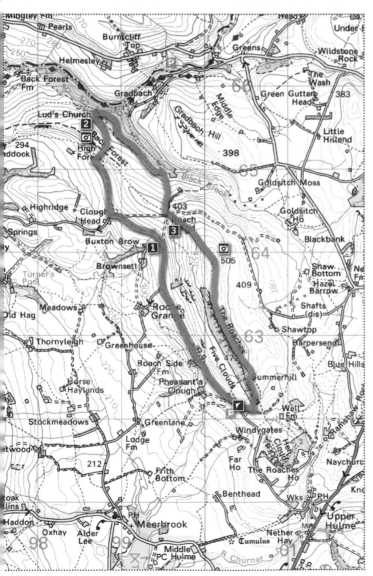

TERRAIN
The route follows lanes, byroads, moorland paths and woodland tracks. Expect mud and wear walking boots and warm clothing for the exposed ridge of The Roaches.

HOW TO GET THERE
BY CAR: The Roaches are beside a minor road just northwest of Upper Hulme, 3 miles north of Leek off the A53. Follow signs for Tea Rooms and park in lay-bys on the right, ½ mile past the Tea Rooms.
BY PUBLIC TRANSPORT:
First Bus 118 Buxton-Hanley service serves Hulme End.

MAP
Ordnance Survey Explorer Map OL24.
Grid ref: SK 004 622

NEARBY EXCURSIONS
Leek has a local produce market each Wednesday and is a centre for antique shops. Oatcakes are readily available in the Buttermarket; there's also a traditional oatcake shop at 2 Haywood Street (open mornings).

The Churnet Valley Railway runs steam and diesel services on a scenic line at Cheddleton, just south of Leek, most weekends, more frequently in summer
☎ 01538 360522
churnet-valley-railway.co.uk

MORE INFO
Leek Tourist
Information Centre
1 Market Place, Leek,
Staffordshire ST13 5HH
☎ 01538 483741
www.visitpeakdistrict.com

The Roaches Tea Rooms
Paddock Farm, Upper Hulme,
Leek ST13 8TY
☎ 01538 300345
www.roachestearooms.co.uk
Open daily 9am-5.30pm
(closes 4pm Nov-Feb)

Route ⎯⎯⎯

Bosley•
Heaton•   Fawfieldhead•
•Biddulph   Warslow•
    Leek•
    ▶ CHURNET
       VALLEY
Bagnall•   Ipstones•
•Stoke-on-Trent

Cheadle •

The Churnet Valley Staffordshire

Distance 8½ miles (13.7 km) **Type** Moderate **Time** 4½ hours

▶ START

Take the rough lane opposite **Cheddleton** station, then the stile on the right, climbing past the farm. Cross a lane and walk the right-edge of several fields. At the road go left to a path, right, for **Ipstones**, up a marshy slope to a driveway. Turn left; in 20m turn right with a fence on your left. At the end look right for a stile into fields. Head slightly right of the distant holly bush, take a stile and walk ahead to the woods. Look carefully for the fingerposted stile into the **RSPB Combes Valley Reserve**; follow the steep path into and out of the beautiful, secluded valley.

▶ The remote Black Lion Inn feels a million miles away from the nearby Potteries conurbation

1 | 1¾ MILES

Beyond the wood's edge pasture, go left on the track to a sharp left-hand bend. Cut right off this, ignore the lowered-fence on your right and remain on a thin path into thick rhododendrons. Persevere here; it's narrow and twisting.

At the far end bear left to a stile into rough pasture. Head two-thirds left, then swing right before a wall to use a gap above a stone barn. Bear left to climb a stile by a walled-up gateway and then right alongside the wall to a stone gazebo at medieval **Whitehough Farm**. Use the stile beyond, cross the drive to another and walk through to a lane. Join the rough track opposite.

Keep ahead beyond the muddy fords, snaking up to cottages and a tarred lane. Keep ahead-left to reach a minor road and turn left to Ipstones church and village centre.

2 | 3½ MILES

Turn right down Froghall Road; then right again for **Cheddleton**. In 600m, at **Little Stones Farm**, join the second waymarked footpath left and amble ahead through three fields. In the fourth, go half-right to the farm road for **Booths Hall Farm**. Immediately over the cattle grid use the stile and bisect the field left to a handgate.

Continue ahead-right around the corner and walk a field path below

the line of cables; bear left at the field-end to **Glenwood House**. Turn left just before it and then right, tracing the field-edge path behind the tennis court to a wooded corner. Look left for a higher corner-gap into **Booths Wood**, then turn right on the woodland path before reaching a rough track. Drop down steps opposite and turn right on the **Caldon Canal** towpath to **Consall Forge**.

3 | 5¼ MILES

This settlement was the heart of an industrial complex, of which tantalising evidence remains; it's also notable for the remote **Black Lion Pub**. For the short

walk, catch a train back to Cheddleton on the Churnet Valley Railway.

Otherwise, continue north through the serene

◙ **Churnet Valley**. Canal and river combine before parting again at **Oakmeadow Ford Lock**. Remain on the towpath to reach **The Boat Inn** and nearby Cheddleton station. An additional mile (return) along the towpath finds

◙ **Cheddleton Flint Mill**, a unique twin-wheeled watermill where flint used in the ceramics industry was powdered before being taken by canal boat to the pottery works of Wedgwood, Spode and Minton in Stoke.

Delve into a car-free Arcadia of woodland nature reserves, old mills, narrowboats and steam trains just a short hop from **The Potteries**

KEY

INFO

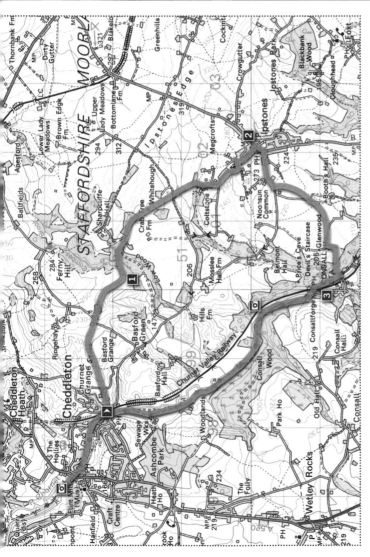

Route

TERRAIN
Muddy field paths, farm tracks, lanes and towpath. The route is convoluted between Combes Wood and Whitehough Farm and waymarking is lacking – look carefully for the features noted in the text. This walk is not one for dogs due to number of stiles and nature reserves.

HOW TO GET THERE
BY CAR: Cheddleton is 2 miles south of Leek on the A520. The railway station is well signposted from this road and there is limited roadside parking.
BY PUBLIC TRANSPORT: Very restricted buses run to Cheddleton from Stoke (Hanley) and Leek.
☎ 0871 200 2233

MAP
Ordnance Survey Explorer Map 258 and 259.
Grid ref: SJ 983 521

NEARBY EXCURSIONS
Churnet Valley Railway
Station Road, Cheddleton
ST13 7EE
☎ 01538 360522
churnet-valley-railway.co.uk
Trains runs each weekend from May to September, plus midweek services in high summer and at other special weekends.

MORE INFO
Leek Tourist
Information Centre
1 Market Place, Leek
ST13 5HH
☎ 01538 483741
www.visitpeakdistrict.com
www.enjoystaffordshire.com

Black Lion Pub
Consall Forge, Wetley Rocks,
Stoke-on-Trent ST9 0AJ
☎ 01782 550294
www.blacklionpub.co.uk

•Birmingham

Bickenhill•

Knowle•

Hockley• ▶ BADDESLEY
Heath   CLINTON

Bedworth•

Hawkes•
End

Coventry•

Warwick•

Baddesley Clinton Warwickshire

Distance 6½ miles (10.4 km) **Type** Easy/Moderate **Time** 3-4 hours

Barely 12 miles from the centre of Birmingham, the National Trust's elegant **Baddesley Clinton** manor house boasts a lineage that stretches back more than 500 years, with its heyday in Elizabethan times when its priest holes were a hideaway for persecuted Catholics. The sense of timelessness is echoed throughout the walk, with **Hay Wood** surviving as a fragment of the ancient **Forest of Arden**. It's believed that Shakespeare dreamt up *As You Like It* while wandering through this peaceful woodland.

▶ Explore this atmospheric Elizabethan house, a haven for persecuted Catholics in the 16th century

▶ START

If you are arriving by train to get to the start point, turn right from Lapworth station, turn left at the end of the road, then left again beyond the canal for the **Heart of England Way** to Baddesley Clinton.

From the Forestry Commission's **Hay Wood** picnic site, follow the wide track into the heart of the woodland. At a junction go second right on the public bridleway. Leave the trees and, via **Wood Corner Farm**, turn left on to the A4141 and right, past **Abbey Farm**, on a bridleway.

At the end, go right along a lane and go right just before the end, across the main road, and enter the grounds of **Wroxall Abbey** on a public footpath. After 400m turn left at a waymarked junction of paths. Head south, with

Wroxall Abbey on your right and a small pond on your left.

1 2½ MILES

Wroxall Abbey was established in the 12th century as a Benedictine priory, and was known as St Leonard's. The chapel was later used by the Shakespeares as their family church. In 1713 the estate was bought by Sir Christopher Wren as his country seat, and after many years as a private school it's now a hotel.

Go straight ahead past the main entrance, and head out across a field to reach **Five Ways**. The pub is on your left, otherwise go right, along the lane, turning right at

the first junction. Follow this to the end.

2 3¾ MILES

Go right for a few paces, over a stile on your left across the field. At the end turn right, cross a metal footbridge and veer right to join the Heart of England Way up to **Rowington Green**. Turn left on to the lane, then right on a bridleway before **Lyons Farm** to eventually emerge by the churchyard of St Michael's.

3 5¾ MILES

Go through the churchyard to reach
📷 Baddesley Clinton hall itself. The atmospheric house retains much of its original character

and is well worth a visit, while the elegant grounds include fishponds and a lake, so be sure to leave plenty of time to explore.

Afterwards, retrace your steps past the church, cross the lane and enter Hay Wood. Turn immediately right for a track back to the start.

However, if you want to extend your woodland walk, continue along the bridleway and turn right at the junction in the middle of the woods. It's a peaceful setting, far removed from the urban hurly-burly. Keep a lookout for the muntjac deer that roam the area and woodland birds such as woodpeckers and nuthatches.

Explore a **medieval manor house** and immerse yourself in peaceful woods on this escape from England's Second City

KEY

▶INFO

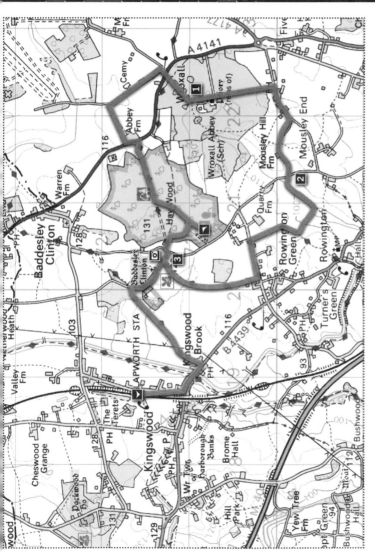

TERRAIN
Woodland and gentle rolling farmland. Can be muddy after wet weather.

HOW TO GET THERE
BY CAR: Located off the A4141 from Solihull, M42 J5, or the M40 southbound J16.
BY PUBLIC TRANSPORT: Lapworth Station, near Kingswood, is on the Birmingham Snow Hill Line

MAP
Ordnance Survey Explorer Map 221.
Grid ref: SP 205 707

NEARBY EXCURSIONS
Enjoy a fascinating towpath wander by lock flights and boatyards at Kingswood Junction, where the Grand Union and Stratford canals meet.

MORE INFO
Baddesley Clinton
Rising Lane, Baddesley Clinton B93 0DQ
☎ 01564 783294
www.nationaltrust.org.uk
Open 11am-5pm, Wed-Sun, 11 Feb-20 Dec.

Route ——————

- Whittington
- Wem
- Shawbury
- Shrewsbury
- Telford
- Church Stretton
- BISHOPS CASTLE
- Ludlow

Kerry Ridgeway Shropshire

Distance 10 miles (15 km) **Type** Moderate **Time** 5 hours

Starting at Middle Woodbatch Farm, this route follows sections of the Shropshire Way, Kerry Ridgeway and Offa's Dyke National Trail. Non-campers can set off from the market town of Bishops Castle.

> This scenic walk takes in the Shropshire Way, the Kerry Ridgeway and the Offa's Dyke National Trail

▶ START

Set off on the **Shropshire Way** from **Middle Woodbatch Farm**; pass between the barns and turn left at a gate. At the waymarker, bear diagonally left across the field, then over a stile. Look back for a wonderful 📷 view over Bishops Castle. Walk around the edge of a field towards a barn and through a gate. Turn left at the road, then right down a track. Bear left, then, as the track turns towards a house, right through a gate. Amazing views open up to the left as you follow the path 📷 downhill, through several gates. Walk left down the hill, then right through trees to a stile.

At the crossing, take the road signed '**Shadwell**', cross a stream and turn left on a footpath. Bear right at the Shropshire Way waymark, then left through a field. Turn left at the road, and left again at **Cowpasture Gate**. Turn right at the waymarker, then follow the path through pine woodland. In the valley on your right is Churchtown – or rather a solitary church with no town in sight! Bear right at the Shropshire Way sign, then join the **Offa's Dyke National Trail**, and follow the path into **Churchtown**.

1 | 3¼ MILES

Cross a bridge and road, then power on up the legendary **Churchtown Hill**, the steepest ascent on Offa's Dyke. Over a stile at the top, cross the road and carry straight on. Cross another road and a stile, then walk down into the valley. Follow the acorn markers over a bridge.

Bear left up the hill, turn right over a stile, and continue uphill past woodland. Bear left, over a stile on your right. When you reach the road turn off Offa's Dyke and follow the road right. You are now on the **Kerry Ridgeway**, an old drover's road between Wales and London.

2 | 5 MILES

Follow the path for 4 miles to Bishops Castle. In the town, take a right down the high street. After the Six Bells pub, turn right, then left along **Church Lane**. Turn right down **Field Lane**, then left after 10m. Walk past farm buildings and over a stile, then on a path with views left over the hills.

Skirt the edge of the field then bear downhill. At the base of the hill bear right on an unclear footpath, keeping the stream on your left. Continue through the next few fields to a road. Turn left and follow the road right to Middle Woodbatch Farm.

▶ THE CAMPSITE

Middle Woodbatch Farm campers are welcome to roll up their sleeves and get stuck in at this working farm, which dates back to the 1700s. With a 10 tent cap and free range over a hefty 170-acres peace is guaranteed, but it is recommended that you call ahead to check the availability of this walker-friendly site, especially in high summer.

Enjoy the **Shropshire** countryside, from ancient earthworks to quirky Bishops Castle and its two micro-breweries

KEY

▶ INFO

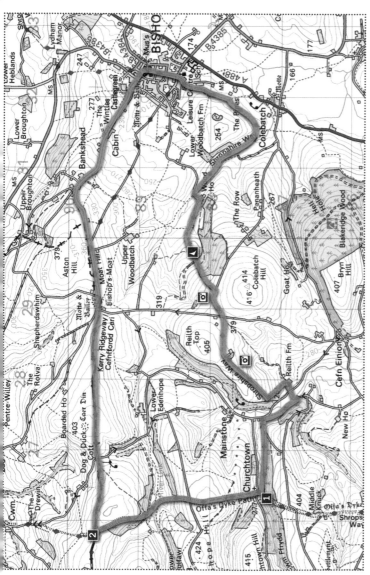

TERRAIN
Waymarked paths, permissive paths through farmland and minor roads.

HOW TO GET THERE
BY CAR: Bishops Castle is 23 miles southwest from Shrewsbury on the A488. Middle Woodbatch Farm is 1½ miles from Bishop's Castle.
BY PUBLIC TRANSPORT: Bus 552/553 runs from Shrewsbury to Bishops Castle.

MAP
Ordnance Survey Explorer Map 216.
Grid ref: SO 297 881

CAMPSITE
Middle Woodbatch Farm Woodbatch Road, Bishops Castle, Shropshire SY9 5JS
☎ 07989 496875
middlewoodbatchfarm.co.uk
10 pitches, no caravans. Open Mar-Oct – call about camping out of season.

MORE INFO
Offa's Dyke National Trail
www.nationaltrail.co.uk/offasdyke

Bishop's Castle Tourist Information
☎ 01588 638467
www.bishopscastle.co.uk

Shropshire Hills AONB
shropshirehillsaonb.co.uk

Route ⎯⎯⎯

Kiddeminster•
•Tenbury   Redditch•
Wells Ombersley•   Studley•
Worcester•   Alcester•
▶ MALVERN
HILLS
Evesham•
•Ledbury
Tewkesbury•

Malvern Hills Worcestershire

Distance 6 miles (9.6 km) **Type** Moderate **Time** 3 hours

They may be only 8 miles long, but what the **Malvern Hills** lack in scale they make up for in drama. These steep-sided hills are an awe-inspiring sight, looming large over the spa town of **Great Malvern**. Pure spring water flows from the hills and the various springs and wells that line the hillsides are fascinating to explore.

▶ START

From the tourist information centre, climb steps past a statue of composer Edward Elgar to **Belle Vue Island**, a terrace of shops. Just below the last few steps look out for Malvhina, a decorated public spring where you can fill up your water bottles for the climb ahead. It was designed in 1998 by sculptor Rose Garrard to represent the three most important periods in Great Malvern's history: its Celtic origins, the coming of Christianity and the growth of the town in Victorian times.

Turn left past shops, then right into **Rose Bank Gardens**. Climb the so-called **99 Steps** (there's 95), following a Worcestershire Way sign. Cross a road and bear left on a public footpath to **St Ann's Well**. The path zigzags steeply uphill and arrives at St Ann's Well and café, where Malvern spring water overspills from a marble font. From 1842 patients taking the famous Malvern Water Cure were

> The Malverns have inspired painters, composers and poets such as W.H. Auden and Edward Elgar

sent up this steep lane before breakfast for their morning drink.

Follow a path that loops behind the well, then turn left after 50m where the path splits. Head up the track, ignoring a left turn. Where the tracks meet, take a left, signposted to the Beacon, up to the ridge. Behind you there are magnificent views over Great Malvern.

1 2 MILES

At the round stone marker, follow the arrow, marked The Dingle, which heads downhill and skirts to the right of the Worcestershire Beacon. Fullow the path into woodland, bear left as the trees thin out and pass by the back of a house, then a car park on your right. Continue on

a track, then at a small lay-by bear left on a path. After a quarry, take either of the small paths to a flat grass plateau, from which there are excellent views towards **British Camp**, an Iron Age hill fort where folklore has it that British chieftain Caratacus made his last stand against the Romans. Continue on the path, through trees, then bear uphill, keeping left.

2 2¾ MILES

At a stone marker, turn left and follow the concrete path to the summit of **Worcestershire Beacon**, the highest point of the Malverns. The views are extensive and there's a toposcope to help you pick out landmarks such as the Wrekin in Shropshire and the Severn Estuary.

3 3¼ MILES

Follow a path down to the circular stone marker. Take the path signed 'Sugarloaf' and climb to the summit of the hill. Keep to the lower path and walk to a crossing of paths. Take the first left downhill, which skirts around the base of **Table Hill** (ignore the path going straight downhill). When you reach another junction, take the right, higher path around the back of the hill. Bear right then continue around the back of **North Hill**. Turn right where the path splits, then follow **Lady Howard Walden Drive**. When you reach a plaque signed to Sugarloaf, turn left downhill. Turn right then retrace your steps back to the town centre.

Blow away the cobwebs on an invigorating walk to the highest point of the **Malvern Hills**

KEY

▶INFO

TERRAIN
Steep, well-marked stony paths. The hills are crisscrossed with paths.

HOW TO GET THERE
BY CAR: Great Malvern is 8 miles southwest of Worcester and an hour's drive from Birmingham. From the north leave the M5 at J7 and take the A44 towards Worcester, before turning left on to the A4440 then left again on the A449. Turn left on the B4208 to Great Malvern, from where several car parks are signed.
BY PUBLIC TRANSPORT: The Hills Hopper Bus Service runs at weekends and Bank Holidays in the summer.
www.malvernhillsaonb.org.uk

MAP
Ordnance Survey Explorer Map 190.
Grid ref: SO 775 459

MORE INFO
Malvern Hills AONB
☎ 01684 560616
www.malvernhillsaonb.org.uk

Visit Worcestershire
www.visitworcestershire.org

Malvern Tourist Information Centre
21 Church Street,
Great Malvern WR14 2AA
☎ 01684 892289

Route ———

HEART OF ENGLAND

• Tewkesbury
Chipping•
Norton
• Cheltenham
•Brockworth
Burford•
•Stroud   ‣ BIBURY
• Cirencester
• Tetbury   Farringdon•
•Malmesbury
Swindon•
•Chippenham

Bibury Gloucestershire

Distance 4 miles (6½ km) **Type** Easy **Time** 2½ hours

‣ Arlington Row is one of the most photographed places in the Cotswolds, and it's easy to see why

Bibury paints one of the prettiest pictures in the **Cotswolds**. William Morris called it "the most beautiful village in England." With ducks to feed and delightful riverside picnic spots it's an ideal starting point for a family ramble.

‣ START

Park alongside the river near The Swan Hotel and head off down the B4425 beside the **River Coln**. Look out for trout in the clear waters, where you'll also find eager ducks to feed! Take the second right to visit St Mary the Virgin church then turn left and return to the road. Turn right down a lane, then right on to a

bridleway (signed 'Coln St Aldwyns'). On your right is the grand facade of Bibury Court Hotel.

Cross a bridge beside a weir and mill. Bear right with the road, past storehouses in Cotswold stone, then bear left uphill. Go through a gate and continue on a lane then bear left through a gate. Head uphill on stony ground and here you can see the underlying Cotswolds stone, a yellow oolitic limestone formed in tropical seas some 210-140 million years ago, breaking through the surface. The stone is rich in fossils – challenge children to find imprints of fossilised sea urchins.

1 1 MILE

Go through a gate and bear left through **Oxhill Wood**. The path can be muddy, but this presents the ideal opportunity for young nature detectives to identify footprints of muntjac, roe and fallow deer.

Go through a gate and head downhill, then climb a stone stile and cross a bridge. The woodland-topped field, which slopes gently down to a stream, makes an ideal place to stop for a picnic.

Walk up the hill to a wooden gate, then on into woodland with thick undergrowth that's teeming with butterflies and wild flowers, and is

perfect for bug hunting.

Bear right between traditional hedgerows. When you reach an opening on your left you intersect **Akeman Street**, the course of a major Roman road linking London to Cirencester. Put your ear to the ground and imagine ancient soldiers marching to London.

2 2 MILES

Turn right at a road and, after 100m, right again on a public footpath. Go through a gate, and bear right through a field, before going through another gate and heading uphill on an overgrown track, bordered by dog roses and elderflower. Continue straight ahead, bearing right at a wheat field, and carry on past crop fields with delightful views left.

At a crossroads, turn right then cross a junction of paths and continue straight ahead. Carry on through a gate to a point where five paths meet. Go through a gate, alongside a row of cottages, and then turn right down a lane. The route takes you alongside the picture perfect **Arlington Row**. Built in 1380 as a monastic wool store, the row was converted into weavers' cottages in the 17th century. Finish the day with a visit to the working trout farm or a refreshing drink in one of the many beer gardens.

This gentle family walk in **the Cotswolds** is perfect for young fossil hunters and nature detectives

KEY

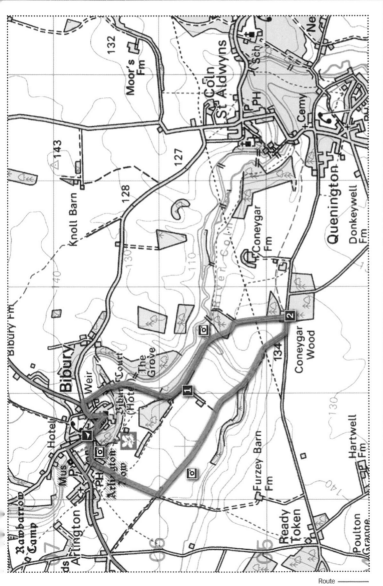

⏴**INFO**

TERRAIN
Public footpaths which may be muddy in places. Two short sections on road.

ACCESS
Rough paths and stiles make this route unsuitable for buggies or wheelchairs.

HOW TO GET THERE
BY CAR: Bibury is 26 miles southeast of Gloucester on the A417 and A429 to Cirencester, then B4425.
BY PUBLIC TRANSPORT: Trains run from Kemble station (which is the one line from Stroud, connecting to Swindon and London) to Cirencester, then catch the 860, 861, 865 or 866 from Cirencester to Bibury.

MAP
Ordnance Survey Explorer Map OL45.
Grid ref: SP 121 068

NEARBY EXCURSIONS
Bibury Trout Farm
Bibury, Cirencester GL7 5NL
☎ 01285 740215
www.biburytroutfarm.co.uk

MORE INFO
Cotswolds AONB
www.cotswoldsaonb.org.uk

Visit the Cotswolds
www.visitthecotswolds.org.uk

Route ⎯⎯

Painswick•

SLAD ▸
Elcombe •

Bisley•

Stroud•   Lypiatt •

Thrupp•   Eastcombe •

Slad Gloucestershire

Distance 5 miles (8 km) **Type** Moderate **Time** 2½ hours

Laurie Lee arrived at the Cotswold village of **Slad** during the First World war, along with his mother, brothers and sisters. It was here he spent the formative years of his life, and collected inspiration for his novel *Cider With Rosie*. The vivid imagery in his writing, deep understanding of the landscape and love for the valley and its people gives a poetic, funny, sometimes sad, but very real picture of a way of life that has all but disappeared.

▸ START

Walk north from **The Woolpack** pub; after 250m you reach a fork in the road. Below nestles **Rosebank Cottage**, Laurie's first home in Slad. Take the right fork and keep right down to **Steanbridge**. **Steanbridge House** was the **Big House** in the book, where Squire Jones throws village parties.

At Steanbridge pond, with its resident ducks, coots and moorhens, take the right-hand path and head uphill into **Redding Wood**. Take the left path leading above a large badger sett with a field boundary on the right. At the next track, turn right and follow the path uphill. Take the next track on the left and then keep straight ahead.

This is **Catswood**, home for the legendary two-headed sheep which, according to local tales found in the novel, lived among the larches and

▸ Rosebank in the Cotswolds village of Slad was the childhood home of poet and author Laurie Lee

was only visible during lightening flashes. It sings in a double voice and can tell you the date and nature of your death, so is best avoided.

📷 The view sweeps across the valley here – keep an eye out for roe and fallow deer – with Snow's Farm nestling on the opposite hillside. Take the next signed footpath on the left to cross the brook then bear left uphill to Snow's Farm. At the farm join an uphill lane, then at the top turn right along a restricted byway.

1 2 MILES

Shortly after entering woodland, take a footpath descending steeply on the left. In

spring you will probably hear greater spotted woodpeckers drumming out their territory and the valley echoing to the cry of the solitary buzzard.

The footpath leads down to the left of a woodland pond and soon joins a well-used track. Turn left and follow the track left on emerging at **Bulls Cross**.

2 3 MILES

Bulls Cross is a wild patch of heathland marking an ancient crossing. In *Cider With Rosie* this is the site of the local gibbct, and Laurie relates the local legend of the ghostly appearance of an ill-fated coach and horses on this spot. From here there is a

lovely view over the valley to the historic village 📷 of **Painswick** on the opposite hillside.

At the crossroads, follow a bridlepath straight ahead through the nature reserve of **Frith Wood**. Keep straight along this track until you reach Worgan's Farm. Just beyond the farm take a footpath over a stile on the left, bearing right at a lower fork to emerge on the road just below Slad village. On entering the village, the school Laurie attended is opposite The Woolpack and his final resting place is in the churchyard of **Holy Trinity Church**.

Experience the beauty and atmosphere of a beautiful **Cotswold** valley, so vividly captured by the poet and author Laurie Lee

KEY ▶INFO

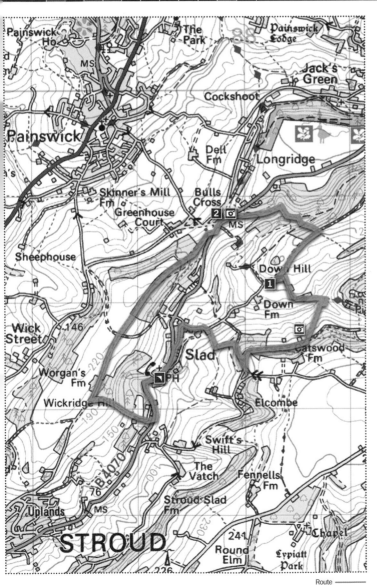

TERRAIN
A hilly walk, mostly on woodland paths and tracks, with some steep inclines. Some sections can be slippery, so walking boots are strongly advised.

HOW TO GET THERE
BY CAR: Slad is 2 miles north of Stroud on the B4070
BY PUBLIC TRANSPORT:
Stroud is on the main London Paddington to Cheltenham train line, with direct services to London in 1½ hours. Regular bus services to Stroud from Cheltenham, Gloucester, Cirencester, Bath and Swindon.

MAP
Ordinance Survey Explorer Map 179.
Grid ref: SO 872 073

NEARBY EXCURSIONS
Rococo Garden
Painswick, Gloucestershire
GL6 6TH
☎ 01452 813204
www.rococogarden.co.uk
Open 11am-5pm 10 Jan-31 Oct.

MORE INFO
Stroud Tourist Information
☎ 01453 760960

Route ———

Nagshead Gloucestershire

Distance 4½ miles (7 km) **Type** Easy **Time** 2½ hours

Ross-on-Wye•
Cheltenham•
Gloucester•
•Monmouth
NAGSHEAD ▸
Stroud•
Lydney•
Cirencester•
Dursley•
Tetbury•
Thornbury•
Malmesbury•
Bristol•
Chippenham•

▸ Bicslade Valley is a remote, lush ravine filled with ferns, birdlife and signs of its industrial hertiage

▸ START

From the Nagshead car park, use the signed Nature Trails and walk up the forestry road for 150m. At the fork, turn left on to a road that rises through the woods.

Many of the trees have nesting boxes; **Nagshead Reserve** is famous for its pied flycatchers. A myriad of other species live here, including rarities such as hawfinch and goshawk. You may see fallow deer at any time, grazing the margins or crossing the track; you'll probably catch a glimpse of them crashing deeper into the woods, flashing their distinctive white rumps. The road threads through some of Britain's best bluebell woods, the azure carpet is at its best in April and May. Remain on the forestry road to reach a gate, stile and junction of roadways.

1 1¼ MILES

Walk ahead along the right-edge of a tract cleared of firs some years ago. Look to the shallow banks for strips of bare earth, a sure sign that deer use this place as a crossing. Their cloven hoof-prints are smaller than those of wild boar and lack the dewclaws. Areas of grassy turf that have been roughly disturbed and turned are evidence of wild boar rooting through the softer soil. Keep right at a fork, and re-enter woodland. In a further 800m you'll reach a set of overhead cables crossing the road. Here, turn sharp right on a wide path beneath the wires. In a further 100m turn left on a lesser path which winds through to a sunken trackway.

2 2¼ MILES

Turn down the **Bicslade Tramroad**, once the route of a horse-drawn tramway which, until World War Two, transported stone to workshops in the valley; the stone sleepers are still in place. This is a beautiful, remote, narrow valley rich with ferns, birds and industrial remains. At a junction beyond huge boulders bear right, shortly passing a mining memorial and sculpture. Adjacent to this is one of the Forest of Dean's unique freemines; a drift mine worked by a few strictly forest-born miners. Remain on the access road to a sharp left-bend.

3 3 MILES

Turn right at the **Gloucestershire Way** waymark over a stile into **Nagshead Plantation**, magnificent oak woods planted for Lord Nelson, who realised that the navy of his successors would not have sufficient timber for their warships. Trace the path uphill; 100m beyond a gate, keep right at the fork and turn left through a higher gate to return along a forest ride to the car park.

▸ WILD BOAR IN THE FOREST OF DEAN

Britain's native wild boar were hunted to extinction by 1700. Today's population probably originate from boar that escaped from a rare breeds farm to the north of the Forest of Dean in the 1990s. Estimates suggest more than 200 now roam the Forest. Look for muddy wallows and tree-rubs with coarse hairs.

Walk amid woodland planted for Nelson's Navy, **carpeted with vivid blubells**, rich with birdlife and home to deer and wild boar

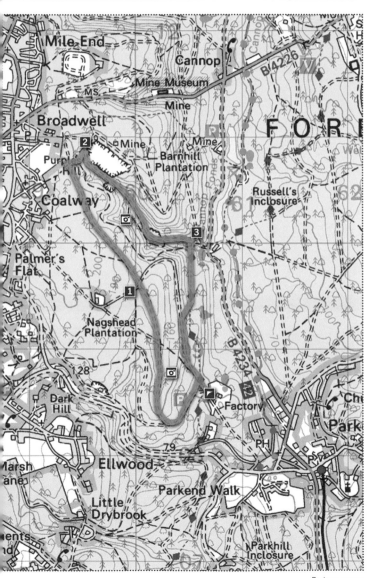

TERRAIN
Forestry roads, woodland tracks and paths. Two long, gentle climbs.

HOW TO GET THERE
BY CAR: Nagshead RSPB Reserve is signposted off the Parkend to Coleford road, immediately west of Parkend. The approach is up a long, unsurfaced forestry road. Note the closing time shown at the barrier.

MAP
Ordnance Survey Explorer Map OL14.
Grid ref: SO 607 084

NEARBY EXCURSIONS
The Dean Forest Railway runs steam and preserved diesel trains between Parkend and Lydney, most weekends from May-Sept, plus some summer weekdays.
www.deanforestrailway.co.uk
☎ 01594 845840

MORE INFO
Forest of Dean Tourism
☎ 01594 812388
www.visitforestofdean.co.uk

Nagshead Reserve
www.rspb.org.uk/reserves

Route ——

WALES

Where do you start in Wales? The wild, jagged coastline of **Pembrokeshire**, packed with cliffs, stacks, islands, coves, golden beaches and a wealth of wildlife? The 136-mile (218-km) wooded valley of **Wye**, home to ancient monastic ruins and hosts of native daffodils? What of the chocolate-box villages, many with their own castles tucked around the back? Then there's the ancient valleys of red sandstone that make up the **Brecon Beacons**, liberally sprinkled with natural and man-made reservoirs? And we haven't even mentioned **Snowdonia** yet!

In terms of landscape, Snowdonia is the undisputed jewel in the Welsh crown. It isn't simply the fact that these peaks, containing some of the highest in Wales or England, stretch over 3,000 feet (914 m) into the often dramatically turbulent sky – it is also extraordinarily beautiful. Tens of thousands of hikers, climbers and extreme sports enthusiasts swarm to the UK's third largest national park month in month out to appreciate its scale and grandeur. The breathtaking nature of the rugged clefts is outstanding, whether you make it by boot and crampon, or via the Snowdonia mountain railway, which provides a less strenuous but by no means less exciting journey up the 3,560 feet (1,085 m) of **Mount Snowdon**. From its summit, you can easily see how this formidable line of defence kept out potential invaders and allowed Welsh culture, including the distinct national language, to survive so well.

If the volcanic remnants of Snowdonia seem a little on the ambitious side for you, then head southwest to Pembrokeshire. We've already mentioned the sublime coastline, which rivals anything Cornwall has to offer. Less well known are the **Preseli Hills**, where you can walk over the very ground that provided the bluestones of Stonehenge, hewn from the tor of **Carn Menyn**. Here too you'll find the **Golden Road**, an ancient track that would have been traversed by tradesmen travelling between the kingdom of Wessex in the South West and Ireland.

Wherever you wander in rural Wales, you can't shake the feeling that the views you encounter are timeless in the truest sense of the word; that here, amidst the waterfalls, winding lanes and defiantly rugged peaks you are walking with the ancients, and experiencing a welcome that transcends time. Wales is a country that draws you back and urges you on to take up fresh challenges and uncover new secrets.

Trellech Monmouthshire

Distance 5½ miles (8.9 km) **Type** Moderate **Time** 3 hours

Trellech was the most prosperous borough in Norman Wales; its remains are now being excavated. Far older are **Harold's Stones** – three standing stones that give the village its name – and a virtuous well, a spring possibly venerated by Druids. The views from **Beacon Hill** are magnificent.

▶ START

From the car park a path marked 'Ffynnon' leads to **St Anne's Well**, still revered as a healing well. Use the nearby gate into the lane, cross left to a bridleway and turn right on this; at its end turn left. On your left is the excavation of the lost village.

Fork left for **Broadstone** and turn left along a greenway opposite the first cottage. At the end turn left through the farmyard to a lane. Turn right, and in 50m go left on the drive (footpath for Cleddon), curving behind cottages on to a woodland track. Keep ahead off a left bend; at the woodland's end turn right down the stony track to a narrow lane. Turn left and walk to a sharp-left bend. Here is ◉ the top of **Cleddon Falls**, where Wordsworth's *Lines Composed a Few Miles above Tintern Abbey* was inspired.

1 2 MILES

Turn left along the **Wye Valley Walk**, a rough lane then a woodland

▷ Trellech's standing stones are named after the Saxon king Harold, yet predate him by 2,000 years

path. Keep left at a fork to reach a complex junction; here take the narrow path (leaving the Wye Valley Walk) beside a bench. This eventually reaches the woodland edge. Cross the forestry road and go left through a gate on to a track rising across **Trellech Beacon**, where heath is being grazed by Welsh mountain ponies and re-established.

Go over a cross-track, rise to use a gate and go half-right on the narrowest path, winding between the trees to reach a wider track. Turn right to the Beacon Hill viewpoint; on clear ◉ days the panorama is phenomenal.

2 3½ MILES

Continue along the track, through a gate and back across the heath. Views now include the Malverns, Cotswolds and Clee Hills. Turn left at the T-junction, cross a cattle-grid and walk a little further to a junction. Turn left to a lane. Go right and use the stile on the left, head across the pasture, falling via stiles to pass just right of the lower barn. Look half-left for a stile on to a level path through bracken, use another stile and drop to a handgate. Don't use this, but bear right inside the meadow to use a stile in 75m; turn right along the track.

Fork half-left after an open gateway to steps at the far corner and walk the lane ahead to the Lion Inn. Trellech's church reflects the former status of the village. Turn left outside the far churchyard wall, along the path past the motte and through a farmyard.

A waymarked concessionary path leads to and from Harold's Stones, three superb ◉ Bronze Age megaliths which give a tangible sense of the history inseparably connected to the countryside here. To return, head back to the car park is at the end of the driveway.

Explore **medieval Wales's largest town**, now lost beneath the ground, less than an hour's drive from Bristol and Cardiff

KEY

▶INFO

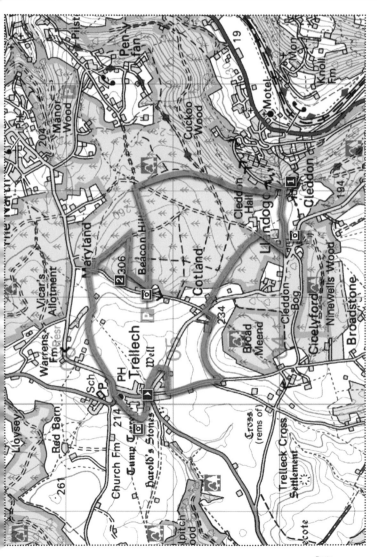

TERRAIN
Lanes, greenways, forestry tracks and paths through gently undulating countryside.

HOW TO GET THERE
BY CAR: Trellech is on the B4293 between Monmouth and Chepstow. The Lion Inn is at the village centre; the small village car park is next to the village hall.
BY PUBLIC TRANSPORT: Buses service 65 runs to Trellech from Monmouth and Chepstow.
☎ 0871 200 2233
www.traveline.org.uk

MAP
Ordnance Survey Explorer Map OL14.
Grid ref: SO 515 038

NEARBY EXCURSIONS
The Nelson Museum
New Market Hall, Priory Street, Monmouth NP25 3XA
☎ 01600 710630
Features a remarkable collection of memorabilia relating to the great naval hero – including his glass eye!

MORE INFO
Monmouth Tourist Information Centre
Market Hall, Priory Street, Monmouth NP25 3XA
☎ 01600 713899
www.visitwyevalley.com

Route ———

Blorenge Monmouthshire

Distance 6 miles (10 km) **Type** Moderate **Time** 3 hours

▷ Blorenge overlooks Abergavenny with views of the Severn Estuary

▶ START

Park at **Keeper's Pond** and enjoy views over the **Black Mountains**. The instantly recognisable 📷 **Sugar Loaf** is the flat-topped peak above **Abergavenny** and on a clear day you can pick out the **Brecon Beacons'** highest peaks, **Pen y Fan**, **Corn Du** and **Cribyn** to the west. The surrounding landscape bears scars from the industrial activity the area is famous for; coal mining has left black furrows in the hillside, evidence of limestone and ironstone quarries litter the landscape and bell pits pockmark the ground behind the car park.

Walk left around the pond and over a bridge, and then bear right on a track. Amazingly, Britain's uplands support 70 percent of the world's heather moorland, a habitat associated with many rare species. Keep an eye out for red grouse,

ring ouzel, hen harrier and merlin. The heather uplands also provide refuge for snipe, lapwing and curlew. Thin mineral soils and peat also support dwarf shrubs like bilberry, which provide an important habitat for nesting stonechats and whinchats.

Stay on the path as it bears right, then at a waymarker turn left downhill on a rocky path.

1 1¼ MILES

As you head downhill the landscape opens up, with views left over to 📷 **Crickhowell** at the head of the valley and the Black Mountains beyond. Drop down to an old tramroad and turn right. You soon pass a tunnel, which marks out the original route of the tramroad.

As well as the upland birdlife, there have been sightings of polecats, foxes and badgers in the area, and the dry stone walls provide nooks and

crannies for adders and common lizards, which in turn attract weasels and stoats, natural predators of the many ground nesting birds.

Bear right around the base of the hill, dipping downhill, and when the path skirts larch woodland, keep your eyes peeled for redstart and redpoll. Carry on with the fence of your left, then turn right through a gate on to a public bridleway.

2 3¼ MILES

You now reach the 📷 **Punchbowl**, a large, wooded glacial cwm with a picturesque man-made lake. Watch out for mallards, herons, green woodpecker and warbler as well as dragonflies and damselflies flitting off the surface of the lake.

Walk left along the shore then take the lower path along the fence line climbing out of the Punchbowl. Walk to a gate, and then carry on

up the now gentler slope. There's a bench a few metres after the gate where you can catch your breath and scan for birds.

At a cattle grid, turn right along the road as heathland opens up again on either side. Look out for ring ouzel and wheatear, which thrive on the tops of exposed upland heaths, nesting in bushes or even disused rabbit warrens.

3 4 MILES

Take a sharp right at the **Carn y Gorfydd** enclosure and follow the path towards the summit of the **Blorenge**. Look east for views towards the **Severn Estuary**. Keep an eye out for hobby, a small, very swift species of falcon seen frequently on the heathland, catching prey on the wing.

Continue on the rocky path to a turf-covered area of limestone spoil mounds, where there are more amazing views over into the punchbowl.

Turn left at a small brick building, and follow 📷 a boggy path to the summit. The boulders at the top mark a Bronze Age burial chamber, and you'll have to scramble up the last few metres to the trig point. Head in the direction of the radio masts on a stony path. Bear right at a path junction to the Foxhunter car park, then turn right along a lane, passing disused bell pits, to return to Keeper's Pond.

Discover a wealth of wildlife within the once industrial landscape
of the **Black Mountains**

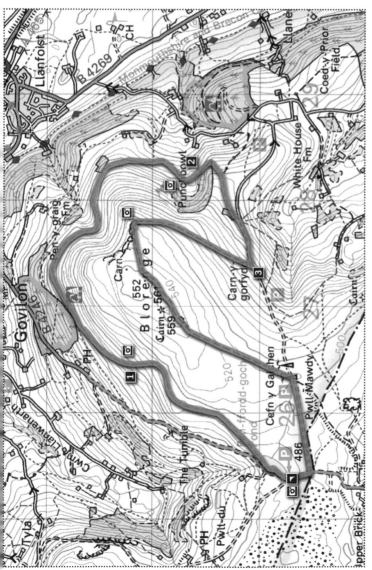

TERRAIN
Well-trodden grassy paths
and old tramways. May
be rocky, steep or boggy
in places.

HOW TO GET THERE
BY CAR: Keeper's Pond
car park is on the B4246
between Abergavenny and
Blaenavon.
BY PUBLIC TRANSPORT:
Abergavenny is on the main
train line between Cardiff and
Manchester.

MAP
Ordnance Survey Explorer
Map OL13.
Grid ref: SO 254 107

NEARBY EXCURSIONS
Big Pit Museum
Blaenafon, Torfaen NP4 9XP
☎ 01495 790331
www.museumwales.ac.uk
Open mid Feb–Nov, Mon-Sun
9.30am-5pm, underground
tours 10am-3.30pm.

MORE INFO
Woodland Trust
**www.wt-woods.org.uk/
thepunchbowl**

Visit Wales
www.visitwales.com

For details of guided walks
contact: Brecon Beacons
National Park Authority,
Plsa y Ffynnon, Cambrian
Way, Brecon LD3 7HP
☎ 01874 624437
www.breconbeacons.org

Abergavenny Tourist
Information Centre, Swan
Meadow, Monmouth Road
Abergavenny NP7 5HH
☎ 01873 853254

Route ———

Rhondda Valley Mid Glamorgan

Distance 8½ miles (14 km) **Type** Challenging **Time** 4½ hours

Merthyr •
Tydfil
Abertillery •
TREHERBERT ▶
Rhondda •
• Abercynon
Ogmore Vale •
Caerphilly •
Bridgend •
Cardiff •

▷ The high point on this walk affords views over former mining communities Treorchy and Cwmparc

Richard Llewellyn wrote *How Green Was My Valley* in 1939. It's the evocative story of a coal mining community in the early 1900s, seen through the eyes of Huw Morgan, the youngest son of a proud mining family. Today the collieries are long gone, but the stunning scenery remains.

▶ START

With your back to **Treherbert station**, take a left along **Taff Street**; the road bears right over a small bridge then left. At the main road turn left along a typical Rhondda valley terrace of stone houses. After a mile, pick up a path that travels along the route of an old railway line that transported coal from local collieries through the now disused **Rhondda Tunnel**.
Continue along the

hedge to a gap opposite. Turn left to the main road then go right, walking through the village of **Blaencwm** (meaning 'top end of the valley'). Go through the gate directly ahead.

1 1½ MILES

The path bears right across an old slagheap, which over time has blended well into the landscape. Follow the main path, and when it splits head left up a steep rocky path. The route climbs through the fir trees and into a wild landscape, with the sound of the river rushing below. Listen out for the distinct call of stonechats in the bracken and skylarks high in the sky. In the book, this is Huw Morgan's daily walk to school, come rain or shine. It's very steep and

rocky here for 150m – look out too for lumps of coal underfoot. Further up, take in the fantastic 📷 view back down the valley to Blaencwm.
Where the path forks, head straight on to a track and turn left. At the crossroads, continue on the track. Walk to a stile and exit **Bwlch Forest**.

2 3¼ MILES

Turn left on to the road. After a mile you reach a gate on your right. Follow the track for 100m to a stile. Head straight on down and over the field – the path is not well defined, but you will pick it up just over the brow. Continue to a sheltered area, which is ideal for a picnic stop and has stunning views down the 📷 **Ogmore Valley**.
The path then becomes no more than

a narrow sheep track, clinging to the edge of a huge drop known as **Craig Ogwr**. There are many well-positioned rocks to sit on, so catch your breath and take in 📷 the views of **Nant-y-moel** and **Price Town** below. Eventually the path descends steeply and you reach the road.

3 6 MILES

Cross the road and walk on to a grassy path that hugs the hillside. When the path splits take a left.
Don't forget to look back at the impressive geology of **Graig Fach** and **Graig Fawr** – the rocky cliff-like edges of the valley.
Pass a radio mast and on to an uneven farm track which descends towards the town, where the sounds of people replace the more natural noises on the hillsides. You can imagine the miners Llewellyn describes leaving the mine at the end of a hard day, singing songs on the way home.
Follow a street to the main road. Turn right; follow the terraced street to the end, then go left and over the bridge. On your right is **Ton Pentre** train station. To complete the loop, hop on one of the trains for a 12-minute journey back to **Treherbert**.

Discover the wilderness surrounding mining towns in the **Rhondda Valley**, as featured in Richard Llewellyn's classic *How Green Was My Valley*

KEY **INFO**

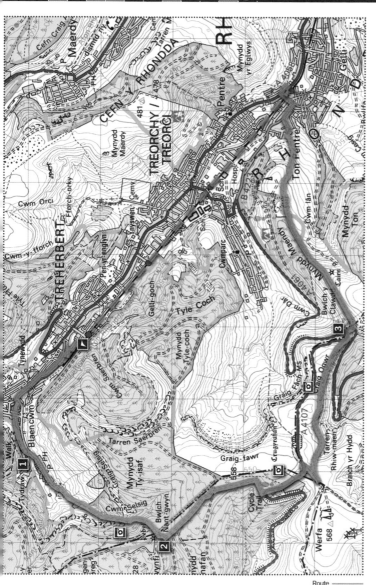

TERRAIN
Uneven, rocky and grass paths and tracks, which are steep in places, and a short section of road walking. Dress warmly, taking a wind and waterproof coat as some areas are exposed, and wear walking boots.

HOW TO GET THERE
BY CAR: From junction 32 on the M4 take the A470 to Pontypridd, then the A4058 to Treorchy and on to the A4061 to Treherbert.
BY PUBLIC TRANSPORT: Buses 120 and 130 from Cardiff travel via Caerphilly to Treherbert. Rail services run regularly between Treherbert and Ton Pentre.
Traveline Cymru
☎ 0871 200 22 33
www.traveline.info

MAP
Ordnance Survey Explorer Map 166.
Grid ref: SS 938 981

NEARBY EXCURSIONS
Rhondda Heritage Park
Coed Cae Road, Trehafod
CF37 2NP
☎ 01443 682036
rhonddaheritagepark.com

Big Pit National Coal Museum
Blaenafon, Torfaen NP4 9XP
☎ 01495 790311
www.museumwales.ac.uk/en/bigpit/

MORE INFO
Pontypridd Tourist
Information Centre
☎ 01443 490748

www.destinationrct.co.uk
www.loopsandlinks.co.uk
www.visitwales.co.uk

Route ———
Train route — — —

133

Ystradfellte Rhondda Cynon Taff

Distance 6 miles (10 km) **Type** Moderate **Time** 3-4 hours

> Discover one magnificent waterfall after another on this exhilarating walk in the Brecon Beacons

▶ START

Park at the lay-by near to **Clyn Gwyn Bunkhouse** and walk down a bridleway. Turn right (signed 'waterfall walk') and follow a wide path. After 500m turn right to a viewing platform over the impressive **Sgwd Isaf Clun Gwyn**. Retrace your steps then turn right and walk through woodlands until you see the **Sywd Clun Gwyn**. Continue on the high path then turn right to the falls. If the water level is low you can explore the moss-covered rocks and even clamber down to the shelf to watch the water cascade into the valley.

Back on the path, take the peaceful route alongside the river. Cross a wooden bridge by a pebbled bank and turn right onto a rocky path. Keep right and walk along the ancient riverbed, evidence of the river's course before it cut further into the limestone. Follow the path right to a viewpoint overlooking **Sgwd Clun Gwyn**.

1 1 MILES

Walk left on a narrow path that weaves over tree roots. Be careful of your step and keep an eye on children near the edge. Descend with the path down to the river, bearing right to look at **Sgwd Isaf Clun Gwyn,** a long curved waterfall dripping with mosses.

Pick your way carefully downstream to a deep pool and a peaceful spot beneath a three-tiered fall that makes for a beautifully composed photo. Amble further downstream to **Sgwd y Pannwr** as the river turns sharply and tumbles into a deep pool surrounded by overhanging trees.

2 1½ MILES

Turn back on yourself and take the path right, then turn off immediately right to follow an unclear rocky path. Take a left steeply uphill and climb out of the valley, then follow the path right. Bear left through lush woodland and dappled sunlight. Turn right and head steeply downhill to a grassy bank, then turn left and follow the river to a two tiered waterfall in a delightfully peaceful spot.

Head back the way you came and rejoin the path, turning right. When the path drops down to the riverside you can walk alongside the river to Wales' best-known waterfall, **Sgwd yr Eira**. Until recently you could walk behind the falls but the path is now closed due to unstable rocks.

3 2 MILES

Turn back and walk up steps. Turn left then take the top route and continue above the tree line. Carry straight on at a junction, then stick to the upper path, bearing right, and turn right to return to the viewing platform at Sgwd Clun Gwyn. Walk uphill, turn left at the top and follow the path back to the bridge.

Carry straight on alongside the river bank until you reach **Cwm Porth**, an eco-friendly information centre, with picnic and toilet facilities. Walk down from the car park to explore **Porth Yr Ogof**, one of the largest cave entrances in Wales. At 20m wide and 3m high you can safely explore the opening of the cave (don't forget your torch). Look out for calcite streaks on the back wall that resemble a white horse, giving the cave its name.

4 4 MILES

Walk back to Cwm Porth, cross the road and retrace your steps. For an interesting detour, turn right through a gate, signed 'Access for Cavers', and walk over the ancient water-worn riverbed to the resurgence pool where the **River Mellte** gushes out from its underwater course.

Back on the path, turn right then left to rejoin the main path. Cross the bridge and follow the path back to the bunkhouse car park.

Discover a world away from the crowds in the **Brecon Beacons** on a spectacular walk in waterfall country

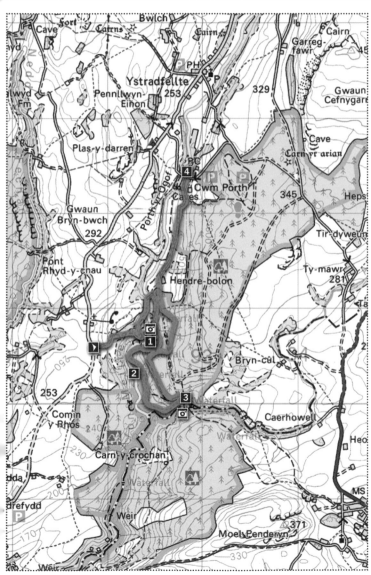

TERRAIN
Steep and rocky paths, challenging in places with some scrambles, steps or tree routes to negotiate. Extreme care should be taken when exploring the opening of Porth yr Ogof. Many people have drowned in these caves and further exploration should only be attempted by well-equipped experienced cavers or under the close supervision of a qualified instructor with excellent local knowledge.

HOW TO GET THERE
BY CAR: Leave the M4 at J32 and take the A470 for 14 miles towards Merthyr Tydfil, then the A465 towards Neath and take the exit for A4109 (signed 'for caves') to Pontneddfechan. Head north on the B4242 to Ystradfellte and the bunkhouse and car park is on this road.
BY PUBLIC TRANSPORT: Aberdare is served by direct trains from Cardiff

MAP
Ordnance Survey Explorer Map OL12.
Grid ref: SN 918 105

MORE INFO
Brecon Beacons National Park
www.breconbeacons.org

Wales Valleys Walking Festival, 5-21 Sept 2008
wisdomandwalks.co.uk

Rhondda Cynon Taff
www.destinationrct.co.uk

Route ———

Penderyn Rhondda Cynon Taff

Distance 8 miles (13 km) **Type** Moderate **Time** 4½ hours

Aberystwyth
Llandrindod •
Wells
•Cardigan   Hereford •
Brecon Beacons•
National Park
▶ PENDYRN
Swansea•

▶ START

Park at lay-by just north of the **Penderyn Distillery**. Cross the road and pick up a footpath leading to a lane; turn left, past farm buildings. Aim for **Moel Penderyn**, a great lump of limestone ahead. Leave the lane and turn right at a bridleway sign, through a gate. Go immediately over a stile on your right and head up the hill for

📷 views over the **Rhondda Valley** and **South Wales Coalfields**. Turn left and follow the path; bear right around the hill, following the fence line. Zigzag up the hill and bear left. From here you can see the **Tower Colliery**, the last deep mine in Wales, which closed in January 2008. Ahead of you you'll also see **Penderyn Quarry**, where limestone is harvested.

▶ On a good day, the views over the central Brecon Beacons are simply stunning

1 1 MILE

Continue over the brow of the hill to a trig point, and more panoramic views over the central **Brecon Beacons**. The largest open cast mine

📷 also lies ahead, as well as a patchwork of reclaimed green fields. Continue along the grassy path and bear left over limestone paving, following the path along the length of the hill. Cut back left via a stile to a bridleway and turn right. Go through a gate and along the footpath, pass through a second gate and descend to **Dinas Rock**.

2 2½ MILES

Turn right and head downhill into woodland, following steps and a rocky path to a beautiful picnic spot where you can pause for a short while before continuing with the walk. Take a quick detour across the bridge to explore the entrance to an old silica mine, now home to a colony of bats. Return across the bridge, then turn left and head back, taking a right back up the steps. Turn left uphill and then bear left. Continue on a well-defined path, then bear right.

Pass Dinas Rock car park and turn right over a bridge then right along a lane, picking up a riverside path that passes the overgrown remains

📷 of an old gunpowder works. Look out for the waterwheels and turbine houses, now covered in moss and camouflaged in

the woodland.

Continue along the track past a white cottage, once home to industry workers. You'll soon pass the remains of an old powerhouse and a waterfall, from which water was drawn for the gunpowder works. When the site was running this area was cleared of vegetation, but since production finished in the 1920s, it is being reclaimed by plant life. Bear left, following the purple waymarkers, and carry on to a pebble bank, next to a stone leat.

3 4 MILES

Head back on the riverside path and return to the waterfall, known locally as **Loonies Leap**. Turn left and cross the bridge then head up the steep path ahead and follow the path right at the top. Turn left at a sign,

continue over the brow of the hill and follow a path along the edge of the valley, through a gate. Cross a footbridge and carry on uphill, past a ruined farm.

Turn right and follow waterfall path markers. Turn left, past another ruin and over a stream. Continue ahead and, at a giant bolder dumped here in the Ice Age, turn left and head uphill, signed 'Penderyn'. Carry on the path, along the fence line and towards the trig point from earlier. Turn left over a stile and follow the fence line to another stile. Bear right, then skirt left, climbing steadily. Turn left at a gate then turn right along a lane past The Red Lion Pub. Take the next left and follow the footpath back to the original starting point of this enchanting ramble.

Discover an enchanting old gunpowder works in the
Brecon Beacons, now reclaimed by plantlife

KEY

INFO

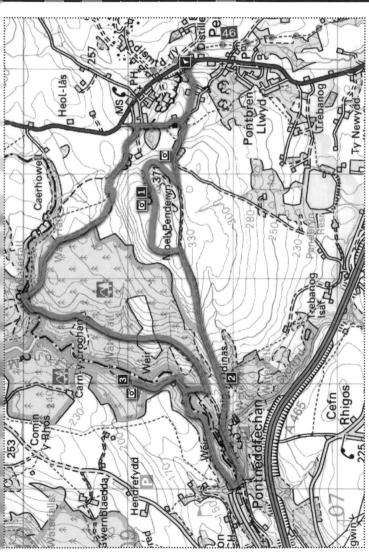

TERRAIN
Mainly footpaths and
bridleways.

HOW TO GET THERE
BY CAR: Penderyn is 32
miles northwest of Cardiff.
Follow the A470 to the
Merthyr Bypass, take the first
exit onto the A465 and follow
this to Hirwaun. Take the third
exit (A4059) to Penderyn.
BY PUBLIC TRANSPORT:
Trains run from Cardiff to
Aberdare, where a bus
connects to Penderyn.

MAP:
Ordnance Survey Explorer
Map OL12.
Grid ref: SN 950 084

NEARBY EXCURSIONS
Penderyn Distillery
Visitor Centre
Penderyn CF44 0SX
☎ 01685 813300
www.welsh-whisky.co.uk

Rhondda Heritage Park
Lewis Merthyr Colliery,
Coed Cae Road, Trehafod
Rhondda Cynon Taff
CF37 2NP
☎ 01443 682036
rhonddaheritagepark.com
Open daily 10am-6pm.

MORE INFO
Loops and Links
Walks in the Welsh valleys
www.loopsandlinks.co.uk

Visit Wales
www.visitwales.co.uk

Destination Rhondda
Cynon Taf
www.destinationrct.co.uk

Route ———

Rhossili Bay West Glamorgan

Distance 9½ miles (15 km) **Type** Moderate **Time** 5 hours

> Behind the bay Rhossili Down rises 180m (600ft) and is blanketed in gorse, grasses and heather

Located at the western tip of **Gower**, the National Trust-owned **Rhossili Bay** is one of the most spectacular beaches in the UK. With breathtaking seascapes and rare wildlife, it abounds in natural wonder.

▶ START
Turn right out of the car park and follow a path behind St Mary's Church. Turn left on to a stony track and continue through a gate, signposted to **Rhossili Down**. Ascend the hill using the wooden steps and follow the main grassy track until you ◎ reach **The Beacon**, Gower's highest point at 193m (632ft), providing exceptional 360° views.

1 1 MILE
Continue along the high sandstone ridge, passing the remains of Stone Age burial chambers on your right. At a fork in the path, bear left past the ruins of a Second World War radar station, before descending steeply to **Hillend**. Continue through a kissing gate and immediately turn left, following the road through Hillend Caravan Park until you reach a car park and access to Rhossili beach. Walk along the beach towards Rhossili village – at low tide the skeletal remains of the shipwreck ◎ *Helvetica*, beached in 1887, are clearly visible.
Climb the steps in the far corner and follow a path that brings you out opposite the car park.

2 5 MILES
Turn right and head downhill past the National Trust Visitor Centre (stop here to check tide times – access to Worms Head is only possible 2½ hours either side of low tide). Continue through a gate on to a surfaced path, passing the remains of an old Iron Age fort on your right. Follow the wide grass track leading to the Old Coastguard Lookout building, today manned by Coastwatch. A path leads down to the start of a slippery scramble across the causeway.

3 6½ MILES
Worm's Head gets its name from the Old English word for dragon (wurm) and its serpent-like shape. It is split into three sections: the **Inner**, **Middle** and **Outer** heads. It's possible to follow a path to the Outer Head, home to a seabird colony. Separating the Inner and Middle head is another rocky causeway, and as you cross to the Middle Head you will see a natural rock arch called ◎ **Devil's Bridge**. Keep a lookout for seals.

4 8½ MILES
Return across the causeway and take the path to the right of the Old Coastguard Lookout. Follow the path inland past the vile, a rare medieval open field system. Continue along the path until you reach a road junction. Turn left into Rhossili village and return to the car park.

▶ WORM'S HEAD

At low tide Worm's Head's limestone causeway provides ample opportunity for rockpoolers to cast their nets and discover an array of marine wildlife such as hermit crabs, coral weed, snake lock anemones, blennies and cushion starfish. Also, look out for a ship's anchor encrusted in the rocks – it's all that remains of one of the many ships fallen prey to the treacherous seas around Gower.

Explore **Rhossili Bay's** historical relics and pristine beach before
crossing to the tidal island of **Worm's Head**

KEY

INFO

TERRAIN
Well-worn tracks across heathland and grassy fields, narrow coastal paths, sandy beach and a rocky uneven causeway that can be slippery. Note the tide times at the National Trust Visitor Centre before crossing the causeway to Worm's Head.

HOW TO GET THERE
BY CAR: From Swansea follow the A4118, then the B4247 signposted to Rhossili. The car park (not National Trust) is situated next to National Trust Visitor Centre.
BY PUBLIC TRANSPORT: The nearest mainline train station is in Swansea (18 miles). The Gower Explorer bus, numbers 118 and 119, run regularly from Swansea. Traveline Cymru
☎ 0871 200 2233
www.traveline-cymru.info

MAP
Ordnance Survey Explorer Map 164.
Grid ref: SS 415 880

NEARBY EXCURSIONS
National Waterfront Museum Oystermouth Road, Maritime Quarter, Swansea, SA1 3RD
☎ 01792 638950
waterfrontmuseum.co.uk
Open daily 10am-5pm, except some days during Christmas and New Year's Day.

MORE INFO
National Trust Shop and Visitor Centre
Coastguard Cottages, Rhossili, Gower SA3 1PR
☎ 01792 390707
www.nationaltrust.org.uk

Route ———

139

Tarrenhendre Gwynedd

Distance 11½ miles (18 km) **Type** Challenging **Time** 6-7 hours

▶ This walk features some fantastic vistas, such as this view of Foel y-Geifr and Tarren y Gesail

With its mountains and high glacial lakes, **Snowdonia** attracts walkers by the busload, but while most of the crowds head to the **Snowdon Massif** and the peaks of the north, the quiet charms of the national park's southern hills are just aching to be discovered.

This walk, starting from the little village of **Pennal** in the **Dyfi Valley** at the southern edge of the park, takes you to the 634m (2076ft) summit of **Tarrenhendre** and a ridge with views encompassing **Cader Idris**, **Pumlumon**, the **Dyfi Estuary** and **Cardigan Bay**. Owain Glyndwr is said to have held court on a mound near Pennal and the church holds

a facsimile of a letter he sent in 1406 to the French King Charles VI.

▶ START

From behind **Pennal Church**, join a road coming from the school and follow it to a fork. Bear left, cross a bridge over **Afon Pennal** and head uphill. After a cattle grid and a gate, bear left to a ladder stile and walk through gorse to a track. Turn left, ignore a right-hand path, and head uphill to the forest corner, where you take a track crossing the hillside.

After a stile, veer to the left, keeping ahead to another stile where you have a valley below on

your left. Continue below **Mynydd Cefn-caer** with views of Tarrenhendre on your left. Emerge on a track and go left around the head of the valley. Pass sheepfolds on your left and walk uphill to the ridge between Tarrenhendre and **Foel y-Geifr**. To your right is **Tarren y Gesail** with Cader Idris behind.

1 | 3 MILES

Bear left, ignoring a right-hand stile, and take the steep path, crossing a stile on the way, to a corner fence. To conquer Tarrenhendre's boggy summit, climb the stile and follow the right-hand fence to a corner where

you cross a makeshift stile on your right. A small pile of stones to your left marks the top. Return to the ridge and continue along the undulating path, passing above steep, narrow valleys on both sides. If the weather is clear you can enjoy exhilarating views. Just beyond the summit cairn of **Trum Gelli** is a large cairn marking the end of the ridge path.

2 | 7 MILES

After a stile, take the path downhill through moorland frequented by meadow pipits and wheatears. From here are views of **Llyn Barfog** above **Cwm Maethlon**, named Happy Valley by the Victorians. Many legends are attached to the lake, said to be the home of Gwyn ap Nudd, the king of the fairies. After a stile lower down, head across a boggy patch and through a gap to a track. Turn left, cross fords, go through a gate across the track and, just before another gate, look for a small Bronze Age stone circle. It is known as **Eglwys Gwyddelod**, or Irishman's Church.

3 | 9¼ MILES

Beyond the gate, you will soon emerge on a shady lane where you bear left to the A493. Turn left to Pennal. There is a grass verge for most of the way.

Climb a mountain and hike along a grassy ridge with glorious views in a little walked area of **Snowdonia National Park**

KEY

INFO

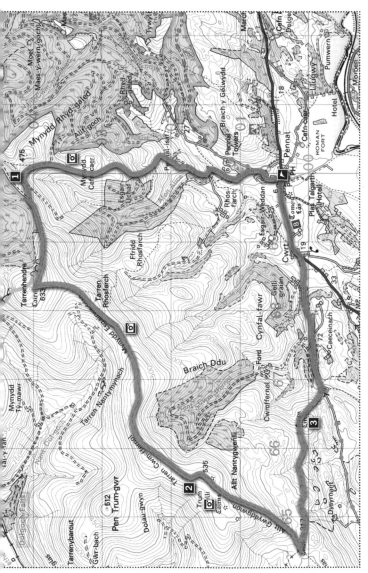

TERRAIN
A long but mainly gentle climb to a grass and heather ridge. A few paths are unclear. The track above Cwm Maethlon may be wet in places.

HOW TO GET THERE
BY CAR: Pennal is on the A493, 3½ miles west of Machynlleth.
BY PUBLIC TRANSPORT: Bus 28 runs from Machynlleth to Pennal.

Machynlleth is served by trains on the Shrewsbury to Pwllheli Cambrian Coast line.
www.thecambrianline.co.uk

NEARBY EXCURSIONS
Centre for Alternative Technology
Machynlleth SY20 9AZ
☎ 01654 705950
www.cat.org.uk

MAP
Ordnance Survey Explorer Map OL23.
Grid ref: SH 699 003

MORE INFO
Machynlleth Tourist Information Centre
☎ 01654 702401

Snowdonia National Park Authority
www.snowdonia-npa.gov.uk

Route ———

Gwydyr Forest Conwy

Distance 5½ miles (9 km) **Type** Moderate **Time** 3-4 hours

The hills on the western side of the **Conwy Valley** near **Llanrwst** have been mined since the 1600s. New machinery in Victorian times led to the establishment of larger mines, but most were unprofitable and closed after a few decades.

▶ START

From the back of the car park, take a marked footpath uphill and, at a waymarked post, bear right. Cross a clearing and follow the path over a bike trail and walk gradually uphill. Bear right on the lower of two tracks and soon turn left. After a few paces, take a path on the right. On your right are two capped mine shafts with grilles allowing access for hibernating bats. Look out for crossbills and coal tits in the forest.

Pass some derelict buildings and another capped mine shaft, then turn left along a track. On your right is a boggy area that was once a mine reservoir. At a right bend, go left on a path marked by an arrow. Pass the remains of the **Vale of Conwy Mill** where below on your left is a buddle, used for separating ore. Emerge on a lane and turn left.

1 1¾ MILES

Turn left on a track just before **Llyn Sarnau** car park and climb a ladder stile. Follow the path around a corner then go left to **Llanrwst**

▶ The remains of the Cyffty Mine buildings and buddle at Gwydyr overlook the peaks of Snowdonia

Lead Mine engine house, where there is an interpretation board. Pass the tall chimney and bear right to a stile. Turn right on a track and, after a barrier, turn left. After joining another track, bear right, crossing a track, and walk downhill towards a house. Before it, climb a stile on the right and follow a path, at first beside a wall then across open ground ◉ with magnificent views, in clear weather, of **Snowdonia**'s mountains. Reach a wall on the left and pass above a house. Cross two tracks and climb a stile then head towards the remains of ◉ **Cyffty Mine**. A path

leads past wheel pits to a mine shaft. Return to continue uphill and bear right, passing a buddle.

2 3¼ MILES

Follow the lane for 300m then go left on a forest track, passing a barrier. On reaching another track, bear right and, at a reservoir on your left, turn right uphill. After a spoil heap, turn right on a path with a blue footprint sign. Walk downhill and on a lower track, at a bend, climb a stile and head downhill, passing the chimney of **Hafna Mine**. Look for the information board explaining the milling process. This was a three-floored mill.

Descend steps and, just before the lane, bear left on a track with a barrier. Take a path on the right that has a miner's pick and hammer sign.

3 5 MILES

Cross a lane and pass the site of the demolished **Parc Mine Mill**. Water, coloured orange by iron, flows from the old tunnels. At a level area, cross a stile on the path to **Kneebone's Cutting**, named after the mine's engineer. Return and emerge on a track where you turn left, passing barriers, to a lane. Turn right then left to the car park.

Discover the remains of abandoned lead and zinc mines on the
hillsides of the beautiful **Gwydyr Forest**

INFO

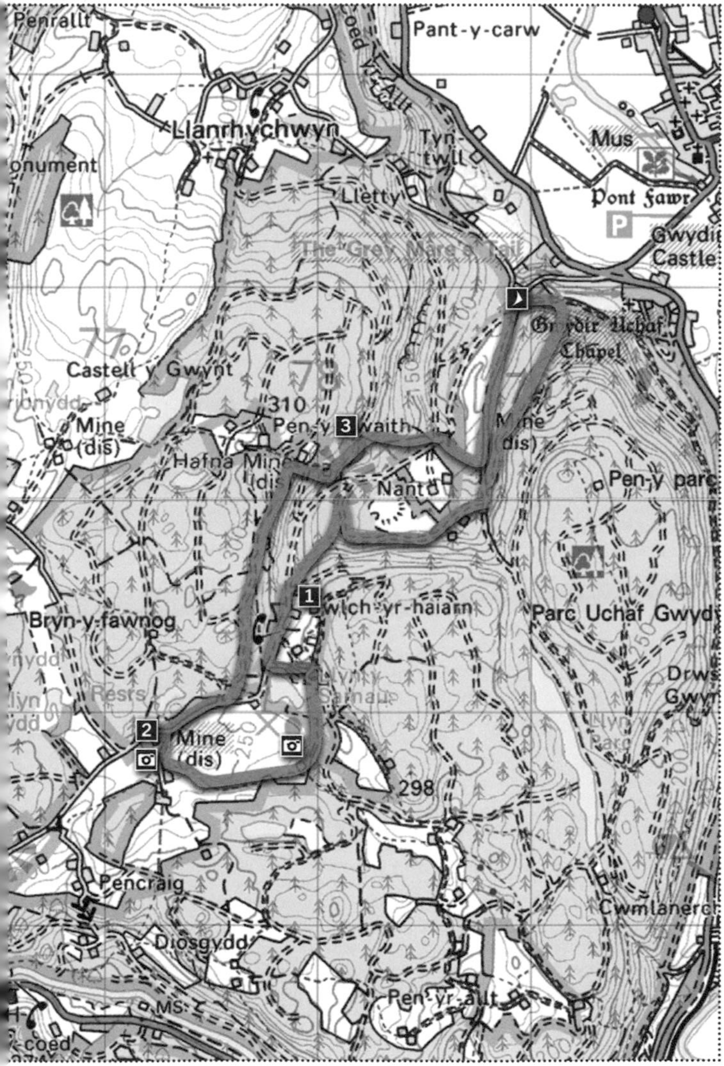

TERRAIN
Mainly forest paths
and tracks, some pasture
and lanes.

HOW TO GET THERE
BY CAR: West of Llanrwst,
leave the B5106 at the
Llanrwst/Betws-y-Coed fork
and take a minor road with
a Gwydyr Forest Park sign.
At a road on the right for
Llanrhychwyn go left to
the Marin car park.
BY PUBLIC TRANSPORT:
Trains on the Conwy Valley
Line stop at Llanrwst, 1 mile
from the start. Buses to
Llanrwst from Llandudno,
Blaenau Ffestiniog, Abergele
and Llangollen.

MAP
Ordnance Survey Explorer
Map OL17.
Grid ref: SH 790 609

NEARBY EXCURSIONS
Trefriw Woollen Mills
Trefriw LL27 0NQ
☎ 01492 640462
www.t-w-m.co.uk

Llanrwst Almshouse Museum
12 Church Street, Llanrwst
LL26 0LE
☎ 01492 642550

MORE INFO
Betws-y-Coed Tourist
Information Centre
Royal Oak Stables,
Betws-y-Coed LL24 0AH
☎ 01690 710426
www.visitwales.co.uk

Route ───────

143

Vale of Clwyd Denbighshire

Distance 6½ miles (10.4 km) **Type** Moderate **Time** 3½ hours

The **Vale of Clwyd** is a peaceful green valley lying between the **Clwydian Range** and the **Hiraethog Moors**. It receives few walkers or visitors because of the popularity of nearby Snowdonia. One of its treasures is the narrow, wooded **Clywedog Gorge**, a different landscape to the broad vale. The walk begins along a riverside track known as **Lady Bagot's Drive**. The Bagot family were local landowners and the drive was a carriage route for Lady Bagot, who loved the gorge.

▶ START

From the main road in **Rhewl**, opposite the lane to Llanynys, take the track signed for Bontuchel. It crosses a bridge over **Afon Clywedog**, a tributary of the River Clwyd, and a house known as Rhyd-y-Cilgwyn on the right, which was part of the Bagot Estate. It retains several timber framed farm buildings.

Continue with the river on your left and enter a wood. In places there are unusual rock formations in the river. You may spot grey wagtails, dippers or a heron.

Pass through a gate and, after a house, ignore a footbridge spanning the river. Bluebells, wood avens and wild garlic cover the woodland floor in spring. Watch for treecreepers and nuthatches. Ignore paths leading off and another

> **Behind Ruthin, the heather-clad Clwydian Range offers tantalising walking opportunities**

footbridge. Further on there are cliffs on your right and a field on the opposite side of the river.

1 2 MILES

Reach a footpath signpost with steps on your right. This is where the walk turns around and heads back to Rhewl, but to see more of the valley continue along the main track to a lane. Bear left for 500m then go left downhill over the 18th-century bridge to **Bontuchel**. The riverside house is a former mill. Turn left then soon go right on a lane. It rises and falls to a right bend where you go left at a parking sign.

2 3 MILES

A right-hand path beside the field leads to a wildlife hide where you may be lucky enough to spot dormice. Return to the main track and follow it over a bridge and through the woods to a junction, where you go left to a road. Turn left to **Bontuchel Bridge** and retrace your steps to Lady Bagot's Drive. Climb the steps seen earlier and take the woodland path to a stile and field.

Keep ahead and follow a short fence into more woods. Ignore a right-hand path and, after a stile, emerge in a field with wide views ahead of the Clwydian Range.

3 5 MILES

Go ahead over a stile and beside a fence with a pond on your left. Continue ahead to follow the left boundary of fields and pass a corrugated barn on your left. At a corner, bear right on a track and walk downhill into a wood, then between fields to the main road. Turn right to cross a bridge where a battle took place between Royalists and Parliamentarians during the Civil War. It is said that Afon Clywedog flowed red with their blood. You will soon arrive back at the start.

Discover the secrets of a **hidden valley** in a little visited area
of beautiful north Wales

KEY

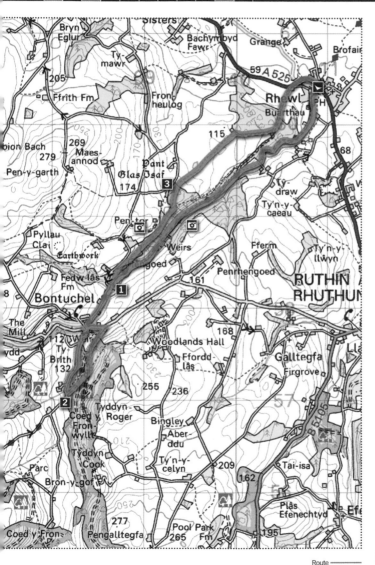

TERRAIN
Riverside and woodland
tracks and paths, fields
and lanes.

HOW TO GET THERE
BY CAR: Rhewl is on the
A525, north of Ruthin. Park
with care in the village.
BY PUBLIC TRANSPORT:
Buses run from Corwen
and Rhyl.

MAP
Ordnance Survey Explorer
Map 265.
Grid ref: SJ 109 604

NEARBY EXCURSIONS
Ruthin Gaol
Clwyd Street, Ruthin
LL15 1HP
☎ 01824 708281
www.ruthingaol.co.uk
Open weekends and school
holidays 10am-5pm.

Denbigh Castle
Castle Hill, Denbigh LL16 3NB
☎ 01745 813385
www.cadw.wales.gov.uk
Open 1 April-31 Oct,
10am-5pm.

MORE INFO
Llangollen Tourist
Information Centre
The Chapel, Castle Street,
Llangollen LL20 8NU
☎ 01978 860828
www.visitwales.co.uk

Route ————

Hope Mountain Flintshire

Distance 6 miles (9.4 km) **Type** Moderate **Time** 3 hours

> The old silica quarries in Waun y Llyn park are now home to stonechat, wheatear and meadow pipit

Caergwrle is only a few miles from the town of **Wrexham** and industrial **Deeside** but the village offers a beautiful escape into upland Wales.

▶ START
From the car park entrance, turn right, passing **Ye Olde Castle Inn**. On the opposite side of the road, a path climbs to the ruins of **Caergwrle**
🖸 **Castle**, a worthwhile diversion for the views as well as the ruins of the masonry castle, built by Dafydd ap Gruffydd. An information board points out features of the remains.

Return to the inn and take a path beside it to Bryn Yorkin Lane. Turn left around two bends and, at a junction, turn right to steps on your left. Walk ahead through the field and cross a drive and another field to a lane. Turn left and, after a bend, go right along Bryn Yorkin drive. An underground passage is said to link the Jacobean mansion with the castle.

1 1 MILE
Before Malt House, bear right beside a wall then bend left to a gate and woods. Turn right and, before a stile, bear left on an ascending path then walk through a field to a lane. Turn right for views
🖸 stretching to Deeside and the Wirral. After passing a lane on your right, go left on a footpath through fields to a higher lane.

2 2½ MILES
Cross directly to a stile and walk uphill. As you pass through the broken wall on **Hope Mountain**, there is a breathtaking panorama of a green
🖸 landscape stretching as far as the **Clwydian Hills**. Go downhill to an old track bordered by trees and old walls. Turn right to a lane. Cross to a bridleway and follow it past a ruined farm and a house.

Take the right-hand stile, entering **Waun y Llyn Country Park**. During the 19th and early 20th centuries, silica sandstone was quarried here. Stonechat, wheatear and meadow pipit may be spotted on the moorland, while snipe

are sometimes seen in the winter months.

On reaching a wider path turn right, passing a small lake, and head uphill at a former quarry site to a viewpoint at the toposcope.

3 4 MILES
Enjoy views of the **Cheshire Plain** and
🖸 **Moel Famau**, the highest summit of the Clwydian range. Face the lake and take a right-hand path towards the left side of a house, where you climb two stiles close together. At a corner in the right-hand fence, head left and soon downhill to a track.

Bear right to a lane junction and cross directly over. Turn left on the lane passed earlier and walk downhill. Go around a bend at the houses and, when the lane turns left, go ahead beside a wall to reach the main road. Turn right for 60m then cross a stile on the left. Keep to the right of the field and go through a right-hand kissing-gate.

Continue ahead to the Derby Arms, where a short diversion leads to a 17th-century packhorse bridge over the **River Alyn**. Packhorse trains crossed it several times a day on the Chester to Corwen trail. Return to the inn and cross the lane to soon emerge on the main road near the car park.

Discover quiet countryside with amazing views on this easily accessible walk near the **north Wales border**

KEY

▶INFO

TERRAIN
Footpaths, tracks and lanes.

HOW TO GET THERE
BY CAR: Caergwrle is on the A541 north of Wrexham. The car park is on the left if you are driving from Wrexham, just beyond Ye Olde Castle Inn.
BY PUBLIC TRANSPORT: Buses run from Wrexham and Mold. Caergwrle has a station on the Bidston-Wrexham railway line.

MAP
Ordnance Survey Explorer Map 256.
Grid ref: SJ 305 574

NEARBY EXCURSIONS
Alyn Waters Country Park
The Visitor Centre, Mold Road, Gwersyllt LL11 4AG
☎ 01978 763140

MORE INFO
Wrexham Tourist Information Centre
Lambpit Street, Wrexham LL11 1AY
☎ 01978 292015
www.visitwales.co.uk

Route ⎯⎯⎯

Chester• Winsford•

Wrexham• Nantwich•

▶ **LLANGOLLEN**
Market Drayton•
Oswestry•

Shrewsbury•

Dee Valley Denbighshire

Distance 9 miles (14½ km) **Type** Moderate **Time** 5-6 hours

▶ Llangollen takes its name from Saint Collen, a 7th-century monk who founded the church beside the Dee

Take the **Llangollen Railway** to Glyndyfrdwy station. The original line to the Cambrian coast closed after the Beeching Report in the 1960s and a preservation society now operates standard gauge trains between **Llangollen** and **Carrog**. This beautiful trip runs much of the way beside the **River Dee**.

▶ START

At **Glyndyfrdwy** station, go out to the road and turn left to cross a bridge over the River Dee. This part of the river is a Site of Special Scientific Interest known for its salmon, trout and otters, and you may also spot birds such as dippers, wagtails and,

possibly, a kingfisher.

At the junction turn right and bear left at a footpath signpost to walk through a field to a small gate in the right-hand corner. Go left a few paces then uphill on a path through trees, bracken, gorse and a field to a lane. Turn left to join another lane. Continue ahead, passing a cattle grid, and walk uphill with great views of the **Dee Valley**. Keep a watch overhead for peregrines, buzzards and ravens. You may spot merlins and hen harriers hunting.

The lane continues through open land to a signpost in a dip, where you turn right.

1 1¾ MILES

Before a cattle grid, bear left and after coniferous trees, go through a right-hand gate. After another gate, the track bends left and soon rises to another track where you turn right.

Pass a farm and turn left on another lane then left on a bridleway. Walk uphill, with views of a valley below and **Llantysilio Mountain** ahead. Grouse inhabit the moors here. At a corner gate, bear right to a footpath signpost at the highest point of the walk. The **Eglwyseg Crags** and **Trevor Rocks** are now in view.

Head downhill beside

a right-hand fence then on a sunken track to an access track. Turn right to a lane and continue ahead, passing the Sun Inn, a 14th-century drovers' inn. A few paces after a chapel, take a footpath on the left.

2 5¼ MILES

Follow the left-hand fence into another field then go right to cross a footbridge and uphill to a kissing gate near houses. Continue to a lane then turn right and take the second footpath on your left. Trace the right side of a field, wood and hillside to a right-hand stile. Head downhill then beside woodland to a lane.

Turn left then left again to a footpath on the right and walk along the left side of a field to the next field and through gates to a lane.

3 6¾ MILES

Turn left to Llantysilio church and go through the kissing gate beside the lych-gate. Walk downhill to the River Dee and **Horseshoe Falls**, a weir created in the 19th century by Thomas Telford to feed water into the **Llangollen Canal**. Join the towpath and follow it past the Chainbridge Hotel to **Llangollen Wharf** then downhill into the centre of Llangollen.

Enjoy some spectacular views and peaceful countryside on this delightful walk along the **Dee Valley Way**

KEY

▶INFO

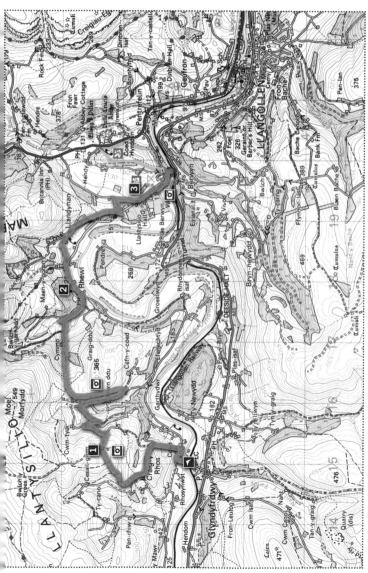

TERRAIN
Rough pasture, woodlands, tracks, canal towpath and lanes, with several climbs. Strong footwear essential.

HOW TO GET THERE
BY CAR: Llangollen is at the junction of the A5 and A539. Several car parks in the town.
BY PUBLIC TRANSPORT: Buses from Chester, Wrexham, Llandudno and Barmouth to Llangollen. Nearest main line station is at Ruabon (on the Chester-Shrewsbury line). Buses run from near the station or Bridge Street to Llangollen. Llangollen Railway Station is close to the bridge over the River Dee. Trains run every day from May to early October and during school holidays plus most weekends.
☎ 01978 860979
www.llangollen-railway.co.uk

MAP
Ordnance Survey Explorer Map 255.
Grid ref: SJ 150 429

MORE INFO
Llangollen Tourist Information Centre
☎ 01978 860828

Visit Wales
www.visitwales.co.uk

Route ——————

149

NORTH WEST

Cumbria, and more specifically the **Lake District**, can safely claim to be the walking capital of Great Britain. It's certainly one of our most hyped areas and for once the reality lives up to the talk. Fourteen major lakes and waters are crammed into an area roughly 30 by 25 miles (50 by 40 km), set against a stunning vista of dramatic fells and mountain peaks. The two largest lakes, **Windermere** and **Ullswater**, are the honeypots here, along with the villages of **Hawkshead** and **Grasmere** – 'the loveliest spot that man hath ever found!' that inspired Wordsworth to wax lyrical about daffodils – the towns of **Ambleside**, **Penrith** and **Kendal** (home of the famous mint cake), and the often-crowded faces of **Helvellyn** and **Scafell Pike**, England's tallest mountain.

Part of the reason for the region's popularity – awe-inspiring scenery notwithstanding – is down to a decidedly eccentric fellwalker, Alfred Wainwright. Between 1952 and 1966 AW, as he's affectionately known to his legions of devotees, climbed 214 summits to compose his seven *Pictorial Guides to the Lakeland Fells*. Since then, millions of hikers have taken to the fells with a well-thumbed copy of one of these tomes, many of them aiming to match AW's achievement and climb all 214 of the **Wainwright Fells**. In the seventh guide, this poet of the fells got it so right when he wrote: 'The fleeting hour of life of those who love the hills is quickly spent, but the hills are eternal.'

Eternal the hills may be, but they are in no way all there is to see in the North West. Head into **Lancashire**, the county that embraced the industrial revolution with more fervor than anywhere else in Britain, where you'll discover the unspoilt beauty of the **Ribble Valley**, an area said to have inspired J. R. R. Tolkein when he created the Shireland of *The Lord of the Rings*, and the **Forest of Bowland**. Just don't expect trees when you explore the 'Forest' – the name refers to a time when it was hunting ground. Today it is an Area of Outstanding Natural Beauty, famed for heather moorland, blanket bog and rare upland birds including the hen harrier.

In contrast to the rugged mountains of Cumbria and the delights of **Lancashire**, the undulating dairy pastures of **Cheshire** form an idyllic backdrop for walking, and of course play their part in making delicious, crumbling Cheshire cheese.

The North West is a mecca for those who love the outdoors, but it is always worth looking beyond the tourist traps to see what other delights are hidden away.

Hilbre Islands Merseyside

Distance 4¼ miles (7 km) **Type** Easy **Time** 5 hours

> This Hilbre Islands walk features some stunning scenery and some equally amazing wildlife too

The **Dee Estuary** was a busy shipping lane for centuries. Packet boats, troops and traders embarked at **Parkgate**, the port for Ireland, until silting scuppered this in Georgian times. With multiple designations as a protected area for nature conservation, it is the estuary's wildlife that is the focus of attention for modern day visitors. Today, shrimping boats and leisure craft follow the channels guarded by the three **Hilbre Islands**. The islands are owned by Wirral Council and managed by the country park rangers, assisted by the enthusiastic Friends of Hilbre volunteers.

This walk is best done across a low-tide period. Leave **West Kirby** 3½ hours after high tide; the walk to the islands takes an hour. Spend a maximum of three hours here before setting off back to the mainland. Do not attempt this walk in poor visibility or adverse weather conditions.

▶ START

The **Dee Lane** slipway adjoins the sailing club at **West Kirby**; tide times are posted on a board here. Sight the Hilbre Islands and aim for the left-hand one, **Little Eye**. The sands are firm, 📷 patterned by current marks and punctured by marine worm casts.

1 1 MILE

Keep Little Eye to your immediate right, turning up its western flank to continue along the string of islets, shortly reaching **Little Hilbre Island**. Spend some time rockpooling here – the shallow pools may hold dab or flounder. Beyond is the southern tip of **Hilbre Island**. In its time this remote outpost has seen a remarkable variety of inhabitants and trades. Tantalising evidence of early visitors has been found, including a few Bronze Age and Roman fragments. The carved head of a cross and a slab grave suggest occupation during the Viking era, while a monastic cell existed until the 1530s. Salt boilers, smugglers, wreckers and telegraphers have all left their mark – there was even a Seagull Inn here in Victorian times!

Today, the Dee Estuary ranger is the islands' sole permanent inhabitant. During spring and summer, Atlantic grey seals travel from the Irish Sea to the bountiful feeding grounds of the estuary. There can be as many as 500, and at low tide the seals haul themselves on to sandbanks just west of Hilbre.

The islands are also famous among Britain's birding fraternity; since 1957 a bird observatory has monitored the bird populations. During spring and summer wading birds such as oystercatcher, knot and dunlin present a 📷 great spectacle, while the giants of the British seabird world, gannets and several species of skua, are regular visitors. Many butterflies also rest here, and plants include the very rare rock sea lavender.

2 2¼ MILES

Reverse your route to return to the mainland, enjoying sublime views across the silvery Dee to north Wales and the distant peaks of Snowdonia. The eye-catching **Mariners Beacon** above West Kirby was erected in 1841 to guide vessels homeward from the treacherous seas of Liverpool Bay, and acts as a useful landmark.

Beat the tide to visit the **Dee Estuary's** sandstone islets, where grey seals thrive and seabirds rule the roost

KEY

▶INFO

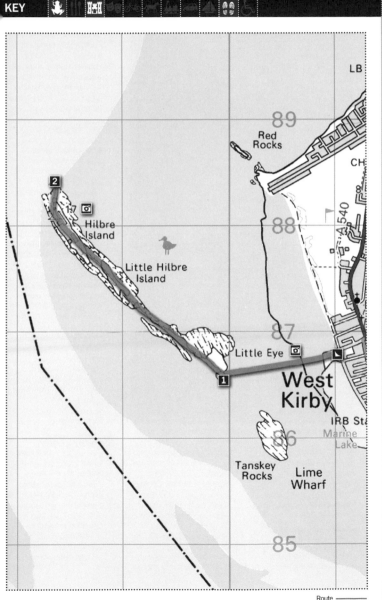

TERRAIN
Firm sand and rocky outcrops. Wear wellies or old walking boots, and pack waterproofs in your rucksack. Take binoculars to spot the wildlife.

HOW TO GET THERE
BY CAR: West Kirby is at the northwest tip of the Wirral Peninsula; park near the Sailing Club or Marine Lake.
BY PUBLIC TRANSPORT: Regular daily trains go to West Kirby on Merseytravel's Wirral Line service from Birkenhead and Liverpool.

MAP
Ordnance Survey Explorer Map 266.
Grid ref: SJ 210 867

NEARBY EXCURSIONS
Liverpool University's Ness Botanic Gardens are 5 miles south of West Kirby and are open daily from 10am.
☎ 0151 353 0123
www.nessgardens.org.uk

MORE INFO
For advice on tides contact the Wirral Country Park Visitor Centre at Thurstaston.
☎ 0151 648 4371
www.deeestuary.co.uk/hilbre
Detailed times are also posted on the noticeboard at the Dee Lane slipway – take heed of the advised time of safe departures from here and back from Hilbre.

Birkenhead Tourist Information
Woodside Ferry Terminal
☎ 0151 330 1000
www.visitwirral.com

Route ⸺

153

Blackburn
Halifax
Rochdale
Bolton
Prestwich Oldham
Manchester
Sale
DISLEY
Macclesfield

The Gritstone Trail Cheshire

Distance 11¼ miles (18 km) **Type** Moderate **Time** 5 hours

The **Cheshire Plain** ends abruptly in the east as waves of gritstone hills and deep valleys, forming the western fringe of the **Peak District**. **The Gritstone Trail** explores this enticing countryside, dipping into **Lyme Park** and threading along ridges offering extraordinary views. This inter-station walk follows it over the hills to join the **Macclesfield Canal** at this old silk-working centre.

▶ START
At **Disley** station (behind the Manchester platform) join the waymarked Gritstone Trail up a long flight of steps. At the lane go uphill and turn left towards the church, then bend right on **Green Lane**, which soon roughens to a track. Keep straight on at Higher Stoneridge Farm along a path to a bridlegate, beyond which a track winds to a gate and cross-lane.

1 1 MILE
Turn right, cross a bridge and enter Lyme Park beside **East Lodge**; follow the drive to **Lyme Hall**, one of England's greatest stately homes.

Beyond the car park keep left at a cattle-grid where the Gritstone Trail is signed through a kissing gate, past which it rises through woodland, prior to climbing steeply up a braided way to reach a moorland track beside Bowstones Farm.

The trail turns right,

▶ Harrop Valley: where the National Park meets the Cheshire Plain

but a short diversion left reveals the **Bowstones**, ancient boundary markers given their name thanks to the legend that **Robin Hood** restrung his bows at this spot.

2 3½ MILES
Return along the track and remain on it. As the wall bends away, keep

ahead along **Sponds Hill** to reach **Bakestonedale Road**; turn right here. Immediately past Brink Farm, go left along a rough track and follow frequent Gritstone Trail discs. Keep left of the old quarry and favour the lower option at a choice of two trail waymarks. Cross a cattle grid and

fork left alongside a wall. Further waymarks show the way down into the
 **Harrop Valley** and up to a back lane. Turn right to a minor road and left to a triangular junction; rise left to a crossroad.

3 7 MILES
Continue ahead along **Oakenbank Lane**. At a left-bend in 500m, keep ahead down steps, tracing trail discs via stiles and gates to a lane. Turn left; in 75m turn right for North End Farm. Just before the second cattle grid, turn left up a path to **White Nancy** monument, a folly built to celebrate victory over Napoleon. Join the path along **Kerridge Ridge**, with huge views across northwest England. After three kissing gates, the path reaches a twin stile and gate. Use both, turn right alongside the wall and drop to a lane. Turn left along the downhill road; keep right at the junction with Swanscoe Lane, then left at the next to reach **Higher Hurdsfield**.

4 9½ MILES
Bear right along **Rainow Road** to reach the canal bridge; slip left on to the towpath and walk beside the **Macclesfield Canal**. In ½ mile leave at bridge 37 and walk down the main road to find **Macclesfield** station through the bridge beyond the traffic lights.

Enjoy the **Peak District's** final, hilly flourish on this linear walk in the fascinating, fractured countryside between Disley and Macclesfield

KEY

▶ INFO

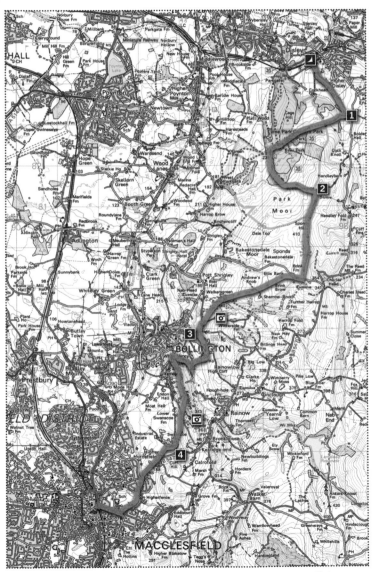

Route ⎯⎯⎯

TERRAIN
Good paths, tracks and lanes, and a towpath. The Gritstone Trail is very well waymarked by fingerposts and frequent discs marked with a black boot-print and the letter G.

HOW TO GET THERE
BY CAR: Disley is on the A6, about 7 miles southeast of Stockport. There is a large car park at the railway station.
BY PUBLIC TRANSPORT:
Regular daily trains to Disley station on the Manchester Piccadilly and Stockport to Buxton line. Frequent trains from Macclesfield to Stockport and Manchester on the West Coast main line.

MAP
Ordnance Survey Explorer Map OL1 and 268.
Grid ref: SJ 973 845

NEARBY EXCURSIONS
Lyme Hall
Disley, Stockport SK12 2NR
☎ 01633 762023
www.nationaltrust.org.uk
This Palladian mansion is set in a 1,300-acre deer park.

Macclesfield's silk heritage is shown in several museums and heritage attractions.
☎ 01625 612045
www.macclesfield.silk. museum/

MORE INFO
Macclesfield Tourist Information
Town Hall,
Macclesfield SK10 1DX
☎ 01625 504114
www.peaksandplains.co.uk

Peak District National Park
www.peakdistrict.org

Forest of Bowland Lancashire

Distance 13 miles (21 km) **Type** Challenging **Time** 6 hours

•Lancaster
Settle•
DUNSOP
BRIDGE
Garstang•
Clitheroe•
Longridge•
Preston•
•Blackburn
Leyland•

North Lancashire's grouse moors and heathery fells shimmer from horizon-to-horizon, cleaved by becks and dappled with rocky outcrops. One such, **Whitendale Hanging Stones**, is equidistant from all 401 islands of Great Britain – the true heart of the realm. Reaching this wild spot requires stamina and determination; your reward is a glimpse of a place few will ever see – sublime seclusion in a stirring landscape that's also home to Britain's rarest raptor.

❯ START

From the car park at **Dunsop Bridge**, turn right and cross the river to the war memorial. Turn right on the lane and follow for 2 miles beside the **River Dunsop**. At **Footholme** waterworks, cross the first bridge and fork left to an Access Land sign. Cross the narrow footbridge and turn upstream. Keep right at a hut, use the gate and then the footbridge and trace the undulating, boggy path to **Whitendale Farm**. Drop to the lane and turn right beside the farmhouse, through gates to join a track above **Whitendale River**. Keep right at a tall waymarker post for **Salter Fell**; beyond a gate the track declines to a wet path and follows the river for 1 mile.

Rising steadily past yellow-topped posts, your company may include wheatears, curlew, red

> Step into the wild: this walk will truly take you into the heart of the UK

grouse and possibly a glimpse of one of Britain's most majestic birds, a hen harrier. This is the symbol of the Forest of Bowland Area of Outstanding Natural Beauty (AONB); it's a fitting emblem as all of England's dozen or so breeding pairs nest in these remote uplands. Remain on the path to reach a moorland track and turn left. This, the **Hornby Road**, and part of the **Salters Way**, meanders across **Croasdale** and **Salter Fells** which, in 2004, were unveiled as the very first areas of Access Land created under the Right to Roam commitment in the Countryside and Rights of Way Act 2000.

1 | 6½ MILES

At the second gate, turn left on your side of the fence and rise alongside it to a cross-fence below **◙ Wolfhole Crag**. Turn left here (near-side of the fence), shortly passing **White Crag** and its noisy lesser black-backed gull colony. Just before the fence bends left, the insignificant outcrop is Whitendale Hanging Stones, the middle of Great Britain. From this unprepossessing spot **◙** are some inspiring views across Bowland's fells and valleys. The area is called Bowland as the uplands are bordered to the east and south by the **River Ribble**, curving in a great bow en-route from the high Pennines to the Irish Sea.

2 | 8½ MILES

Use the gate just past the stones and walk directly away from the fence, alongside a line of shooting butts on your right to reach a distinct stony outcrop. Look beyond this for a faint vehicle track (not the shallow valley ahead-left) that bends right and curls past posts across the boggy terrain to meet a shooter's road. Turn left along this and remain with it to a gate at the edge of Access Land. Cross the nearby bridge and walk via **Brennand Farm** back to Footholme, then Dunsop Bridge.

Enjoy a vigorous walk to the very centre of Britain, amid the
secluded cloughs, moors and crags of Lancashire's **Bowland**

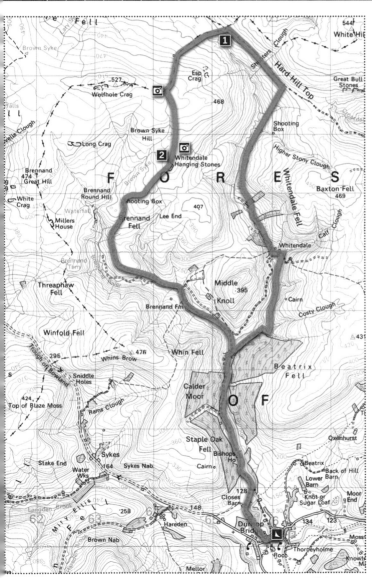

KEY

▶INFO

TERRAIN
Lanes, paths and tracks, but
with section across moorland
with faint or no paths. Some
stretches may be extremely
boggy, so try to do the walk
during a dry spell of weather.
The walk is lengthy rather
than steep. Take a map,
compass, torch, whistle,
food and plenty of fluid –
mobile telephone reception
is very patchy in this area.
Not suitable for dogs due to
ground-nesting birds.
Parts of this route may be
subject to some access
restrictions during the grouse
season (12 August to 10
December), so before setting
out, check the website
www.openaccess.gov.uk
or call 0845 100 3298.

HOW TO GET THERE
BY CAR: Dunsop Bridge
is 10 miles southeast of
Lancaster. Take the Trough of
Bowland Road from the city,
or approach from Preston via
Whitewell or from Clitheroe
via Newton-in-Bowland.
The car park is in the village
centre.
BY PUBLIC TRANSPORT:
Buses B10 & B11 to Dunsop
Bridge from Clitheroe,
Monday to Saturday.
☎ 0871 200 2233
transportforlancashire.com

MAP
Ordnance Survey Explorer
Map OL41.
Grid ref: SD 660 501

MORE INFO
Bowland Visitor Centre
Fell House, Goosnargh,
Preston PR3 2NL
☎ 01995 640557
www.forestofbowland.com

Route ———

157

NORTH WEST

Clitheroe •
Colne •
Burnley •
Blackburn •
▸ ROSSENDALE
Edenfield •
Ramsbottom •

Rossendale Lancashire

Distance 6 miles (9.7 km) **Type** Moderate **Time** 3 hours

Rossendale's Irwell Valley was a powerhouse of the Industrial Revolution, famed for its textiles and footwear. Less-known were the immense stone quarries, which provided the flagstones that paved many of England's towns. The stirring remains of such litter the enclosing moors, a mini-wilderness threaded by old tramroads, dappled by workings, dotted with wind turbines and possessed of extraordinary views.

▸ START

Walk ahead 50m from the car park entrance before bearing right up the tarred lane. At its end, pass between the houses and bend left up a fenced track, continuing beyond a stile on an ever-rising way to reach some ruins. Use the stile, right, to join an old track that circles the flank of **Cowpe**
📷 **Lowe**. Excellent views stretch out across the moors here.

At a fence corner with Access Land and RW (Rossendale Way) discs, walk to the tall gateposts. Aim ahead-right to walk the right-hand embankment of the small reservoir, and from the far end keep ahead along the nearby old track. To your left are the first delvings of the many quarries of the **Cowpe**, while ahead the horizon is broken by your first sighting of the wind turbines on **Scout Moor**. At a leaning fingerpost, fork left, cutting across to

▸ Explore a mini wilderness, dotted with industrial remains and awash with outstanding views

a gateway and stile amid tumbled walls.

1 | 1¾ MILES

Use the stile and continue along the track. Its origin as a cartway soon becomes obvious, with deep ruts etched into the flagstones. The higher track – you can follow either – was one of the many tramroads threading these remarkable workings.

At a Pennine Bridleway fingerpost go ahead for **Top of Leach**, gradually climbing **Foe Edge**. This rises to and through the gaunt, strangely appealing landscape of **Crag Quarry**. To your

left immense views
📷 open out, from the sharp profile of Pendle Hill in the foreground to Pen-y-Ghent and Whernside further on.

2 | 4 MILES

The track eventually reaches another Pennine Bridleway fingerpost. The trail heads left, but first divert right along the worn cartway for 90m, then go right across the moor to gain the trig pillar at Top of Leach, with a memorable
📷 panorama across the roof of England.

Return to the fingerpost and start a steep descent towards **Stacksteads**. In just

under a mile and, before the farm, go through the gate and fork left here, through another gate, then bend left on the field road for 90m. Turn right beside a fence and drop to a cross-fence. Look right for a broken stile, use this and double-back to a lower stile, then walk down the sunken path to a gate on your left. Walk through the yard, past **Higher Boarsgreave Farm**, and continue to a tarred road. Turn right and walk through Cowpe, past the Buck Inn to find the picnic site access road on the left opposite Green Bridge South terrace.

Explore the memorable moors and cloughs of **Rossendale**, where remnants
of the quarrying industry lie amid formidable South Pennine scenery

▶INFO

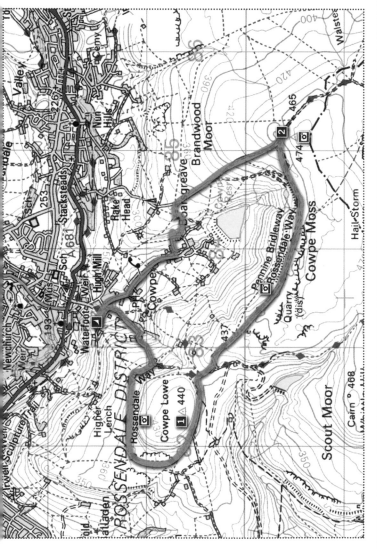

TERRAIN
Mostly good moorland tracks,
but expect mud in places.
There's an initial steady climb,
otherwise the trail features
level or downhill walking.
Don't attempt this walk in
misty conditions. The trail is
good for dogs, but keep them
on a lead when requested.

HOW TO GET THERE
BY CAR: Waterfoot is halfway
between Rawtenstall and
Bacup on the A681. Turn
south up Cowpe Road (at
mini-roundabout, signed for
Health Centre and picnic site)
and follow signs to the picnic
site, up a cobbled lane on
the right.
BY PUBLIC TRANSPORT:
Rossendale Transport bus
service 464 (Accrington to
Rochdale via Rawtenstall)
runs frequently via Waterfoot.
☎ 01706 390520
www.rossendalebus.co.uk

MAP
Ordnance Survey Explorer
Map OL21.
Grid ref: SD 834 215

NEARBY EXCURSIONS
Helmshore Mills
Textile Museum
Holcombe Road, Helmshore,
Rossendale BB4 4NP
☎ 01706 226459
Open daily from 1 April-31
Oct, noon- 4pm.

MORE INFO
Rossendale Tourist
Information Centre
Rawtenstall Library, Queens
Square, Rawtenstall,
Rossendale BB4 6QU
☎ 01706 252411
www.visitrossendale.co.uk

Route ———

Crook O'Lune Lancashire

Distance 3¾ miles (6 km) **Type** Easy **Time** 2 hours

> Scan the riverbanks for the flash of blue of a passing kingfisher

Crook O'Lune, where the **River Lune** meanders in an impressive oxbow, has long been admired as the quintessential English landscape. Painted by Turner and described by Gray and Wordsworth, it has lost none of its charm and picturesque beauty over the years. It has been included in the **River Lune Millennium Park**, stretching from Caton to Salt Arye, on Lancaster's coast. The park was created to provide opportunities for leisure and recreation away from the hustle of city life around Lancaster, providing cycleways, footpaths and green spaces for public enjoyment, including artworks, and information on the local wildlife and history.

▶ START

Start from the car parking area at Crook O'Lune park and pick up the tarmac footpath near the main road (the line of the disused Morecambe to Leeds railway). Before you leave the car park however, you might want to linger and take in the landscape before you. Yorkshire's three peaks (Pen-y-ghent, Whernside and Ingleborough, with its distinctive table-top) are visible on the eastern horizon.

The Crook O' Lune itself was immortalised by Turner in paint and much admired by successive generations of poets, including Wordsworth (although Ruskin preferred Kirkby Lonsdale's eponymous Ruskin's View), while contemporary artist Colin Wilbourn has contributed a carved artwork, one of three within the Millennium Park.

Back to the railway path, follow it east (turn left) across the old bridge over the River Lune. Soon you will pass the village of **Caton** on your right. Past Caton village, cross **Artle Beck** and look out for Wilbourn's third carved picture, (the first is back westwards towards Lancaster itself).

1 | 1 MILE

Continue to a lane crossroads and turn left, following the footpath sign. A gate and stile are immediately on the left.

Over the stile, continue to the banks of the River Lune. Follow the river north as it meanders back and forth and look out for river and estuary birds that might be around. Kingfishers, oystercatchers, sand martins and redshanks are all frequent visitors along here. You may also see salmon and trout in the river.

2 | 2 MILES

Eventually you will come to a large waterpipe bridge straddling the river. Cross over and turn left, heading back west, towards the starting point.

The path skirts Burton Wood, a nature reserve where bluebells and wild garlic can be seen in spring. The return walk to Crook O'Lune is a simple matter of following the river bank – or, of course, you may choose to do the walk in the reverse direction if you prefer. Back at the car park, the mobile catering van Woodies is well regarded if you feel that you've earned yourself a bacon butty.

Escape to **Crook O'Lune**, one of Lancashire's best picnic spots, where a quintessentially English landscape meets breathtaking views

KEY

▶**INFO**

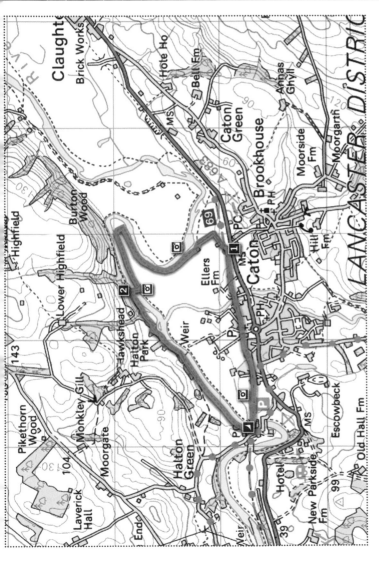

TERRAIN
Easy, flat walking on well surfaced footpaths, but also muddy riverbank paths. Wellies or walking boots are recommended.

HOW TO GET THERE
BY CAR: Take the M6 J34 on A683 east (towards Kirby Lonsdale) to Halton (2 miles from J34). Crook O' Lune car park is on the left just before Caton Village
BY PUBLIC TRANSPORT: There is a regular bus service through the Trough of Bowland between Lancaster and Kirkby Lonsdale.
www.catonvillage.org.uk

MAP
Ordnance Survey Explorer Map OL41.
Grid ref: SD 521 648

NEARBY EXCURSIONS
Lancaster City Museum
Market Square, Lancaster
LA1 1HT
☎ 01524 64637

MORE INFO
Crook O' Lune Country Park
LA2 9NB
☎ 01524 32878
citycoastcountryside.co.uk

Visit North West Tourism
www.visitnorthwest.com/
lancaster/crookolune.htm

Visit Lancashire
www.visitlancashire.com

Route ⎯⎯⎯

Windermere •
CONISTON ▸
Kendal

Burrow-in-
furness

Coniston Cumbria

Distance 9 miles (14½ km) **Type** Challenging **Time** 5 hours

> ▸ The climb up to Bethecar Moor affords excellent views to the hamlet of Nibthwaite on Coniston Water

Arthur Ransome's *Swallows and Amazons* stories have endured for three-quarters of a century and show no sign of dipping in popularity any time soon.

This walk, magically combined with a lake cruise, immerses you fully in the atmosphere of the tales and the scenery that inspired them. And even if you're not yet a fan, the open spaces of the moors and the sensational views over lake and fells are reason enough to relish this magnificent outing.

▸ START

Between March and October, cruise down the lake on a Coniston launch to **Water Park**, passing **Peel Island** (Wild Cat Island) with Its secret harbour. (Alternatively, take bus X12 to **Water Yeat** then lanes and a field path to Nibthwaite).

From the jetty, walk up

the path to the road and turn right. Entering the hamlet of **Nibthwaite**, a signed footpath offers a short detour to Amazon-like boathouses.

Retrace your steps and turn up the lane by the phone box. On the left is **Swainson's Farm**, where Ransome stayed as a boy. His memories of magical summer holidays were a major inspiration for the books. Go through a gate and follow the path on the right up and around the slopes of **Brock Barrow** to **High Bethecar Farm.**

1 1 MILE

Head left onto **Bethecar Moor,** a rolling expanse reminiscent of Ransome's Swallowdale. Another clear track joins from the right. Tamely following wide tracks is not in the *Swallows and Amazons* spirit so, providing the

weather's still clear, leave the track where it dips into a marshy hollow. Climb on to the steep ridge of **Arnsbarrow Hill** and follow a slim path along it. The path aims towards the nearby edge of the forest, then begins to bear left, passing just above Arnsbarrow Tarn. Leave the path and go straight ahead up a broad slope to Top o'Selside. There's a cairn on its western top.

Head northwest on easy open slopes, which soon become a broad ridge; follow this down to the ruins of **High Parkamoor**. Descend a good track and then turn right to the abandoned farm of Low Parkamoor.

2 4 MILES

Follow a fine green track across the moor to **Park Crags**, a great viewpoint, before entering the

forest. A muddy track leads you to a forest road.

Go left for 500m, and then take a narrow rough path down to the isolated house of **Lawson Park**.

3 4½ MILES

Go left, then right on a footpath marked by a white arrow. At a fork go left, descending gently across the slope until you reach a stone hut (The Dogs' Home, central to Ransome's *The Picts and the Martyr*s). Just below this a clear path forks off right, marked by a mauve-topped post. Follow this waymarked path down through the woods to **Machell's Coppice** car park. Turn right, following the shore, and then the road, to **Brantwood**.

4 5½ MILES

Continue along the road for 600m. Bear left on a footpath through the fields, past Low Bank Ground to High Bank Ground; as **Holly Howe,** this featured at the opening of *Swallows and Amazons*. Find a narrow walled path then cross a large open field below Lanehead, home of the Collingwood family (Ransome unsuccessfully proposed to two of their daughters). Rejoin the road and follow it left. Walk along the shore round the head of the lake then follow a sheltered footpath alongside the road back to Coniston.

Explore the rippling lake, wild moors and lush woods that inspired
the famous *Swallows and Amazons* stories

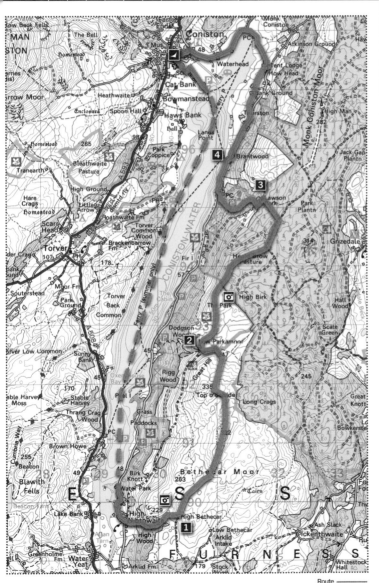

TERRAIN
Wild, open moorland,
woodland paths and lanes.
One muddy section demands
decent boots.

HOW TO GET THERE
BY CAR: Coniston is
southwest from Ambleside on
the A593.
BY PUBLIC TRANSPORT:
Bus X12 runs from Ulverston
to Coniston, the 505 runs
from Ambleside to Coniston.
**www.stagecoachbus.com/
northwest/index.html**

MAP
Ordnance Survey Explorer
Map OL6 and OL7.
Grid ref: SD 305 975

MORE INFO
Coniston Tourist
Information Centre
Ruskin Avenue, Coniston
LA21 8EH
☎ 01539 441533
www.conistontic.org

Route ————
Add-on ferry route — — —

Eskdale Cumbria

Distance 7 miles (11½ km) **Type** Moderate **Time** 4 hours

Caldbeck•
• Maryport
• Cockermouth
•Workington
Keswick •

The Lake District •
National Park

• Gosforth
▶ ESKDALE
Coniston •

Of all the remote and dramatic landscapes in the **Lake District**, Upper Eskdale's **Great Moss** must be one of the most beautiful – and the best thing is you can reach it without arduous climbing or complicated navigation. In fact it's just a pleasant walk along the valley floor, following the tumbling waterfalls of the **River Esk**.

▶ START

Park at the foot of **Hardknott Pass**, at **Brotherilkeld** (if you travelled to Eskdale via the passes of Wrynose and Hardknott your day will already have been scenic and adventurous!). The farm at Brotherilkeld is accessed via the gate beside the telephone box. Pass through the farmyard, staying right, and ignore the path across the footbridge. Follow the footpath on the right of the valley that leads through the farmyard and picks up a path beside the field wall. Climb over a number of stiles before traversing the fellside, a little way above the river flowing along the valley bottom. You may notice **Birk Dub** and **Kail Pot** marked on the map – these are natural holes in the river, which were once used to dip sheep; dubs and pots are often found marked on Lakeland rivers. After passing Kail Pot, climb a final stile out on the fell with the river Esk flowing swiftly by your side.

▶ The wild and remote beauty of Upper Eskdale is irresistible

1 1 MILE

Follow the well-marked path alongside the river along the valley floor to a conspicuous Y-junction in the river at **Lingcove**, where a beautifully constructed ancient packhorse bridge crosses the river. The River Esk becomes rockier and narrow as you approach Lingcove and the water constricts into a series of waterfalls, with crystal clear plunge pools ready-made for a dip on a hot day. These pools invite exploration, photography or at least a moment of quiet reflection.

2 2 MILES

Lingcove bridge is at the confluence of **Lingcove Beck** and the River Esk; cross the bridge and from here the route continues to **Throstle Garth** and winds steeply past **Throstlehow Crag**. The Esk is now hidden within a deep gorge and the path continues up to a craggy area, known as **Scar Lathing**, before suddenly turning the corner to reveal the true identity of Eskdale's Great Moss. The river cuts a meandering, multi-channelled path through this high plateau, sheltered all around by the mighty crags of **Sca Fell**, **Esk Buttress** and **Bowfell**. These are the high, central fells of Lakeland and relatively few visitors will see these mountains from this perspective – stark, lonely and dramatic.

3 3 MILES

Footpaths around Great Moss have a habit of becoming unreliable due to the shifting, boggy ground and the preponderance of sheep trods, so the best course is to walk next to the river. Follow the river to a crossing point where **How Beck** descends in waterfalls from Sca Fell itself, where it is possible to cross the river and investigate the lower falls.

4 3½ MILES

Spend some time exploring Great Moss – many walkers cross over Great Moss and pick up the return path behind Scar Lathing, forming a little circuit of this grassy combe. When you are ready, return to Eskdale by retracing your steps back down to Lingcove Bridge, again enjoying the waterfalls, until you see Brotherilkeld farm.

Explore the wild beauty of Upper Eskdale's **Great Moss**

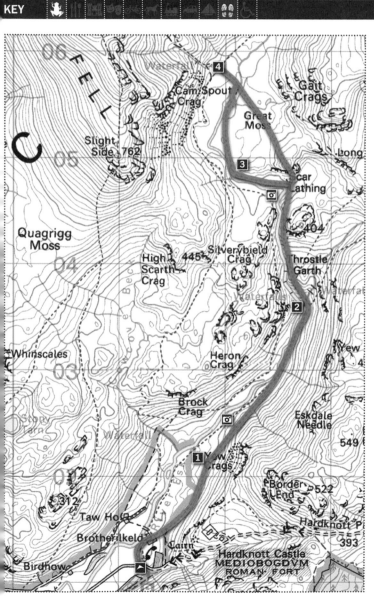

TERRAIN
Pleasant valley bottom and open fell on good footpaths, then short steep sections of narrow fell path followed by flat, open and sometimes vague footpaths on short grass and gravel. Navigation is very straightforward if the river is kept in sight, however, poor weather and hill fog can lead to a difficult navigation crossing Great Moss – so be prepared with map and compass and check the weather forecast. Dress appropriately for remote hill walking.

HOW TO GET THERE
BY CAR: Eskdale is 15 miles west of Ambleside via Little Langdale, Wrynose Pass and Hardknott Pass. Park at the bottom of Hardknott Pass, near Brotherilkeld Farm.
BY PUBLIC TRANSPORT: Take the Ravenglass and Eskdale Railway from Ravenglass to Boot and then walk (approx 2 miles) to Brotherilkeld.
www.ravenglass-railway.co.uk

MAP
Ordnance Survey Explorer Map OL6.
Grid ref: NY 212011

MORE INFO
Cumbria Tourism
www.golakes.co.uk

Lake District National Park
www.lake-district.gov.uk

Route ————

St Bees Head Cumbria

Distance 7 miles (11 km) **Type** Moderate **Time** 4½ hours

Maryport •
Penrith •
Keswick •
Whitehaven •
ST.BEES HEAD ▶
• The Lake District
Windermere •
Ulverston •
Lancaster •

▶ Blow away the cobwebs on a walk to St Bees Head and the largest seabird colony in the northwest

The red sandstone headland of **St Bees** is a surprising feature, jutting out into the Irish sea between **Whitehaven** and **Egremont**, on the Cumbrian coast. There are no other significant cliffs on the whole of the northwest coastline and this uniqueness seems to have gathered about it a host of other features. Gemstones on the beach attract beachcombers, while birdwatchers flock to the RSPB viewpoints along the cliff-top path to try and spot guillemots, kittiwakes, fulmars and razorbills.

Dolphins and porpoises may be watching you from the foaming sea – and views stretch as far as the Isle of Man on a clear day.

If you spend some time exploring the red sandstone boulders covering the beach you will discover hundreds of years of carved names and messages inscribed in the soft red rock; it's a fascinating place.

▶ START

Park at the beachside car park at St Bees and spend a few minutes admiring the golden curve of sand of St Bees beach, which is particularly 📷 beautiful at low tide. Go past the lifeboat station and the caravan park, and over a small bridge to gain the start of the cliff-top path at **South Head**, just 100m away from the car park. Climb steeply at first and then more gently, up the sandy cliff path with expanding views over the surrounding beach and St Bees village. Continue to follow the path around South Head, known locally as **Tomlin**. There is an information board here to help identify the views. Ahead you will see the path dip and the shingle beach of **Fleswick Bay** come into view below. Continue to a path junction at the north corner of Fleshwick Bay, where it's possible to descend down to the bay and search for gemstones like agate, carnelian and jasper.

1 | 1¾ MILES

Regaining the cliff top path, continue north towards the lighthouse, which has stood here since 1822 and is still in use today. The cliffs are up to 91m (300ft) 📷 high at **North Head** and are an internationally important seabird-breeding site and RSPB reserve, particularly active in the spring. The sea cliffs are also popular with climbers.

2 | 2¼ MILES

Continuing north from the lighthouse, the path zigzags along the line of the field boundary to the end of the RSPB reserve, until you reach **Birkhams Quarry**. At this point the path follows the quarry access track back inland to a surfaced road, which is followed to another road junction.

3 | 4¼ MILES

Turn right at the road junction to a crossroads after 100m where you will see a radio mast. At the signpost for Fleswick Bay, turn left to gain **Hannah Moor Lane**. At the end of this lane you will encounter four ladder stiles before the path goes diagonally across the field to the far left corner. Following the field boundary, the path takes you downhill to meet the waymarker post above Fleswick Bay, from where you can easily retrace your steps back over Tomlin to St Bees beach and the car park.

Experience one of the most dramatic natural features on the **North West coast**, where the largest seabird colony in the region resides

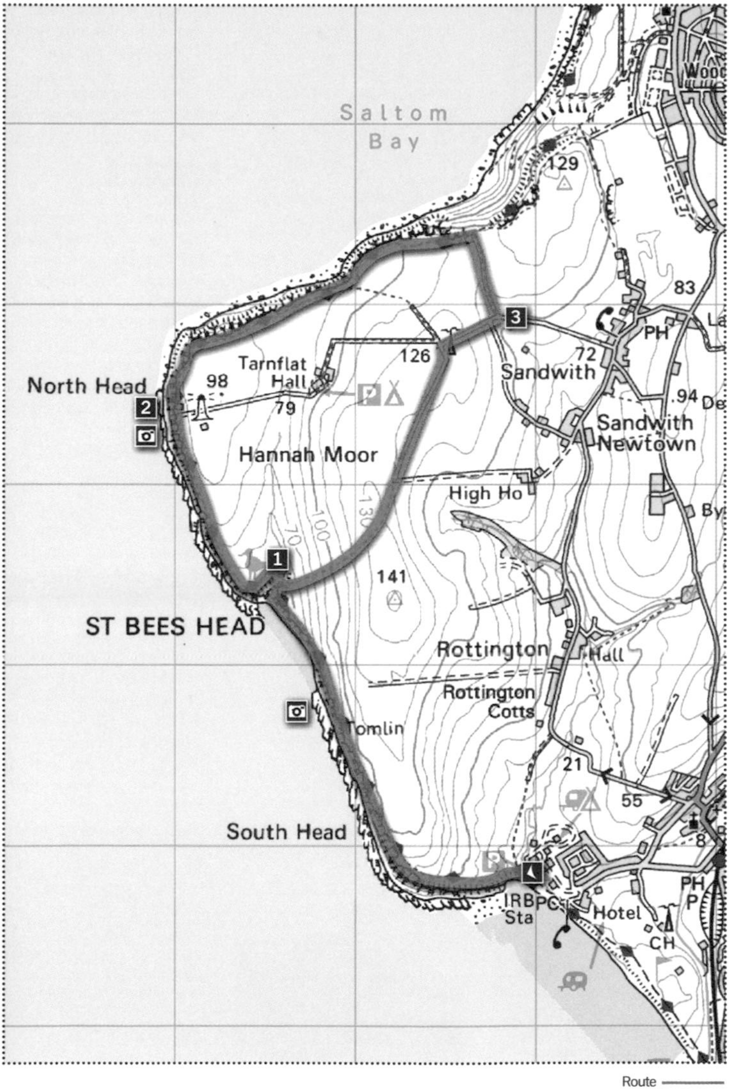

Saltom Bay

129

Wood

83

3

72

PH

94 De

North Head

98

Tarnflat Hall

126

Sandwith

2

79

Sandwith Newtown

Hannah Moor

High Ho

By

1

130

141

100

70

ST BEES HEAD

Rottington Hall

Rottington Cotts

Tomlin

21

55

South Head

IRBPCS Sta

Hotel

PH P

CH

TERRAIN
Cliff-top paths with some steep climbs. Do not walk too close to the cliff edge.

HOW TO GET THERE
BY CAR: Leave the M6 at Penrith J40 and follow the A66 through Keswick. At Cockermouth, take the A595 towards Whitehaven, then the B5345 to St Bees.
BY PUBLIC TRANSPORT: Buses run from Penrith, West Cumbria or Windermere. By train take the West Coast Main Line to Carnforth from the south or Carlisle from north, then change on the Furness west coast line to St Bees.

MAP
Ordnance Survey Explorer Map 303.
Grid ref: NX 959 117

NEARBY EXCURSIONS
The Beacon Museum
West Strand, Whitehaven
CA28 7LY
☎ 01946 592302
thebeacon-whitehaven.
co.uk

MORE INFO
Cumbria Tourism
www.golakes.co.uk
www.visitcumbria.com

St Bees Tourist Information
www.stbees.org.uk

Whitehaven Tourist
Information Centre,
Market Hall, Market Place,
Whitehaven CA28 7JG
☎ 01946 598914

St Bees Head RSPB reserve
☎ 01697 351330
www.rspb.org.uk

Route ———

- Cockermouth
- Keswick
- **BUTTERMERE**
- The Lake District
- Windermere
- Bootle

Buttermere Cumbria

Distance 8 miles (13 km) **Type** Challenging **Time** 6 hours

> This walk traverses the base of the imposing Fleetwith Pike

START

Leave **Syke Farm** campsite and follow the bridle path leading down to **Buttermere**'s shoreline. Follow the tranquil water edge to the head of the lake at **Lower Gatesgarth**, and then follow a short stretch of road to **Gatesgarth Farm**. The quiet fell road, which is the end of **Honister Pass**, leads past the farm to **Gatesgarth Cottages**. Follow a footpath south to **Warnscale Bottom**.

1 2 MILES

The path leads to

Warnscale Bottom, traversing the base of the mighty **Fleetwith Pike**, the dominating pyramid at the head of Buttermere. At an obvious junction follow the path right to a footbridge across **Warnscale Beck**.

2 2½ MILES

After crossing the bridge the path rises steeply, zigzagging up the fell with Warnscale Beck to the left and **Black Beck** to the right. The going is steep but rewarding, with fine views over the numerous waterfalls.
As the path meanders

around between steep crags, the summit draws near and the industrial heritage of the area reveals itself in the form of abandoned quarry workings. Slate quarrying remains an important part of Lakeland life and **Honister Slate Mine** is still active and open to the public.

3 3½ MILES

The footpath levels out on a summit littered with old quarrying spoil and abandoned workings. **Blackbeck Tarn** is 500m to the west in a hollow, surrounded by crags and boulders. The outflow, **Black Beck**, plunges down the fellside, revealing the magnificent panorama of the Buttermere and **Crummock Valley**.
It's now only 500m across the fell to the famous **Innominate Tarn** (the "tarn without a name") where Wainwright had his ashes scattered. The path is rocky and complicated in poor visibility, so a bearing will be required. This vantage point allows

a clear view all the way across the **Solway Firth** to **Galloway**; **Great Gable** lies to the south, while **Ennerdale** and the mighty **Pillar Mountain** are directly behind you.

4 4 MILES

After 500m a cairn marks the summit of **Hay Stack**. From here a steep path drops down to the crossroads of **Scarth Gap**, a pass that was once a busy packhorse route linking Buttermere with Ennerdale. Turn left and descend back to the valley floor and the west shore of Buttermere at **Peggy's Bridge**.

5 5½ MILES

Turn left beside a wall and head into **Burtness Wood**, either along the shore or on a bridleway that passes through the wood. At the path junction turn right over a footbridge and follow the bridleway back into Buttermere. Once in the village you have a difficult choice – The Fish or The Bridge. Either way you will have earned that pint.

THE CAMPSITE

The campsite at **Syke Farm** offers a no frills site in a stunning location, within reach of Red Pike, Buttermere and Honister and with views to die for. The two hotels in Buttermere village, The Fish and The Bridge are just two minutes walk away and the farm itself makes its own ice cream.

This challenging and scenic walk explores **Buttermere**, culminating in a visit to Innominate Tarn, Alfred Wainwright's final resting place

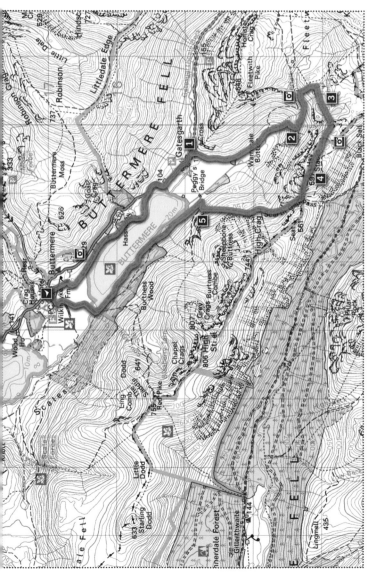

TERRAIN
Valley floor footpaths and bridleways leading to high fell paths and mountain terrain. These are good footpaths but care is required and navigation skills are necessary, particularly in poor weather. Take mountain-walking equipment suitable for the expected weather forecast. Weather proofs, good walking boots, navigation equipment, food and drink, spare clothing and a first aid kit are all essentials.

HOW TO GET THERE
BY CAR: Buttermere is reached via Newlands Pass from Braithwaite (Keswick, A66) or Honister Pass from Borrowdale (Keswick, A66) or Cockermouth (A66, B5289 Lorton Vale, Buttermere road).

MAP
Ordnance Survey Explorer Map OL4.
Grid ref: NY 178 167

CAMPSITE
Syke Farm Campsite
Buttermere CA13 9XA
☎ 01768 770222
40 pitches, no caravans.
There are toilet and shower facilities and a stone shelter to cook in if needed. Dogs are allowed if on a lead.

MORE INFO
www.golakes.co.uk

Cool Camping
www.coolcamping.co.uk

Route ——————

Derwent Water Cumbria

Distance 11 miles (18 km) **Type** Moderate **Time** 5 hours

Carlisle •
Penrith •
▶ **KESWICK**
• Whitehaven
The Lake
District
National
Park
Windermere •
• Ambleside
• Kendal

❯ Don't forget your camera: the view over Derwent Water from Cat Bells is truly spectacular

This circuit of **Derwent Water** offers an evolving panorama over **Borrowdale** and makes an exceptional introduction to the ever breathtaking beauty of the **Lake District**.

▶ START

Leave **Keswick**'s Market Square and walk north to a mini roundabout where the pedestrian zone ends and the busy A5271 heads out of town. Walk right along the road for a short distance to the **Cumberland Pencil Museum** and a bridge over the **River Greta**. Follow footpath signs for the **Cumbria Way** and **Allerdale Ramble**, which both follow the north bank of the Greta for 100m before heading across open fields and picking up a cycle path. Follow this west across the River Greta and into **Portinscale**.

1 1 MILE

Follow the road through the village for 600m until a footpath allows you to regain the Cumbria Way just past the entrance to **Nichol End Marina**. Enjoy the walk through deciduous woodland, eventually emerging at **Derwent Bay**. Take a short climb up the road to a cattle grid, a small lay-by and the start of the ascent of **Cat Bells**.

Follow the path as it ascends the steep shoulder beside the road to **Skelgill Bank**, with views over Skiddaw, Keswick and Derwent Water. Continue along the spine of the ridge to the summit of Cat Bells.

2 3½ MILES

The descent to **Mart Bield** is fairly easy. Soon a shallow coll or saddle intersects with a broad, well-used bridleway.

Turn left at an obvious crossroads and head steeply back down to the lake. When you reach the road take a detour beside a wall to traverse the fell.

The path leads to **High Close**, a little wooded plantation, and **Swanesty How**. Continue around the field system, avoiding the road, and pick up a track that leads back into **Grange** village, where there's a lovely picnic spot by the old arched bridge over the **River Derwent**.

3 6 MILES

Having now reached the bottom end of Derwent Water, the route heads back towards Keswick via the east shore. Walk for 900m along the fell road then pick up the Cumbria Way on your right across fields. The path meets a wall and caravan park and follows

the wall to a stile. Over the wall, fork left then right, heading towards **Great Bay** at the foot of Derwent Water. Soon the ground becomes marshy, with boards over the worst affected areas, until you reach a wooden bridge leading over the lake's source, the River Derwent. Soon you reach the Borrowdale Road near the Lodore Hotel.

4 7½ MILES

Walk up the road past the Lodore Hotel then use a permissive path on the right, at a small bridge over **Watendlath Beck**. The overhanging canopy of woodland trees provide welcome shade as the path winds beside the road for 500m before regaining the pavement at **Strutta Wood**. A shoreline path leads around to **Barrow Bay** and then hugs the water's edge below Borrowdale Road. The lakeside path takes you all the way to **Calfclose Bay** and on to **Stable Hills** opposite **Lords Island**.

5 10 MILES

From Stable Hills, follow a wall to access a small wood, **The Ings**, on a well-marked footpath. The path takes you around the shoreline of **Strandshag Bay** to an extremely photogenic spot at **Friars Crag**. Back in Keswick, pass the redeveloped Theatre By The Lake to return to the town's Market Square.

A complete circular tour of one of Lakeland's best-loved lakes,
Derwent Water

KEY

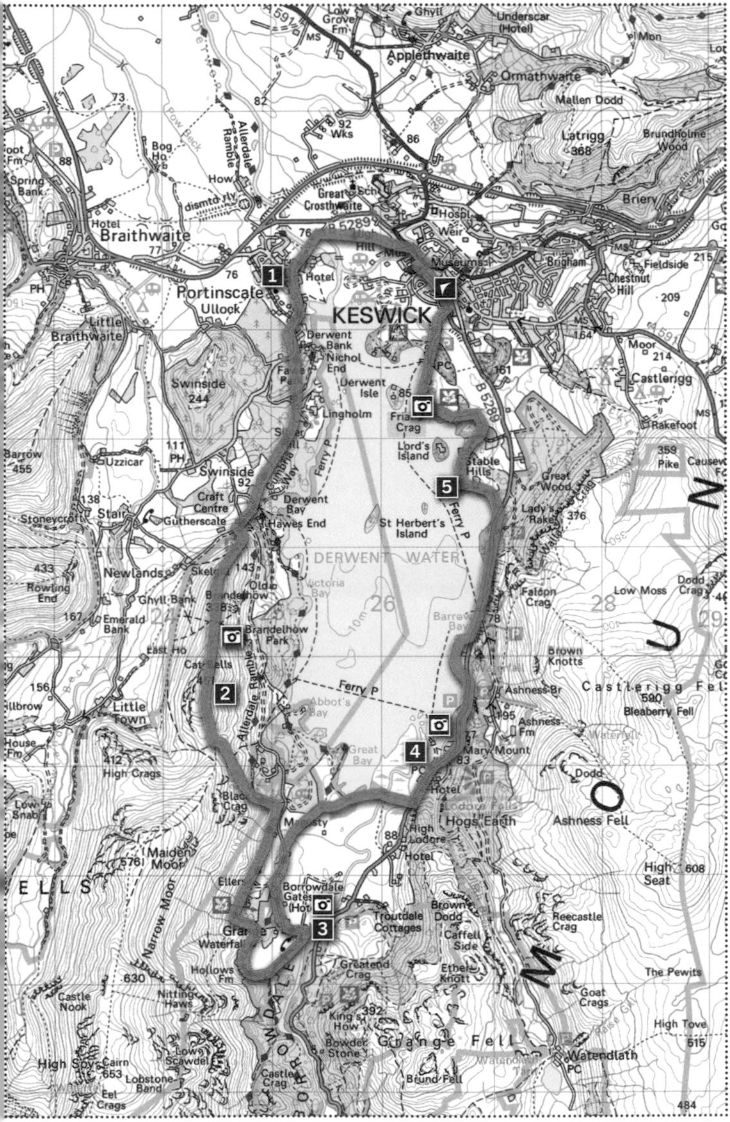

TERRAIN
Short sections of road, wooded paths, open fields and well surfaced footpaths at low level, to open fell and steep fell paths in ascent and descent. Comfortable walking boots or shoes are a must, as is waterproof clothing in a comfortable day-sack.

HOW TO GET THERE
BY CAR: From M6 North, take Penrith J40 then follow the A66 to Keswick.
BY PUBLIC TRANSPORT: Buses run from Penrith, West Cumbria or Windermere. There is a West Coast main line station at Penrith, then take a bus to Keswick.

MAP
Ordnance Survey Explorer Map OL4.
Grid ref: NY 264 235

NEARBY EXCURSIONS
Theatre by the Lake
Lakeside, Keswick
CA12 5DJ
☎ 01768 774411
www.theatrebythelake.
co.uk

MORE INFO
Cumbria Tourism
☎ 01539 822222
www.golakes.co.uk

Keswick Tourist Information
Moot Hall, Keswick
CA12 5JS
☎ 01768 772645
www.visitcumbria.com

Lake District National Park
☎ 01539 724555
www.lake-district.gov.uk

Route ————

Ullswater Cumbria

Distance 10½ miles (17 km) **Type** Easy **Time** 6 hours

Carlisle •
Wigton •
▶ ULLSWATER
Keswick •
The Lake District •
National Park
• Windermere

Morecambe •

Ullswater has a tranquil and secluded atmosphere and the shoreline footpath is scenic, easily navigated and ideal for a family walk. Add an exciting steamer service and you have all the makings of a remarkable day out around one of the most beautiful lakes in England.

▶ START

From the south side of **Pooley Bridge** car park take the footpath to the shoreline beside the boat landings. The shore has eroded quite badly here and tree roots pepper the way, adding fun obstacles for children to scramble over. You soon reach a launching ramp for boats. Continue into the campsite through a gate and walk beside the shoreline. Walk on raised planks over a boggy area and into a second camping ground. When the path meets a single-track lane at **Waterside House** farm, follow signs through the farmyard.

1 1 MILE

Walk along the road for 500m, then take a left on a farm track signed 'Seat Farm'. Proceed right on a path that traverses the fells above the lakeshore. There are a number of distinct paths across the fell and all eventually lead to Howtown Bay. Walk through fields linking farms and cottages to **Swarthbeck**, where a short climb reaches a broad bridleway to **Howtown Bay**.

> Whether on foot or aboard a paddle steamer, beautiful Ullswater is sight to behold

2 4½ MILES

At **Howtown Outward Bound Centre**, descend to the road to the Ullswater steamer pier in a secluded bay overlooked by the 📷 impressive **Hallin Fell**.

Continue on the path around Hallin Fell, hugging the shoreline. A gated footpath beside the boat ramp leads to a short but steep climb to the path proper, then a scenic route leads around Hallin Fell, under the canopy of beech, ash and oak trees, over boulders and craggy outcrops and leads eventually to a broad, grassy field – the 📷 perfect place for a picnic.

3 6 MILES

Walk to the top of the picnic field to a gate and footpath. The track leads back to the road. After 50m, take a path off to the right, following a wall, and cross the fell until you reach a beck. When the path divides, take the bridleway that continues around the fell and eventually descends to the lakeshore. At **Silver Point** you pass through a large copse of woodland. Once out of the trees the path splits – follow the right-hand path as it descends to the shoreline at Silver Crag.

4 8½ MILES

Keep on the path as it passes a house at **Blowick** and continues into another campsite. Walk between walls and continue to **Side Farm** at the entrance to the campsite. Find a path on the right that passes through the farmyard and heads over fields towards **Patterdale** village, seen in the distance.

At the head of the lake, cross the river over a plank bridge and continue on the path right into **Patterdale**. Turn right at the main road and follow it back towards **Glenridding**. At the steamer pier, board the boat to Pooley Bridge and relive the day's walk from the comfort of the steamer as it ploughs majestically up the lake – a fine end to a grand day out circumnavigating one of the finest lakes in England.

This gentle amble along the banks of **Ullswater** offers a variety of delightful picnic spots for family gatherings

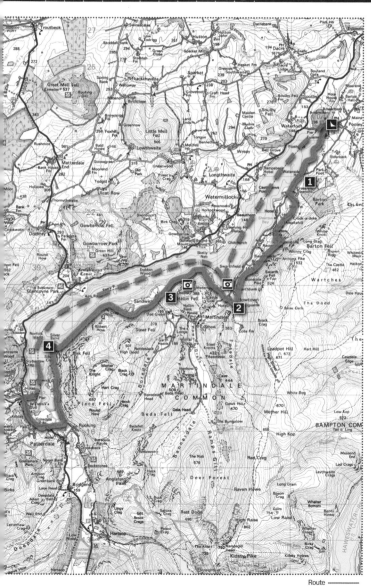

TERRAIN
Scenic shoreline footpath and some easy fell walking across open fells.

HOW TO GET THERE
BY CAR: Pooley Bridge is accessed from the north via Penrith (M6 J40) or from south (Kirkstone Pass via Ambleside) or from Keswick (A66).
BY PUBLIC TRANSPORT:
There is a regular bus service to Pooley Bridge from Penrith but no train.

Ullswater Steamers
The Pier House, Glenridding
CA11 OUS
☎ 01768 482229
ullswater-steamers.co.uk
Cruise any three stages of the lake between Glenridding, Howtown and Pooley Bridge.

MAP
Ordnance Survey Explorer
Map OL5.
Grid ref: NY 470243

MORE INFO
Cumbria Tourism
www.golakes.co.uk

Route ————
Steamer route — — — —

173

Martindale Cumbria

Distance 10 miles (16 km) **Type** Challenging **Time** 6 hours

> Wild, remote and well off the beaten track, the Martindale Horseshoe with its magnificent view over Angel Tarn, is difficult to resist

▶ START

A footpath sign points to a right of way behind Martindale's **Church of St Martin** in **Christy Bridge**. The path is obvious at first – follow it along the line of the field wall to an old galvanised farm gate. Go through the gate and continue on a rising traverse across the fell, ducking under low tree branches. The footpath becomes narrower and indistinct under the growth of bracken in summer, but persevere and you will notice a cave marked on the OS map, not far ahead. This is a good waymark to watch for. More trees follow, the path becomes more indistinct and then the cave, an old quarry working, appears on the left.

Continue over a small scree slope, with the ridge-line coming in view just ahead at **Gowk Hill**, then cross the top wall and follow the path between two sheep shelters. The Roman road known as **High Street** is to the east, but follow the path with the wall on your right, traversing the fell to **Wether Hill**. Cross the wall and continue south to **Red Crag** and **Raven Howe** and finally **High Raise**. At 802m (2,631ft) this is the highest point on this section of the High Street. This is a ◎ great vantage point to sit and scan the forest for red deer.

1 | 3¼ MILES

From **High Raise**, round the head of the valley at **Rampsgill Head**, a dramatic cliff of turrets and crags that guards the head of Rampsgill. There are superb views north towards Ullswater at Sandwick Bay. Cross over to the **Straights of Riggindale** at a junction with Haweswater to the east, High Street to the south, and Hayswater to the west. **The Knott** is your next goal, east of Rampsgill Head following a broad, bridle track. The top wall serves as a decent navigation aid in poor weather all the way to **Satura Crag**. From here you are able to view ◎ **Bannerdale**, having rounded **The Nab**.

2 | 6 MILES

◎ Pause at **Angle Tarn**, once populated with fish for sport fishing, to appreciate what a truly magnificent Lakeland tarn this is, complete with peninsulas and an island. Walk around the tarn to pick up the well-worn **Patterdale** path around the base of **Angletarn Pikes** towards **Boredale**

Hause; navigate carefully to stop at **Stony Rigg**. At this point the path makes an abrupt curve around the head of **Dubhow Beck**, making it obvious as a waypoint. Leave the path and strike out across the boggy fell northeast for 250m and pick up a track that leads to the **Freeze Beck** bridleway.

3 | 7¼ MILES

Not far below Freeze Beck, where this track meets the bridle path at a small cairn, turn back on yourself to continue up a bridle path, heading east and then northeast to **Bedafell Knott** before descending the fell side of **Beda Fell** across **Martindale Common** all the way down to Dale Head farm. From here you are once more back on the Martindale road and it's an easy stroll back to the church.

Wild, remote and host to England's oldest herd of wild red deer, **Martindale** and **Bannerdale** offer a wonderfully scenic excursion

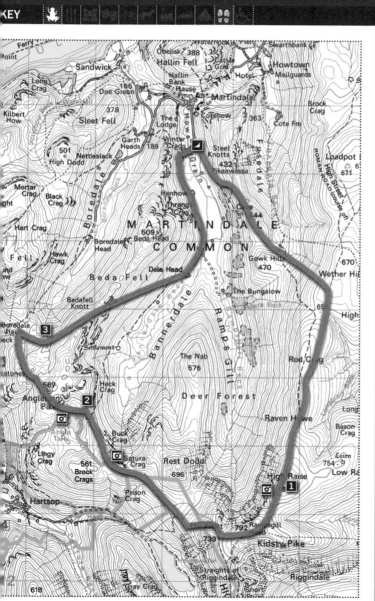

TERRAIN
High, scenic, circular fell walk. There are some strenuous sections, but they're not unduly so once the summit ridges are gained. Most paths are well worn and easily navigated. Some wet or boggy sections require waterproof footwear in wet weather and the general high level nature of this walk will dictate good quality hill walking equipment and clothing, coupled with competent navigation and map reading skills. Dress for mountain walking and check the weather forecast.

HOW TO GET THERE
BY CAR: Pooley Bridge is accessed from the north via Penrith (M6 J40) or from the south (Kirkstone Pass via Ambleside) or from Keswick (A66). To access Martindale, follow the Howtown road from Pooley Bridge, continuing over the fell road past the Parish church of St Peter at the summit to the old church of St Martins in Martindale. Park at Christy Bridge next to the church.
BY PUBLIC TRANSPORT: There is a regular bus service to Pooley Bridge from Penrith but no train.

MAP
Ordnance Survey Explorer Map OL5.
Grid ref: NY 434 184

MORE INFO
Cumbria Tourism
www.golakes.co.uk

Route ⎯⎯⎯

175

NORTH EAST

When the population of **Yorkshire** describe the region as God's Own Country, they're only half joking. However, the present landscape of the Yorkshire Dales was crafted more by the hand of man than that of a divine creator. While the **Dales'** distinctive limestone, millstone and sandstone landforms were carved by glacier ice, their character is our doing. What most people think of as natural scenery is cultivated land: forest areas were cleared to create hay meadows in the valley bottoms and sheep were introduced to graze on the steep fells. The barns and dry stone walls that now pattern the Dales landscape, came about gradually as landowners enclosed the open fells for their livestock. In contrast to the browns and ochres of the heathery summits, the lush green valleys blaze with colour in the summer when the sheep are led away to let the buttercups take hold. This is **Wensleydale** cheese country, a living landscape made famous by James Herriot's hilarious stories of life as a young vet in Thirsk.

But the Dales are only one part of Yorkshire's story. To the west, the breathtaking beauty of the **Pennine Hills** once kept the ancient enemy of the Lancastrians firmly at bay but now the two sides are firmly united by the **Pennine Way**. Sweep east across the country and you're up in **North Yorkshire**, bejeweled with stately homes, castles and abbeys, testament to the former fortunes made from wool, before you reach the wild, isolated grandeur of the **North York Moors**, a vast expanse of heather where often the only sound is the lonely cry of a curlew. Each turn of the roads that cling perilously to the edge of the lonely ridges brings spectacular views that render you awestruck, a landscape that captures your heart – even stops it for a split second. Still higher drama awaits on the east coast where the moorland abruptly ends in the form of lofty cliffs that seem to plummet into the pounding North Sea.

But if Yorkshire is God's Own Country, many searched for Him on the coast of **Northumberland**, with monks arriving on **Lindisfarne** in AD 635. Cut off from Scotland by **Hadrian's Wall**, Northumberland is England's final frontier, a wilderness untamed by humankind. From the tranquil peace of the **Holy Island** to the dark presence of the **North Pennines**, walking here can feel like crossing into another world, epic in scale and as far removed from the genteel idylls of the south as is possible. This is countryside to stir and strengthen the spirit.

Mickelton•
Kirky Stephen•
Richmond•
▷ SWALEDALE
Hawes• Leyburn•
• Yorkshire Dales
National Park
• Ingleton

Swaledale North Yorkshire

Distance 6 miles (10 km) **Type** Moderate **Time** 4 hours

▷ **Take a meandering path through the hay meadows of Swaledale**

Traditional hay meadows are a distinctive part of the **Yorkshire Dales** landscape, and this walk in stunning **Swaledale** offers a chance to explore a fascinating landscape where wild flowers bloom and traditional barns dot the hills. Skirting along the banks of the River Swale, the route allows a real glimpse of the region's delightful character and age-old traditions.

▷ START

From the car park in **Muker**, cross the bridge and turn left, then take the first right beside the **Literary Institute**; it was built in the mid-19th century for the local leadminers. Bear left and right to a sign by **Corner Cottage**, signed 'Gunnerside'.

Go ahead through a gate and into the traditional hay meadows. The importance of the meadows for local farmers is recognised by the Yorkshire Dales Millennium Trust **Hay Time Project**, which

is working to restore upland and lowland hay meadows to their former glory. The meadows help maintain the wide variety of wild flowers, as well as supplying winter fodder for the animals.

Cross the meadows in single file on the paved way, through several stiles, to reach the riverside. Turn right and cross the footbridge. Ascend steps and turn left, signed 'Keld'. Follow the river along a clear track until it curves right around **Swinner Gill**.

1 | 1¾ MILES

Go over a footbridge by the remains of a small lead smelting mill that served mines at nearby Beldi Hill and Swinner Gill. Go through a wooden gate and uphill. The track eventually bends left then right round a stone barn. Swaledale barns – there are more than 60 within ½ mile of Muker – stored the cut hay to feed animals that overwintered inside, saving the farmer the need to move stock. Go downhill through two gates to the top of **Kisdon Force**.

2 | 3 MILES

Go over the bridge then bend left, signed 'Pennine Way'. Descend to cross the footbridge below the fall, then follow the bend right up the hill.

At the top of the slope turn left. Just after a wooden gate, turn right through a green-painted

metal gate, then bear half left to cross the field to the right of a barn to a gap in a wall. Cross to another gap, follow the wall on the right and go through a gap in it towards a gate beyond a barn. Descend through a gate and down to a track. Turn left and follow the track steeply uphill. The track, which has six gates, becomes grassy, taking you high on the side of the conical hill known as **Kisdon**.

There are views towards the village of **Keld** – its name is Old Norse for a spring. Far below the path there are more hay meadows; these are particularly beautiful in June, when they shine with a multitude of wild flowers including buttercups, meadow vetching, globe flower, pignut and wood cranesbill along the valley of the **Skeb Skeugh**, a tributary of the **Swale**.

3 | 4¾ MILES

As the track begins to descend it swings right, with spectacular views of the Swale valley that are well worth savouring for a while. The track then descends between walls to a signpost. Bear left, downhill to another sign for Muker. Follow the track downhill through two gates into the village. Turn left at the T-junction, then head right, back to the village centre and the car park to complete this pleasant route.

Discover the hay meadows of the **Yorkshire Dales** as you walk alongside the River Swale, with dramatic hilltop views

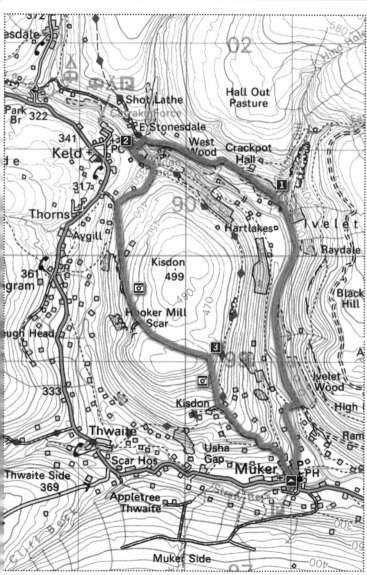

TERRAIN
Meadow and riverside paths, fields and hillside tracks, with some steep ascents and descents.

ACCESS
The hay meadows at Muker are accessible to wheelchairs and pushchairs.

HOW TO GET THERE
BY CAR: Muker is on the B6270 between Richmond and Kirkby Stephen.
BY PUBLIC TRANSPORT: Buses run from Richmond to Keld, every day except Sundays and bank holidays.
www.traveldales.org.uk

The nearest railway station is Kirkby Stephen, which is on the Settle to Carlisle line.

MAP
Ordnance Survey Explorer Map OL30.
Grid ref: SD 905 975

MORE INFO
Yorkshire Dales National Park
☎ 01969 652300
www.yorkshiredales.org.uk

Yorkshire Dales Millennium Trust Hay Time Project
www.ydmt.org/page.php?page=haytime

Route ————

HEBDEN
BRIDGE
Mixenden •
Halifax •
• Mytholmroyd
Sowerby •
Bridge
Rishworth •
Moselden •
Height

Calderdale West Yorkshire

Distance 9½ miles (15½ km) **Type** Challenging **Time** 5½ hours

▶ START

Walk eastwards from **Hebden Bridge** Visitor Centre on the main road. Turn right at Station Road, then left to the canal towpath. Follow it into **Mytholmroyd**, crossing the main road near a tunnel.

Ted Hughes and his friends fished for loaches in the canal – pike, the subject of one of his poems, were also found here. In Mytholmroyd, go up steps beside a modern bridge and left up Midgley Road. Ted Hughes's birthplace is on the corner of Aspinall Street to the left; his bedroom had a view of Scout Rock on the opposite hillside.

1 1½ MILES

Beyond the school on Midgley Road go left on a signed footpath, then right beside a house. At a

▶ Top: Churn Milk Joan; **Above:** The Stubbing Wharf

metal gate the right-hand stile leads to a walled path, often taken by Hughes on his boyhood adventures. Follow the waymarks and continue uphill to a stile.

Turn left on the road. Turn right, signed '**Calderdale Way Link**', then, where the track divides, bear right to a stile. The track curves to wild, open moorland around Crow Hill – Hughes's poem of the same name tells of the

harshness of farming on these sodden hills. Go left at a yellow-topped post and uphill to **Churn Milk Joan**, an ancient stone that is the subject of a poem in Hughes's *Remains of Elmet*.

2 3 MILES

Turn left and follow the **Calderdale Way** for a mile and a half. Across the valley is Heptonstall; Hughes's parents lived there from 1952. After a length of wall, bend left towards houses. After a reservoir and another farmhouse, go under telephone lines and turn left down a waymarked track to a lane. Turn left and, in trees, sharp right by an ornate cottage. Go through a field and between houses to a lane, then turn left. At a road turn right, then left, down to a stile. Go down a field to another road.

Turn right then left, go steeply downhill, over a stile, then bear right to a fence gap. At a crossing path turn left, downhill into **Midgehole**.

3 6½ MILES

Turn right at the road, then left down a slope. At the second bend take a footpath right. Cross the bridge, then at a signpost turn left. Continue steeply uphill, eventually bearing left into tight-knit **Heptonstall.** Turn right into Towngate. Off to the left, in a detached part of the churchyard, is the grave of Hughes's wife, American poet Sylvia Plath, who committed suicide in 1963. Beyond the school take a path left, signed 'Lumb Bank'.

Cross two fields on to a metalled lane. Bear left, downhill, to the corner of a wall with a low window. The wall surrounds **Lumb Bank**, bought by Hughes in 1969 and given to the Arvon Foundation three years later.

4 7¾ MILES

Turn left, downhill, alongside the wall. Follow this path downhill to a junction. Turn right to a road, then left to reach the A646. Turn right, go left over a bridge, past the **Stubbing Wharf** pub, where Hughes and Plath would often drink, and join the canal towpath back into Hebden Bridge.

The narrow valleys and wild moorland of **Calderdale** were always
the vital inspiration for poet laureate Ted Hughes

KEY

‣INFO

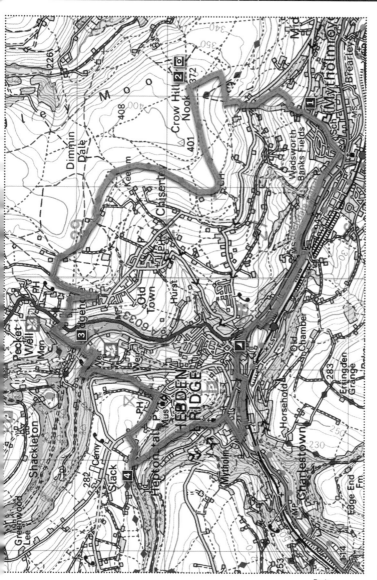

TERRAIN
Canal towpaths at start and
finish, with very steep, rough
paths and open, exposed
moorland. Walking boots,
warm, waterproof clothing
and refreshments are
essential.

HOW TO GET THERE
BY CAR: Hebden Bridge is
on the A646, 13 miles east
of Burnley and 7 miles west
of Halifax.
BY PUBLIC TRANSPORT:
Trains from Manchester
Victoria (about 45 minutes)
and Leeds (about 50 minutes)
run to Hebden Bridge. Bus
592 runs from Burnley to
Hebden Bridge, while bus
594 runs from Halifax to
Hebden Bridge.

MAP
Ordnance Survey Explorer
Map OL21.
Grid ref: SD 985 275

MORE INFO
www.hebdenbridge.co.uk
www.caldervalley.co.uk

Route

Sutton Bank North Yorkshire

Distance 8¼ miles (13¼ km) **Type** Moderate **Time** 4½ hours

The **North York Moors** offer an incredibly varied landscape, from ancient woodland and grassy dales to towering sea cliffs and miles upon miles of richly coloured heather moorland. This route to **Sutton Bank** provides walkers with one of the finest views in Yorkshire and a chance to see the national park's varied scenery from up high on the escarpment edge.

▶ START

Cross the main road and take the path opposite, by the milestone, signed 'Thirsk'. Follow the path for 1¼ miles. The view over the **Vale of York** was vet and author James Herriot's favourite; look for the towers of **York Minster**. You will reach **Kilburn White Horse**, which is 100m (352ft) long and was completed in 1857 by the local schoolmaster. Beyond the horse descend steps to a car park. Turn left, cross the road and climb the verge on to a crossing path. Turn downhill.

1 | 1½ MILES

At a crossing track turn right, cross the road and follow the forest track opposite, keeping left where it divides. Where a green waymarker points left go straight ahead, then take a path right, signed 'Hood Grange'. Across the field, go left by the farm, then right through a gate and over a footbridge. After another gate, cross the track to a scissor stile.

▶ The view of Hood Hill and the Vale of York from Roulston Scar was James Herriot's favourite

2 | 3 MILES

After two more stiles turn right beside the A170 for 135m, then cross to a stile by a gate. Go slightly right, uphill, and then cross a hedge at a waymarked stile. Bear left then go left through two waymarked gates into a farmyard. Turn right between buildings, then left (waymarked) behind a shed. Just beyond a wooden gate go straight ahead, signed 'Southwoods'. **Gormire Lake** is to your left. It's the only lake in the national park and was formed after the last Ice Age, when glacial meltwater found its way blocked. Accessible only on foot, it is edged in summer with a wide variety of plants. It is

said that at dusk you may hear the sound of horses' hooves as the ghost of a knight who plunged to his death over Whitestone Cliff is pursued by the devil. Walk beside **Gormire Lake**, eventually swinging away from the water. At a crossing turn left, then left again at a signpost to a house. Bear right through a gate to follow a track to a wooden gate, by the entrance to **Southwoods Hall**.

3 | 5 MILES

The hall was the former home of vet Donald Sinclair, or Siegfried Farnon in the Herriot books. Follow the track; beyond a gate the route bends right. After three more gates bear left

towards a gate next to **Tang Hall**, the site of a moated medieval manor. Turn right, signed 'Greendale', along a winding track. By the farm bear left through a gate and cross to another gate. Turn left and climb through trees. Beyond the next gate turn right, uphill, then go through a gate, walk to another, and carry on straight ahead at a crossing track. Follow the path uphill through trees to a wooden gate by open ground. At the **Cleveland Way** turn right and follow the ridge for 2 miles to Sutton Bank, passing across the top of **Whitestone Cliff**.

Dramatic views, a white horse, a hidden lake and deep woodland combine on the edge of the **North York Moors**

TERRAIN
Clifftop paths, tracks, farmland paths and woodland. The ascent of the escarpment is gradual, with a few steeper sections.

ACCESS
The section of the walk from the visitor centre to the White Horse is accessible to wheelchairs and pushchairs.

HOW TO GET THERE
BY CAR: Sutton Bank Visitor Centre and car park is at the top of Sutton Bank, on the A170 between Thirsk and Helmsley.
BY PUBLIC TRANSPORT:
From 16 March-26 October the Moorsbus service (supported by the national park) runs every Sunday and bank holiday, plus Tuesdays and Fridays from 1 July-18 July and 2 September-30 September, and daily from 21 July-30 August. The nearest railway station is Thirsk (7½ miles)

MAP
Ordnance Survey Explorer Map OL26.
Grid ref: SE 517 831

MORE INFO
Sutton Bank Visitor Centre
☎ 01845 597426

North York Moors
National Park
☎ 01439 770657
www.northyorkmoors.co.uk

Yorkshire Wildlife Trust
www.ywt.org.uk

Route ——

North •
Yorkshire
Moors
▶ OSMOTHERLEY
The Grange •
Snilesworth •
Fangdale
Beck
Kepwick •
Hawnby •
Kirby •
Knowle
Old Byland •

Corpse Road North Yorkshire

Distance 6½ miles (10½ km) **Type** Moderate **Time** 3-4 hours

This part of the Cleveland Way takes you across some superb open moorland, such as Scarth Wood Moor

The **Lyke Wake Walk** is a demanding 40-mile crossing on foot over the **North York Moors** between **Osmotherley** and **Ravenscar**. The name Lyke is from the Old English for corpse, and Wake means to watch over the body, and together they remember the funeral journeys in which corpses were carried from remote communities to the nearest church so that they could be buried in consecrated ground.

Further back still it was also associated with the idea that the dead were transported over the moors for burial at the highest point. The routes taken were often known as corpse or coffin roads and you can also find them on the Pennines and Cumbrian fells. The journey is commemorated in *Lyke Wake Dirge*, a popular folk song which has its roots in the mournful recitations chanted for departing souls.

> **Above: Osmotherley church;
Below: Lyke Wake Walk marker**

▶ START

Leave Osmotherley and walk northwards up the main street towards **Cod Beck Reservoir** and the youth hostel. Turn left on to **Ruebury Lane** and follow the **Cleveland Way** out across the hillside. A path on the right leads to **Lady Chapel**, built in the 1960s on the site of a medieval shrine and still hosting regular services and pilgrimages to this day.

1 1½ MILES

When you reach **Arncliffe Wood**, fork right uphill (still the Cleveland Way). Emerging from the conifers at the top, go past a telecommunications station until you reach a trig point in the corner of the field. This is the official starting point for the Lyke Wake Walk.

Continue across the open moorland ahead, with wonderful views of the moorland escarpment and the conical **Roseberry Topping** in the far distance, then follow the bridleway as it swings right and down to the road at the bottom.

2 3 MILES

Turn right and walk along the lane as far as the bend by the ford. To your right is a car park, opposite which is a marker stone for the Lyke Wake Walk. However, your route is across the ford or footbridge and up the wide track opposite.

Continue over the moors then along the side of a plantation on a wide, easy track. This is **High Lane**, an old drovers road once used by cattle drovers to move their herds to market at Malton and York. The track eventually emerges on an open lane where you turn left to reach the **Chequers Tea Room**.

3 5 MILES

Chequers is a former drovers' inn, now offering tasty homemade refreshments for hungry walkers, so is a perfect place to stop off for a bite if you're feeling the strain. Just along the lane from here take the path downhill to the right. At the bottom turn right on to the Cleveland Way and follow this back into Osmotherley.

Stride out on the Lyke Wake Walk as it follows the ancient journey of the dead across the **North York Moors**

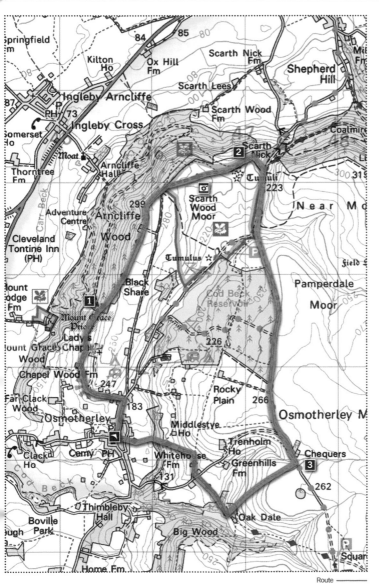

TERRAIN
Variety of woodland paths and moorland tracks, some potentially muddy and slippery.

HOW TO GET THERE
BY CAR: Osmotherley is on the far east edge of the North York Moors. Leave the A1 for Thirsk (A168) then A19 to the Osmotherley turning.
BY PUBLIC TRANSPORT: Buses 80 and 89 run from Northallerton to Stokesley, stopping at Osmotherley (Mon-Sat only).

MAP
Ordnance Survey Explorer Map OL26.
Grid ref: SE 455 975

MORE INFO
North York Moors National Park Centre
The Old Vicarage, Bondgate, Helmsley,
York YO62 5BP
☎ 01845 597426
www.northyorkmoors.co.uk

Route ————

Newcastle
upon Tyne
• Gateshead
CHOPWELL
WOOD
Sunderland •
Stanley•
Lanchester •
Durham •
Bowburn •

Chopwell Wood Tyne and Wear

Distance 1½ miles (2½ km) **Type** Easy **Time** 1½ hours

› **A wildlife haven within minutes of Tyneside, Chopwell Wood offers the ideal place to unwind**

This Forestry Commission walk offers access to a diverse range of flora and fauna in ancient woodland just 15 minutes from the conurbation of **Tyneside**.

There are four alternative waymarked routes, ranging from the **Easy Access** trail to the challenging **Boundary Walk** – this route is suitable for wheelchairs and families with buggies and offers a great chance to observe a variety of wildlife species.

›START

Start at the free central car park and from here on keep your eyes peeled for **red kites**, which are enjoying a revival here after some 150 years. This magnificent bird of prey has a distinctively forked tail, russet plumage and a wingspan of about 2m so it's well worth keeping an eye out for. Head northwest on a compacted gravel path through dense conifer woods.

After 150m, the tree growth changes on the left to broadleaf, and 50m away you'll see a wood carving of a **tawny owl** – just one of the many species that inhabit this woodland. Their haunting screech at night is heard more often than their brown feathers are seen. Carry on along the path as it swings left to a clearing – you might hear the loud laughing or yaffle call of the **green woodpecker** or see that darting grey flash of the much-maligned

grey squirrel. With the prevalence of the grey, you'll not see the red at **Chopwell**.

Just a few steps further forward, you'll join the former railway line. Look right to spot two original wagons returned to their former glory, courtesy of the **Friends of Chopwell Wood**. These wagons regularly rolled along this route with coal from Chopwell colliery, en route to the industrial heart of Newcastle between 1894-1961. Turn left and head off into the distance along 750m of former railway line turned path, lined with conifers and mixed woodland. There are brambles and

rhododendron bushes here, the perfect cover for **rabbits** and **badgers**.

In **Chopwell Wood** you might well spot signs of badger activity – heavily worn badger paths with distinctive five-toed footprints and claw marks on trees, but being nocturnal you'll probably not see them on the walk.

1 ½ MILE

At the end of the rail line route, turn left. After 100m take a relatively steep path to the left, through mixed broadleaf and pine woodland – a landscape that is being reinstated as a broadleaf plantation as it was nearly 1,000 years ago. The woodland floor is carpeted with colour throughout spring – **bluebells**, **wood anemone** and **lesser celandine** are a delight.

At the bottom of the hill, turn left and you'll see some trackside drainage ponds. In and around these ponds, as with other water bodies around the walk, live two species of **newt** as well as **frogs** and **toads**. After 200m you'll meet the forest tarmac road.

2 1¼ MILES

One short steep hill runs past the wood's two fattest trees – gigantic **beeches** with girths of over 4m. From this point, you are about 450m from the car park.

Discover a wildlife haven in one of Britain's rarest ancient woodland, only 15 minutes from **Tyneside**

KEY

▶INFO

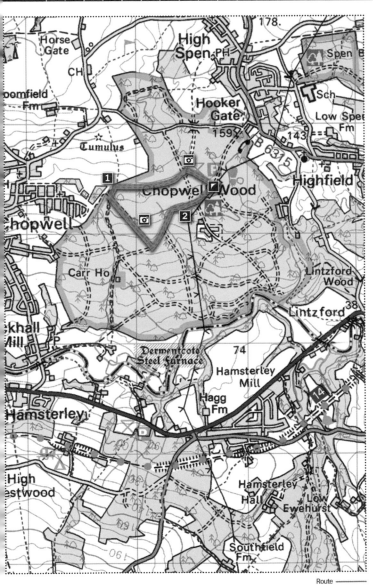

TERRAIN
All relatively smooth paths with no off-track routing – you'll be best with comfortable lightweight boots and waterproofs in uncertain weather.

ACCESS
Cross-country tyres and good gloves are recommended for wheelchair users.

HOW TO GET THERE
BY CAR: From the A1, take the A694 west, signposted Rowlands Gill, then take the B6315 signposted Ryton. On to High Spen and the entrance is off Hookergate Lane on the left.
BY PUBLIC TRANSPORT: Buses to and from Gateshead alight and pick up at the entrance to Chopley Wood. Service numbers 10, 47 and 47A connect High Spen to Newcastle and services X66, 95 and 96 connect to the Metro Centre – change here to services 10, 47 and 47A to reach High Spen.
☎ 0845 6060 260
www.simplygo.com

MAP
Ordnance Survey Explorer Map 316.
Grid ref: NZ 137 584

MORE INFO
Forestry Commission Ranger Chopwell Forest Office, Chopwell Wood, Rowlands Gill NE39 1LT
☎ 01388 488312
www.forestry.gov.uk

Friends of Chopwell Wood
www.jadz.demon.co.uk/focw

- Otterburn
- Bellingham   Morpeth
- Blaydon ... Newcastle Upon Tyne · Blyth
- Dudley
- **BLAYDON** ▸ ·
- Consett ·   Sunderland·
- Durham ·
- Crook·
- Hartlepool·

Derwent Valley County Durham

Distance 10 miles (16 km) **Type** Moderate **Time** 4 hours

The **Derwent Valley Railway** operated from 1867 to 1962, carrying coal, iron ore, bricks and up to half-a-million passengers each year between Consett and Newcastle. Shadowing the **River Derwent**, the disused line is easily accessible by bus from Newcastle upon Tyne.

▸ START
Take a bus to **Swalwell Visitor Centre**. Walk past **Blaydon Rugby Club** and along a track lined with tall trees. After 1½ miles follow the sign to Riverside Meadows down a steep staircase and across a footbridge over the river. Turn left on to the road that loops around **Clockburn Lake**, through hay meadows rich with buttercups, ox-eye daisies, clover, vetches and yellow rattle. The lake is home to mute swans, coot and moorhens, and is visited by grebes, cormorants and herons.

During the 18th and 19th centuries this area was the site of Crowley's Ironworks – at the time, the largest in Europe. It was later replaced by Derwenthaugh Coke Works. The road rejoins the **Derwent Walk** at the start of the **Nine Arches Viaduct**. Crossing high over the river and trees, this is one of the best places to see red kites. Between 2004 and 2006, the Northern Red Kites Project introduced 94 of these magnificent

⟩ Dense undergrowth at the side of the disused railway line shelters roe deer and foxes

birds of prey into the **Derwent Valley**. Many bred successfully, and the kites are now well established, with younger generations spreading out into the nearby North Pennines. The trail re-enters woodland and continues, joining the road at **Rowlands Gill**.

1 3 MILES
Turn left and walk to a fork in the road. Take a left, toward Burnopfield, and at the bottom of the hill, turn right. A track at the side of the car park leads immediately on to the second viaduct.

Beyond this, the trail re-enters woodland. Old railway walls are just visible through thick

undergrowth of holly, hazel, bramble and woodland flowers. Follow the path past **Lintz Green station** which, in 1911, was the scene of an unsolved murder of the station master. Two more viaducts follow, with views over the canopy of **Pontburn Wood**. Between these is the newly planted **Ajax Wood**, part of the Trafalgar Woods Project, which commemorates the naval battle. Follow the track as it descends to a road near **Hamsterley Mill**.

2 5½ MILES
Cross the road and continue for ½ mile to the next road. Re-enter the

wood beyond and follow the track in a long curve, crossing a road. As you approach the picnic site above **Ebchester**, you're treated to extensive views over the Derwent Valley.

In AD80, the Roman fort of Vindomora was built here to guard the supply route of Dere Street, which linked York with the Firth of Forth.

3 9 MILES
The walk now curves gently southward, crossing another road. From the **Shotley Bridge** picnic area, cross the road and walk downhill. A number 45 bus will take you back to Newcastle.

Explore a once busy railway track through the stunning
Derwent Valley, now home to deer, otters and red kites

TERRAIN
Ash and rubble track, generally well surfaced, but can be muddy in places. Strong footwear and waterproof clothing recommended.

ACCESS
The section from Swalwell to Rowlands Gill is accessible to wheelchair users.

HOW TO GET THERE
BY CAR: Take the West Road out of Newcastle. Turn south on to the A1 and follow this across the River Tyne, taking the first turn-off after the bridge. Turn right on to the Consett road at the first roundabout, then left at the second. Then turn right at Blaydon Rugby Club and go to a car park at the Swalwell Visitor Centre.
BY PUBLIC TRANSPORT:
Go North East run buses 45, 46 and 46A from Eldon Square and Newcastle to Blaydon Rugby Club and Swalwell via Gateshead Metro Centre. These services also return from Shotley Bridge and from Ebchester, Hamsterley Mill and Rowlands Gill should you wish to curtail the walk at any of those points.

MAP
Ordnance Survey Landranger Map 88.
Grid ref: NZ 199 621

NEARBY EXCURSIONS
Thornley Woodlands Centre
☎ 01207 545212
www.gateshead.gov.uk

MORE INFO
Swalwell Visitor Centre
☎ 0191 4142106

Visit County Durham
www.visitcountydurham.com

Route ——————

189

Hadrian's Wall Northumberland

Distance 3½ miles (5½ km) **Type** Moderate **Time** 2-3 hours

> Discover more than 1,800 years of history with this walk along part of this great Roman construction

▶ START

Access the main part of the walk by turning right out the campsite and walking up to the **Military Road**. Follow this road west for a few hundred metres then take the road northwards until you reach **Caw Gap**, with **Hadrian's Wall** becoming increasingly visible on the horizon.

Constructed in the second century AD, the wall was as much a frontier as a continuous fortress. Running from **Wallsend** in the east to **Bowness-on-Solway** in the west, it stood at the centre of a military zone marked by a ditch to the north and another ditch bounded by two mounds, one on either side – known as **the Vallum** – to the south.

There were crossing points on the ditches, which usually accessed pass-through points in the wall – almost a form of Roman passport control. The Romans governed those living to the south and either made treaties with or fought those living to the north.

1 ¾ MILE

At Caw Gap, turn left off the road at the first fingerpost, signed 'Cawfields Quarry 1 mile', and follow the low-level route to the quarry car park and picnic area.

As you progress you are following the route of the old Roman **Military Way**, with the Vallum just to your left. The tarmac Military Road you see below you is far more modern, constructed on the orders of General Wade after Bonnie Prince Charlie's 1745 Jacobite Rebellion, for the purpose of moving troops swiftly cross country in the event of another invasion from the north.

Pass the disused water-filled quarry on your right to reach **Cawfields Quarry** car park and picnic area (including a public WC). Note how these crags form an impressive natural defensive structure.

2 1¾ MILES

Take the wall path back eastwards from the quarry. This passes to the north of the quarry and forms part of the **Hadrian's Wall Path National Trail**, running just to the south of the wall. Take time out to look at **Milecastle 42** as you pass. Milecastles were positioned along the wall at every Roman mile (shorter than a statute mile). They were manned by small groups of soldiers who were normally stationed at the larger forts.

3 2¾ MILES

Once you see Caw Gap again, turn off the trail and you will be able to follow your original road route back to the campsite. If you have a thirst, you can always take a ½ mile stride down the road to the Military Road and the Milecastle Inn. Once refreshed walk back up the road and complete the circuit.

▶ THE CAMPSITE

Hadrian's Wall Camping and Caravan Site and Bunk Barn is an intriguing site situated a few hundred metres south of the 18th century Military Road. Here you can camp out almost as the Romans did and experience the rugged, wild atmosphere of a spot that was once a far-flung outpost of their great empire.

Walking along **Hadrian's Wall** is a must for anyone with a sense of history and a vivid imagination

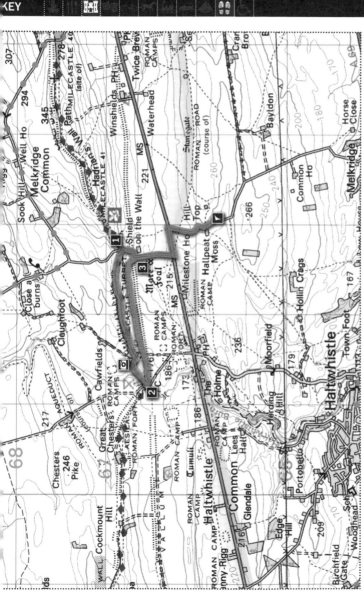

TERRAIN
Road and paths through rugged and undulating countryside. Stout boots and waterproof clothing recommended. The walk is suitable between May-Oct. The National Trail team ask walkers not to use the route between Nov-Apr, as during the winter months the ground is waterlogged and this is when risk of damage to the monument is at its greatest. Walking side by side rather than in single file not only helps to protect the grass path but also any buried archaeology that lies underfoot.

HOW TO GET THERE
BY CAR: Haltwhistle is 36 miles west of Newcastle. The starting point is off the main A69 route northwards at Melkridge village.

MAP
Ordnance Survey Explorer Map OL43.
Grid ref: NY 732 658

CAMPSITE
Roman Wall Camping
Melkridge Tilery, Haltwhistle
NE49 9PG
☎ 01434 320495
romanwallcamping.co.uk

MORE INFO
www.hadrians-wall.org

Hadrian's Wall National Trail
www.nationaltrail.co.uk/
hadrianswall

North East England
visitnortheastengland.com

Route ———

Simonside Hills Northumberland

Distance 7 miles (11½ km) **Type** Moderate **Time** 3½ hours

Embleton
Alnwick
Northumberland
National Park
SIMONSIDE
HILLS
Cramlington
Newcastle
Upon Tyne

The fell sandstones of the **Simonside Hills** were deposited from a river delta some 330 million years ago. Weathering and erosion have led to their dominant aspect, which makes them recognisable throughout the county. Their spiritual significance to the Bronze Age people, 5000 years ago, is evident in the burial tombs and rock carvings that adorn the slopes and summits. The blanket peat bog is an important carbon store and a habitat for plants such as cranberry, bog asphodel, butterwort and cross-leaved heath. It is also home to adders and red grouse.

▶ START

Follow the forest roadway gently uphill from the car park. At the first junction, take the right fork, past a communications tower, and on to the next fork, where you go left. A signpost indicates the proximity of **Little Church Rock**, which is worth the short detour to examine the cup markings that decorate its base. Back on the main trail, carry on to a bend where a rough track leads up to the left. Follow this through trees to more open moorland and a first sight of the wind-sculpted ◙ **Simonside Crags** on the left.

1 | 1½ MILES

At the edge of the next section of forest you will come to another rubble road. Turn right on to this

▶ In summer the Simonside Hills are covered in rich purple heather

and follow it to its end, where it breaks into three footpaths. The middle path leads to a stile at the corner of the forest. Cross this and continue for about 200m to a cairn. About 50m to the right of this is the **Ravensheugh** escarpment and one of ◙ the finest views in the whole National Park, across rock pinnacles, towards the **Coquets** and **Cheviots**.

▶ Look out for ancient carvings!

Return to the stile. Take the track that runs between the wire fence and the forest, past a huge boulder and on to a break in the forest. Follow this gently downhill to another rubble road, turn left and carry on to a junction at the forest edge. Turn right and then ascend the rough, bouldery track that leads steeply past the crags to Simonside summit and another fine viewpoint, ◙ this time extending as far east as the coast.

2 | 3½ MILES

A series of stone slabs lead eastward across the bog to the wonderfully contorted summit of **Old Stell Crag**, crowned by a large cairn that itself stands on top of an ancient stone barrow. A mud track cuts down to a broader footpath, which leads over **Dove Crag** and **The Beacon** before making a final descent to the metalled road and **Lordenshaws** car park.

3 | 5½ MILES

Follow the track that runs from the northern side of the car park. This leads to a hilltop occupied entirely by the remains of ◙ a Bronze Age settlement. A short distance below this is a large boulder decorated with ancient carvings. Return to the road and follow this for a mile back to the start.

KEY

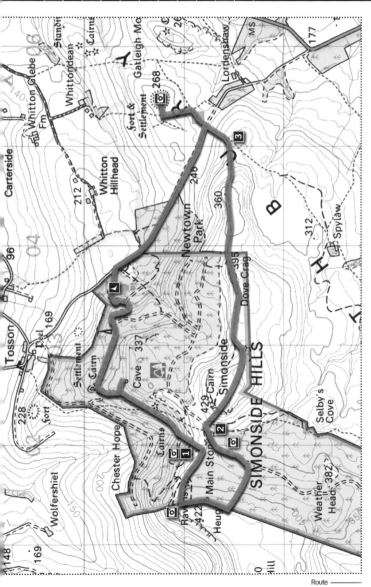

▶INFO

TERRAIN
Meadow and riverside paths, fields and hillside tracks, with some steep ascents and descents.

ACCESS
The hay meadows at Muker are accessible to wheelchairs and pushchairs.

HOW TO GET THERE
BY CAR: Muker is on the B6270 between Richmond and Kirkby Stephen.
BY PUBLIC TRANSPORT: Buses run from Richmond to Keld, every day except Sundays and bank holidays.
www.traveldales.org.uk

The nearest railway station is Kirkby Stephen, which is on the Settle to Carlisle line.

MAP
Ordnance Survey Explorer Map OL30.
Grid ref: SD 905 975

MORE INFO
Yorkshire Dales National Park
☎ 01969 652300
www.yorkshiredales.org.uk

Hay Time Festival
www.yorkshiredales.org.uk/
hay_time_festival

Yorkshire Dales Millennium Trust Hay Time Project
www.ydmt.org/page.
php?page=haytime

Steel Rigg Northumberland

Distance 3½-7 miles (5.5-11 km) **Type** Moderate **Time** 2½-4 hours

❯ A sycamore, made famous by *Robin Hood: Prince of Thieves*, stands proud in a dip in the Whin Sill

Hadrian's Wall is built upon one of the most distinctive geological features in the country – the **Whin Sill**. This great sheet of hard volcanic rock stretches from Teesdale to the Farne Islands. The Romans' use of the escarpment is one of the most impressive ways that man has exploited the earth's geology to fortify human defences.

❯ START

Park at Steel Rigg or hop off the bus at Once Brewed National Park visitor centre and follow the road north to Steel Rigg. Go through the gate at the back right of the car park. The

📷 dramatic **Steel Rigg** appears immediately to your left. Continue along the path and turn left through a gate to follow the **Hadrian's Wall National Trail** left, beside the Roman wall. Emperor Hadrian built this rampart around AD122 to control the border of Roman Britain.

Follow the path downhill then left down steps. Head uphill on a steep path, and cross a stile at the top. You are now stood on top of the Whin Sill. This layer of hard rock was created 295 million years ago, when magma was forced between layers

of limestone, sandstone and mudstone, and it cooled in thick sheets of dolerite. This high point gives great views over the surrounding mires. These ancient areas of peat bog harbour rare sphagnum mosses and grasses.

From now on it's a matter of following the wall and the national trail as it dips and rises along this Whin Sill. Every Roman mile (a distance of 1,000 paces) you'll come across a milecastle, a fortified gateway built to protect weak points along the wall. After a mile you'll come across **Sycamore Gap**, a dip in the landscape with a

sycamore growing in the middle, made famous by the film *Robin Hood: Prince of Thieves*.

1 | 1 MILE

Continue along the trail, and as you climb the dramatic **Highshield Crags** you'll see the glacial **Crag Lough** to your left.

Cross over a farm road and follow the signpost 'National Trail Housesteads 1½ miles'. Hotbank Farm is on your left; keep to the path uphill. The crags here are **Hotbank Crags** and **Cuddy's Crags**.

Follow the wall past Milecastle 37 and go through the woods on **Housesteads Crags**. At the end of the wood go through the gate, downhill to the evocative ruins **Housesteads Roman Fort**.

2 | 3½ MILES

From Housesteads you have three choices to complete the loop: catch the Hadrian's Wall Bus to Once Brewed, return on foot by retracing your steps along the wall, or take the path that runs north of the wall, following signs for the Pennine Way, which gives you a great view of the escarpment. Looking 📷 across Crag Lough you get the Picts' view of the Wall and a dramatic sight of the Whin Sill. Turn left at a road to return to Steel Rigg car park.

With one of the North's most dramatic natural features, a spectacular Roman fort and a famous film location, this is one of the most exciting sections of **Hadrian's Wall**

KEY 　　　　　　　　　　　　　　　　　　　　　　　　　▶INFO

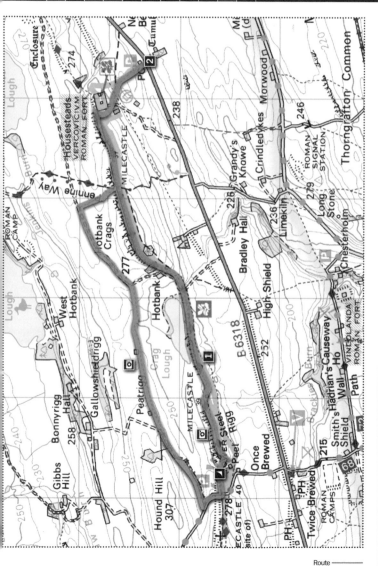

TERRAIN
To conserve the Roman wall, between Nov-Mar and when the ground is wet, take the Roman Military Way which runs to the south of the wall or the path that runs to the north beyond Crag Lough.

HOW TO GET THERE
BY CAR: Steel Rigg and Housesteads are accessible from the Military Road (B6318) 15 miles east from Brampton.
BY PUBLIC TRANSPORT: The AD122 Hadrian's Wall Bus runs between Easter-Oct. The bus departs from Housesteads Information Centre and drops you off at Once Brewed visitor centre.

MAP
Ordnance Survey Explorer Map OL43.
Grid ref: NY 751 677

MORE INFO
National Park Visitor Centre, Once Brewed, Military Road, Hexham NE47 7AN
☎ 01434 344396

Hadrian's Wall National Trail, **www.nationaltrail.co.uk/ hadrianswall**

Northumberland National Park **www.northumberland nationalpark.org.uk**

Visit North East England **visitnortheastengland.com**

Northumberland Tourism **visitnorthumberland.com**

Route ─────

Coquet Valley

Coquet Valley Northumberland

Distance 8 miles (13 km) **Type** Moderate **Time** 5 hours

> The Cheviot Hills in the Upper Coquet Valley offer a remote and wild landscape with far reaching views

The **Upper Coquet Valley** marks the geological boundary between the heather-clad fell sandstones to the south and the older volcanics of the northern **Cheviots**, covered largely by bracken and grass. The boundary is particularly marked at **Coquet Gorge**, where the intervening cementstone layers are well exposed.

▶ START

From the bridge at **Carshope**, take the track that runs steeply uphill to the north. At the top, this joins the public bridleway known as **The Street**. Together with **Clennell Street** to the east, this was a route along which cattle and sheep were driven, both legally and illegally, over the Scottish border. The crossing points were also meeting places at which disputes would be resolved by Wardens of the March, appointed by the respective monarchs.

Follow the bridleway across **Hindside Knowe** and around **Swineside Law** to a saddle. There are wonderful views to either side into the deep, narrow valleys that are characteristic of this northern limit of England's backbone, and across the interlocking ridges that sweep into the Coquet Valley itself. Several tracks run up from the saddle in various directions, but all lead to a junction with the **Pennine Way**.

1 3 MILES

Follow the line of large stone slabs that run parallel to the border fence, to the summit of **Mozie Law**. From here you can look across to **Windy Gyle** in the east and beyond to **Hedgehope Hill** and **The Cheviot**. Over the border, the Scottish valley system displays a more intricate pattern.

The undulating track continues along the border, over the summits of **Beefstand Hill** and **Lamb Hill**. Watch out for the herds, sometimes more than two dozen strong, of long-horned, shaggy-coated feral goats that roam freely across this border region. The descent from Lamb Hill leads to **Yearning Saddle**, and the refuge hut. There are no facilities here, but the bothy will provide around six people with a dry night's rest, free of charge. As with a similar structure just below The Cheviot, the only requirement for visitors is that the hut is left clean and tidy, ready for the next visitors who require a night's shelter from the cold.

2 5 MILES

Take the footpath that runs east. After a short distance, the track forks. Follow the left fork, marked at intervals by wooden posts, down into a tributary of **Blind Burn**, then up again, across **Carlcroft Hill**. A final descent leads to the Coquet Valley road at Carlcroft Farm. Follow the road for 1½ miles back to Carshope. The right fork leads to the valley at Blindburn Farm, adding another 1½ miles to the return to Carshope.

▶ THE BOTHY

A **bothy** is a one-roomed hut, usually unfurnished and without facilities, that can be used as a temporary refuge. Originally referring to a remote Scottish dwelling (bothan means hut in Gaelic) or shooting cabin once frequented perhaps by a shepherd or gamekeeper, the word is generally applied to any isolated building in which shelter can be found, but little else.

Stunningly beautiful in its bleakness, the **Upper Coquet valley** is one of the most remote parts of Northumberland

KEY

INFO

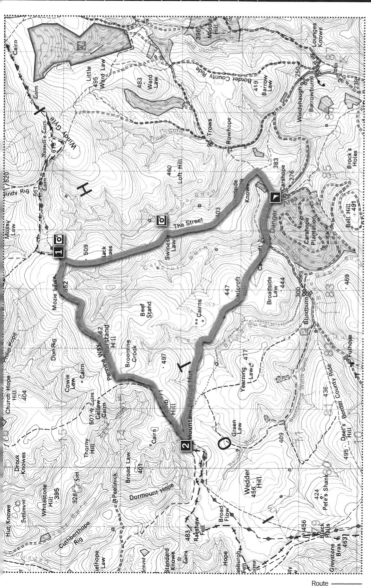

TERRAIN
Mountain footpaths – parts are likely to be boggy. Most of walk is exposed and windswept, so boots and windproof/waterproof clothing are necessary.

HOW TO GET THERE
BY CAR: Take the B6341 west from Rothbury for 4 miles, then turn right on to a minor road through Harbottle and Alwinton.
BY PUBLIC TRANSPORT: Two buses each day travel from Rothbury to Alwinton. Carshope is a further 5 miles with no public transport.

MAP
Ordnance Survey Explorer Map OL16.
Grid ref: NT 846 115

MORE INFO
Rothbury Tourist Information
☎ 01669 620887
www.visit-rothbury.co.uk

North East England
visitnortheastengland.com

Route ——————

SCOTLAND

How to sum up Scotland on a single page? Open a map and see how big the country is. Then consider that the vast amount of that massive landmass is still largely rural and wild. Scotland is one of Britain's – actually, scratch that – one of Europe's last great wildernesses, and can be separated into three distinct parts.

Two-thirds of the country is dominated by the **Highlands**, a monumental succession of mountains and ice-gouged valleys, rushing rivers and lochs, isolated inlets and craggy coastline. Even the wildlife is huge in the Highlands. Red stags stand proud and iconic in the glens, whales and basking sharks patrol the waters off the west coast, while overhead are sea eagles, reintroduced in the 1970s, massive birds – like flying barn-doors. It's almost as if the word remote was invented to describe the region, and it still doesn't seem to do it justice. From the **Cairngorms** to the **Western Isles**, the **Grampians**, **Orkney** and **Shetland**, the people of Scotland have always prided themselves on their self-sufficiency, owing to the isolation of communities, either over land or sea.

In the **Central Lowlands**, defined by two great fault lines to north and south, the main conurbations of Scotland have sprung up – **Glasgow**, **Edinburgh**, **Dundee** – fuelled by the iron-bearing rocks and coal of the valley. Today, nearly 80 percent of the Scottish population lives within this belt of land.

Heading towards the English border you meet the **Southern Uplands**, where lush forests sweep around mountains, their canopies sheltering an abundance of wildlife, giving way to coarsened moorland, vibrant with pink heather in spring, and rich in purple in the colder months. Here the red squirrel maintains its hold against the invading grey, and arctic hares scramble over the hillsides.

Everywhere you roam, you can almost feel the history beneath your feet. Here clans fought for honour and the throne, and Vikings invaded to conquer. In the Highlands abandoned crofters' dwellings betray the cruel clearances of the mid 18th–19th centuries, when thousands of tenant farmers were swept from their homes, an action that still impacts on Scottish culture to this very day.

Yet to many people who live south of **Hadrian's Wall**, Scotland is only seen through the camera lens of a hundred films and television series. But to walk Britain without experiencing the grandeur of Scotland is a waste, if not a complete tragedy.

Ellisland Dumfries and Galloway

Distance 2½ miles (4 km) **Type** Easy **Time** 3 hours

Mickelton•
Kirky Stephen•
Richmond •
▷ SWALEDALE
Hawes•   Leyburn •
• Yorkshire Dales
National Park
• Ingleton

> **Above:** Stroll by the River Nith;
> **Left:** Ellisland Farm buildings

The poet and songwriter Robert Burns came to Ellisland in the latter part of his short life. He opted for the poetic surroundings of this stony farm because he found it more inspirational for his writings. Burns made little success of his agricultural exploits here but his Ellisland writings have gained lasting acclaim.

Walking beside the bonnie banks of the River Nith you can enjoy that same stimulating countryside and you can also visit the farm where the poet wrote *Auld Lang Syne*.

> Today, the farm is a museum

▷ START

Start at the visitor car park at **Friars Carse Hotel**, which is named after the Cistercian

monks who once stayed here. This is where Burns met Francis Grose, who inspired him to write his famous witch poem *Tam o' Shanter*. Turn right and follow the tarred road to where a track is joined that leads behind the house.

This avenue is lined with stunning mature parkland trees where red squirrels dart among the branches. At the northeastern corner of this remarkable sandstone mansion a green track leads to the **River Nith**. Turn right on to the riverside footpath, heading southwards under some ancient oaks until you reach a metal stile just before the **Mains Burn**.

Cross the stile and head up the east bank of Mains Burn to cross left over another metal stile. Follow a grassy track over the burn that leads up to two small hunting gates. Here E-marked signposts for Ellisland show the way. Once on the shoulder of the hill you'll find yourself on the fields once worked by the poet.

1 1 MILE

Linger to think about what life must have been like for Burns during his three rather barren years on this worn-out farm.

Yields from the farm

may have been poor but the bard spent one of his most productive periods of writing here, inspired by the idyllic Dumfries and Galloway countryside.

Follow the line of posts and eventually you will come to the farmhouse Burns built for £300. Today the place is a museum with displays of Burns memorabilia.

Buzzards cartwheel and mew overhead as you take the Tam o' Shanter walk along the Nith. It was in one of the fields here that Burns saw the wounded hare now famed in one of his poems. Tradition also has it that it was in this leafy lane that he composed his celebrated *Tam o' Shanter*.

2 1½ MILES

Take the **South Walk** along the riverbank, where you might see people fly fishing for salmon, or sawbilled goosanders fishing more successfully in one of the pools as you head past Ellisland on the **North Walk**. The route ends in a series of steps climbing back up to the field marker posts.

Follow the H-marked signs this time, up through the woods to the **Hermitage** where Burns mused in this tiny retreat. From here follow the meandering tracks back to **Friars Carse**.

Wander in the footsteps of **Scotland's national bard** and discover where he wrote some of his most famous works

KEY

INFO

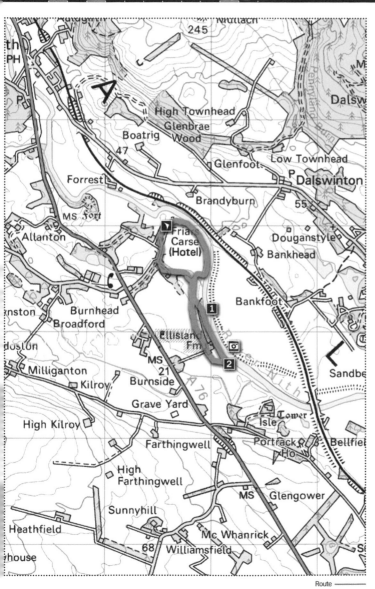

TERRAIN
Woodland tracks, farmland and riverside paths.

HOW TO GET THERE
BY CAR: Ellisland is off the A76 between Dumfries and Auldgirth.
BY PUBLIC TRANSPORT: Buses runs between Dumfries and Ayr.
www.swestrans.org.uk

MAP
Ordnance Survey Explorer Map 321.
Grid ref: NX 924 849

NEARBY EXCURSIONS
Ellisland Farm, Holywood Road, Auldgirth, Dumfries DG2 0RP
☎ 01387 740426
www.ellislandfarm.co.uk
Open all year (closed Sundays and Mondays in winter).

MORE INFO
Visit Scotland Dumfries and Galloway
☎ 01387 253862
visitdumfriesandgalloway.co.uk

Visit Scotland
www.visitscotland.com

Route ————

Bannockburn Trail Stirling

Distance 3 miles (5 km) **Type** Easy **Time** 1½ hours

"We fight for freedom which no good man surrenders but with his life." With these fateful words Robert the Bruce, King of the Scots, planted his standard on a rise above the **Bannock Burn** on 23 June 1314 and awaited the arrival of his English foes. By the following day history had been made, as the government's army was routed. This was a bitter battle for the English, who were prevented from a retreat by a gorge on the river; for the Scots it was one of their greatest victories.

▶ START

Begin at the National Trust for Scotland's **Bannockburn Heritage Centre** car park. The circular route gives
📷 commanding views over the Stirling area and is ideal for history buffs or those simply looking for a varied stroll. Make your way uphill to the eye-catching rotunda.

1 ¼ MILE

The Scottish Saltire flies from the centre of the rotunda – the spot where Bruce is said to have stood. There is also a striking statue of the mounted king, behind which you can see the
📷 stronghold of **Stirling Castle**. Although this area saw some fighting, the main battlefield site is believed to lie a mile or so to the north; the exact location is still disputed by historians and shows no sign of being settled.

▷ A statue of Robert the Bruce on the eve of his defeat of the English

Retrace your steps to walk down a narrow path on the right. At the bottom turn right on to a road for **Chartershall**. At an old bridge over the Bannock Burn, take the very muddy path left, signed '**Whins of Milton**'. Cross a road

and continue to Glasgow Road. Follow a road signed 'Milton Farm' behind a garage, and turn left on to Colliers Way. After the old renovated farm, take the first right. The road soon branches – take the lower option to cross the Bannock Burn.

2 1 MILE

King James III, an ancestor of Bruce, is said to have been assassinated by this ford after the nearby Battle of Sauchieburn in 1488. However, like many distant historical events the truth may have been embellished. One story tells of how James was given a powerful steed for the battle, but the horse threw the king, who either died as a result of his injuries or from a soldier's sword.

Continue to walk above a wooded gorge. At a junction go right, signed '**Coal Wynd**'. At the following junction, go left to climb steeply up the wynd.

3 1¾ MILES

From the top there are excellent views of
📷 the **Ochil Hills**, which display a 30-mile long steep scarp face above the flat **Forth Valley**. Walk downhill to meet the Brae in **Bannockburn** and turn left. Before a bridge, go left on a path, signed '**Milton**'. The area was once famous for its tartan weaving mills, the remains of which can be seen here.

Follow the surfaced path, ignoring side-paths, to recross the river on a bridge above a weir. A track leads on to a road that leads to Milton Farm. From here follow the main road back to the heritage centre.

Experience the landscape that put Scotland on its road to freedom under **Robert the Bruce**

KEY

▶INFO

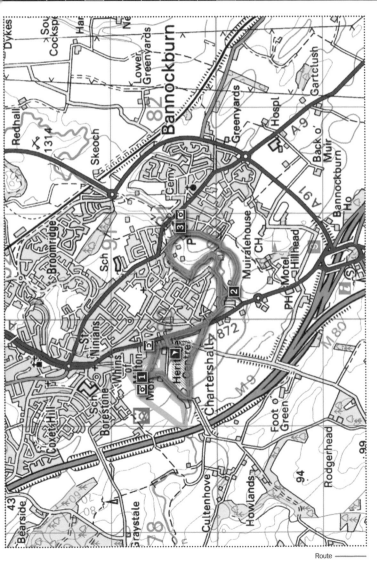

TERRAIN
Minor hills, muddy paths and footpaths.

ACCESS
The walk is only wheelchair accessible for the first ¼ mile.

HOW TO GET THERE
BY CAR: The National Trust for Scotland's Bannockburn Heritage Centre is well signed off the A872 in Stirling. Nearest motorway junction is J9 on the M9.
BY PUBLIC TRANSPORT:
Take bus number 81 from Stirling Bus Station (Goosecroft coaches) to Glasgow Road, Whins of Milton. Stirling is well served by trains and buses.
www.travelinescotland.com

MAP
Ordnance Survey Landranger Map 57,
Grid ref: NS 799 905

NEARBY EXCURSIONS
Bannockburn Heritage Centre Glasgow Road, Stirling FK7 0LJ
☎ 0844 493 2100
www.nts.org.uk
Open daily 1 Mar-31 Oct. Grounds open all year.

Stirling Castle
Esplanade, Stirling
FK8 1EJ
☎ 01786 450 000
www.historic-scotland.gov.uk
Open daily 1 Oct-31 Mar, 9.30am-5pm; 21 Mar-30 Sep, 9.30am-6pm.

MORE INFO
Stirling Tourist Information
41 Dumbarton Road, Stirling
FK8 2LQ
☎ 08707 200620
visitscottishheartlands.com

Visit Scotland
visitscotland.com/white

Route ———

Sheriffmuir Perthshire

Distance 8 miles (12.9 km) **Type** Moderate **Time** 3½ hours

Crieff • • Perth
▶ **SHERIFFMUIR**
Bridge of Allan•
Kirkcaldy•
Dunfermline •
Cumbernauld• Edinburgh•
• Glasgow
• East Kilbride

▷ The Gathering Stone commemorates the Battle of Sheriffmuir, which took place in 1715

The sense of space on **Sheriffmuir** is fantastic, especially in the summer. The muir, or moor, sits high above the Stirlingshire town of Dunblane and runs into the adjoining fertile county of Perthshire. Here the lowlands are blessed with unspoilt rivers, while the uplands have a lifetime's worth of excellent walks with views to the Highlands. This route explores some of the fine natural attractions the area has to offer.

▶ START

Start in the attractive cathedral town of **Dunblane** which, for many centuries, was an important religious centre. From the train station walk into town and up **High Street**, turning left on to **Smithy Loan**. Where this joins the busy **Perth Road**, turn right, past the Dunblane Hydro Hotel, and first left, up **Newton Loan**.

Continue uphill as this becomes a path. Cross a road and, still heading uphill, follow a road into **Ochiltree**. After crossing a second road, take the uphill tarmac path ahead. At the top, carry on to join another tarmac path on the left. This joins a road. Go right then left, up **Leighton Avenue**, to reach the Sheriffmuir-signed track.

As you gain height a patchwork of fields appears below. At a converted farm steading, follow the road, which slants left uphill to access a path by the edge of a field. This leads into woods where foxgloves thrive. Further on, the path joins a wide track that leads to a T-junction.

Keep straight ahead to follow the path.

1 2¼ MILES

Views of the **Ochil Hills** open up as you break out from the trees. Listen out for the uplifting song of lapwings as the path leads to the roadside **Clan MacRae Monument**. This memorial was erected by the clan to commemorate members who died at the 1715 Battle of Sheriffmuir between the Jacobites and government forces.

2 2¾ MILES

To visit the gathering stone, where the Jacobites' standard is said to have been planted, follow the signed path. Bear left at a fork to reach the stone, which is protected by a ribbed iron cage. Return to the road

and turn left for the inn. You may see roe deer by the woods and hares too, if you're lucky.

3 4½ MILES

The inn appears as you top a crest and is as welcome a sight as it was to the travellers of yesteryear. Behind the inn, the rounded Ochil Hills rise and there are paddling pools where the road crosses the **Wharry Burn**. Further downstream, there's a fantastic plunge pool which you can get to from the road opposite **Cauldhame**. After you've cooled down, the return is back the same way – now all downhill!

▶ SHERIFFMUIR INN

Rustic charm abounds in this late 17th-century droving inn, which was an eagerly awaited stopping point for the drovers, or cattle herders, who travelled from the Highlands to the lowland markets. Set high on Sheriffmuir, the inn is the perfect place to enjoy a drink while taking in the scenery, or relax in the comfy interior and enjoy the delicious Scottish fare.

The **Sherrifmuir Inn** awaits thirsty walkers in a stunning moorland setting, packed with wildlife and history

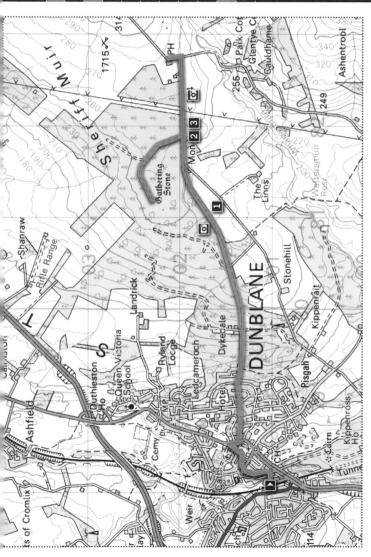

TERRAIN
Easy to follow track and path (with boggy sections) to reach the moor, followed by quiet road section.

HOW TO GET THERE
BY CAR: Dunblane is off the M9 (J11), north of Stirling.
BY PUBLIC TRANSPORT: Dunblane is well served by trains and buses from across central Scotland.
www.travelinescotland.com

MAP
Ordnance Survey Landranger Map 57.
Grid ref: NN 827 021

NEARBY EXCURSIONS
The National Wallace Monument Abbey Craig, Hillfoots Road Causewayhead FK9 5LF
☎ 01786 472140
www.nationalwallace monument.com
Open all year; extended summer opening times daily from 10am–5pm.

MORE INFO
Stirling Tourist Information, 41 Dumbarton Road, Stirling FK8 2QQ
☎ 01786 475019
visitscottishheartlands.com
www.visitscotland.com

The Sheriffmuir Inn Sherrifmuir, Dunblane FK15 0LN
☎ 01786 823285
www.sheriffmuirinn.co.uk

Route ——————

Aberdour Fife

Distance 3¾ miles (6 km) **Type** Easy **Time** 2-3 hours

Map locations: Milnathort, Kennoway, Lough Leven, Glenrothes, Buckhaven, Dunduff, Kirkcaldy, Dunfermline, **ABERDOUR**, Queensferry, Edinburgh

▸ Aberdour's Silver Sands is one of the cleanest and prettiest beaches in Scotland... great for paddling and picnics too!

Only six beaches in Scotland are deemed worthy of the prestigious Blue Flag, and two of them – **Silver Sands** in Aberdour and **Burntisland** – are just a few miles apart.

▸ START

Start from the village of **Aberdour** and turn down a side-road following the signs to the beach. Pass **Aberdour Castle**, which dates back to the 13th century. The quiet road runs down to Silver Sands. This 500m stretch of golden sands offers some superb

📷 views to the islands of Inchcolm, Inchmichery and Inchkeith, and is a popular spot for summer picnics and paddling.

1 ½ MILE

From the car park, the **Fife Coastal Path** (which is clearly signposted) runs along the top of the beach until it crosses a small footbridge over a burn. For the next ½ mile, follow a clear path sandwiched between a wooded railway line and the sea. Across the Firth of Forth you can clearly see Edinburgh Castle. The path is solid but there are a couple of short but relatively steep sections which present no problem for a motorised wheelchair but may mean hard work if you're self-propelling or pushing.

2 1½ MILES

At a narrow arched bridge the path goes under the railway before turning right into a wooded section. You soon reach a small castellated bridge over the **Starley Burn**

📷 **Waterfall** where the lime-rich water gives the rocks an unusual colour.

The next section of path runs between narrow stone walls until you pass a radio mast on the left. On the right you can see the outskirts of **Burntisland**. The path becomes a wider tarmac track and passes through an estate of new houses.

3 2½ MILES

Just before a road, turn right (following the Fife Coastal Path signs) through a passageway under the railway track. Pass a pond then turn left until you meet a quiet road. Turn right to climb steeply then turn first left and keep climbing. After passing a shop you reach **Rossend Castle**, which was built in the 12th century for the Abbots of Dunfermline but is now used as offices for the firm of architects that restored it in the 1970s.

Beyond the castle, start to drop downhill, passing through a stone archway which is a remnant of Burntisland's ancient town walls. After the road crosses the railway again, turn right at a T-junction and drop down to High Street.

4 3 MILES

Turn left and follow the High Street until you reach the entrance to the park. A smooth path runs straight across the grass. Where it splits, take the left fork and follow it for 250m to a ramp under the railway that takes you to the promenade. At high tide the waves come right up to the path, but when the tide is out the beach becomes an enormous

📷 expanse of sand fringed with rockpools.

For the return journey, there's a bus-stop beside the entrance to the park or a train station down from the High Street.

Walk between two of **Scotland's best beaches** on this wheelchair-
accessible and family-friendly jaunt in fife

KEY ⚓ ⛩ 🏰 ⛪ 🐎 🏛 🚗 ⛺ 👣 ♿ ▶INFO

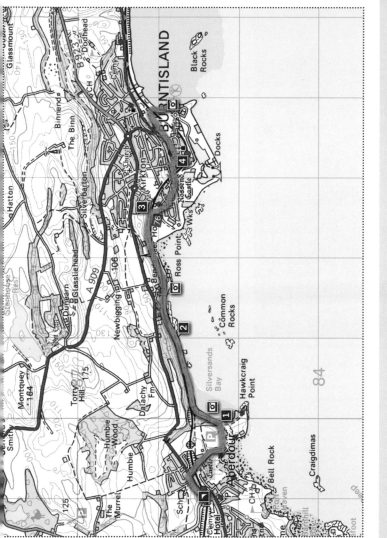

TERRAIN
The entire route follows either
tarmac or solid cinder paths
so is wheelchair accessible
and good for pushchairs and
buggies. Some sections are
steep, which is no problem
for a motorised wheelchair
but hard work if you're self-
propelling or pushing.

HOW TO GET THERE
BY CAR: Take the A921
along the Fife coast
between the Forth Road
Bridge and Kirkcaldy.
BY PUBLIC TRANSPORT:
Stagecoach Fife bus
number 7 runs between
Rosyth and Leven.
☎ 01592 261461
www.stagecoachbus.com

Regular trains run from
Edinburgh. Aberdour is on
the Fife Circle Line.

MAP
Ordnance Survey Landranger
Map 66 or Explorer Map 367.
Grid ref: NT 192 854

NEARBY EXCURSIONS
Aberdour Castle
KY3 0SL
www.historic-scotland.gov.uk
Open: 1 Apr-30 Sept, all
week, 9.30am-5.30pm; Oct,
all week, 9.30am-4.30pm;
1 Nov-31 Mar, not Thurs or
Fri, 9.30am-4.30pm.

MORE INFO
Visit Fife
☎ 01383 720999
www.visitfife.com

Fife Coastal Path
☎ 01592 656094
www.fifecoastalpath.com

Route ⎯⎯⎯⎯

Inverurie •
Aberdeen •
Banchory •
▶ GLEN CLOVA
Montrose •
• Kirriemuir
• Blairgowrie
• Arbroath
• Dundee

Glen Clova Angus

Distance 9 miles (14.5 km) **Type** Challenging **Time** 4-5 hours

▶ **Enjoy views over the deep and brooding waters of Loch Brandy**

The **Glen Clova Hotel** has been offering refreshment to weary travellers since the 1850s. Built on the once busy cattle drove road linking Braemar with Angus, it continues to revive visitors to **Glen Clova**. It also marks the starting point for an upland circuit to two coire lochans, **Loch Brandy** and **Loch Wharral**.

▶ START

Just over the old stone bridge, on the single-track road to **Glen Doll**, there's a small walkers' car park.

With boots on, cross back over the bridge and head left, through the hotel car park, passing a bunkhouse, to reach a gate. Go through and a path rises into a sheltered copse of woodland, emerging on to open moorland higher up. It is a stiff ascent but the path is good and height is quickly gained, offering superb views over Glen Clova. There's more climbing before the gradient eases and the route strikes out across heather that blooms bright pink in the summer. Seek out the juicy blueberries that grow here for a refreshing snack, though do be sure you've got the right berries before you eat any.

1 1½ MILES

A final short pull reveals Loch Brandy, a deep pool nestling in a rocky chasm surrounded by high cliffs and brooding crags. It is a good spot for a paddle or an invigorating wild swim, but take care as the water is deep and can remain cold even on the hottest summer day.

From the loch, follow the path up on to the **Snub**, a shapely shoulder separating Loch Brandy from Corrie of Clova, and progress round the top of the cliffs. The way dips to cross a stream before rising on to **Green Hill**. The plateau is home to red deer, mountain hare and you may also spy the elusive dotterel in summer.

2 3 MILES

The path splits beyond Green Hill. Take the left fork for ½ mile then leave it and strike out over open moor, heading for the trig point on the summit of **Ben Tirran**. Enjoy panoramic views from the top of this Corbett, then head south along the shoulder and descend west to pick up a path descending to Loch Wharral. This is an equally dramatic spot, a head wall of craggy cliffs overshadowing the water, a popular spot with pike fishermen.

3 6 MILES

From the southernmost point of the lochan, a path descends to the **Adrielinn Plantation** and a path skirts down the west side of the trees. Turn right just before you reach the road on another path that rises and falls over a series of low mounds. This runs parallel with the road for a way to reach a pond in trees and, beyond this, it curves round to join the B955. Follow the road back to the Glen Clova Hotel for some well-earned refreshment.

▶ THE GLEN CLOVA

The Glen Clova Hotel's cosy climbers' bar is the perfect place to end a day in the hills. Adorned with mountaineering photos and old bits of kit, and serving a range of cask ales and fine malts, there's a log fire to relax in front of. Live music is a frequent treat, whether organised or impromptu, and there are often special events such as barbecues and spit roasts.

Discover two hidden mountain lochans on a circuit that ends at an historic drovers' inn

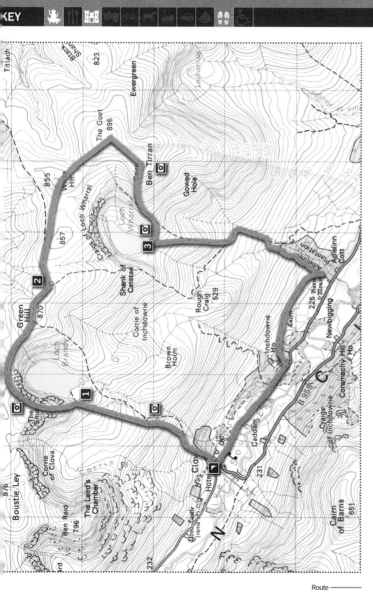

TERRAIN
Hill walking boots recommended. The route follows good paths and tracks over open moor and hillside. On a clear day route finding is easy but if cloud descends a compass and map are invaluable aids. Above Loch Brandy the walk runs close to steep cliffs – don't wander too close to the edge and keep children and dogs in check. Pack warm clothing and waterproofs – even in summer – just in case the weather deteriorates and take some food and drink to keep you going.

HOW TO GET THERE
BY CAR: From Dundee, follow the A90 north and, at Forfar, branch left on the A926 (signed for Angus Glens). At Kirriemuir, take the B955 (signed for Glen Clova) and follow this north, via Dykehead, to Clova. Use the walkers' car park rather than the hotel car park.
BY PUBLIC TRANSPORT: The daily (except Sun) Royal Mail postbus (route 220) leaves Kirriemuir post office at 8.30am, arriving at Clova at 10.10am. Return service departs Clova at 3.55pm.
☎ 08457 740740
www.postbus.royalmail.com

MAP
Ordnance Survey Landranger Map 44.
Grid ref: NO 326 731

MORE INFO
Kirriemuir Tourist Information Centre
1 Cumberland Close,
Kirriemuir DD8 4EF
☎ 01575 575479
www.angusanddundee.co.uk
www.visitscotland.com

Glen Clova Hotel
Glen Clova, near Kirriemuir
DD8 4QS
☎ 01575 550350
www.clova.com

Route ——————

Schiehallion Perthshire

Distance 6 miles (10 km) **Type** Challenging **Time** 4-6 hours

SCHIEHALLION
Dundee
Glenrothes
Stirling
Edinburgh Dunbar
Glasgow East Kilbride

In 1774 **Schiehallion** was chosen as the site for a pioneering experiment to measure the weight of the earth. The Astronomer Royal Nevil Maskelyne needed a geometrically-shaped hill that would be easy to measure, and picked Schiehallion for its triangular outline. He camped at various spots around the mountain for four months, dangling pendulums and measuring how far they were drawn by the gravitational pull of the hill.

Another of his colleagues surveyed the mountain (making Schiehallion the first hill ever to mapped with contours) and between them they used their calculations to measure the volume of the mountain and the power of its gravitational attraction. With some fiendish number-crunching they used their results to work out the earth's weight – proving conclusively for the first time that the world wasn't hollow.

While the Maskelyne experiment became one of the most famous in the history of science, Schiehallion went on to become one Scotland's best-loved hills for walkers. It's a whopping 1,083m (3,553ft), although those who regularly bag Munros (Scottish peaks over 3,000ft) consider it one of the easier hills, thanks to straightforward navigation and a new path leading across the lower, boggier, sections. Stout boots are vital: it's easy to sprain an ankle crossing the boulderfield en route to the summit.

> Views west along Loch Rannoch to the distant peaks of Glencoe

Schiehallion is a popular mountain, so you might have to share the summit. Luckily, the views from the top are big enough to share.

▶ START

Park at **Braes of Foss**, just off the narrow Schiehallion Road running between Loch Kinardochy and Kinloch Rannoch. Pass through a stone gate at the far end, past an information board, then on to the path. Leaving the forestry plantation behind you, follow the track over heathery slopes on a well-made path. Schiehallion ◎ rises up on the right. From here the mountain doesn't resemble the distinctive pyramid that you see from the west – instead you'll see a long sloping ridge rising to a distant summit.

1 ½ MILE

After 10 minutes you reach a crossroads where the path crosses a rough track. On the left are the stone remains of crofters' cottages. From here the climb begins in earnest. Conservation charity The John Muir Trust bought East Schiehallion in 1999 and began replacing a badly eroded boggy track with a properly constructed path. Using 3,450 tonnes of aggregate and 400 tonnes of stone (plus

£817,000) they built a 3.5km-long track that zigzags up the hillside. Purists might argue it detracts from the wilderness experience, but it's definitely a joy to walk on. A moderate gradient with sections of rocky steps takes you to a height of about 860m (2,821ft).

2 1½ MILES

The ground then flattens out and the well-built path simply stops. From here, follow the obvious ridge of the hill upwards and westwards over the boulderfield. Aim for the giant cairn jutting into the skyline. A faint path picks its way through the rubble, but otherwise it's a case of treading carefully through loose rocks. Follow the obvious line of the broad whaleback ridge as it climbs over a frustrating series of false summits.

3 3 MILES

Eventually the rubble gives way to a series of huge stone blocks and with an easy scramble you're at the top. There's no trig point, but the ◎ views are superb. To the west lies **Loch Rannoch** while **Loch Tummel** is east. To the north are the first giant hills of the **Cairngorms**; the mighty **Glen Lyon** Munros lie south. Retrace your steps to return, taking care over the rocks.

Schiehallion's distinctive conical shape earned it a place in
scientific history – and also makes it a great mountain day-trip

KEY ▲INFO

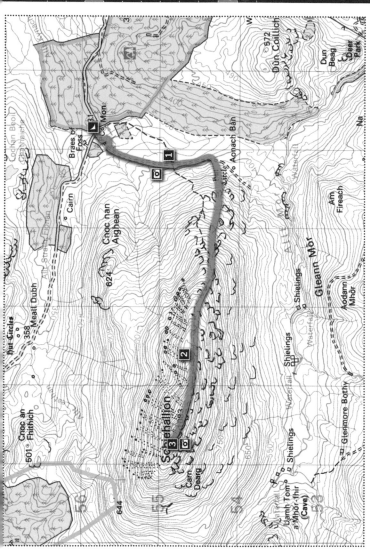

TERRAIN
Well-made path, then it's
a rough boulderfield for
the remaining climb to the
summit. A map and compass
are essential, as are solid
walking boots.

HOW TO GET THERE
BY CAR: From the northbound
B846 between Aberfeldy and
Tummel Bridge, turn left on to
the signposted Schiehallion
Road. After 2 miles you reach
the large Braes of Foss car
park (with toilets).
BY PUBLIC TRANSPORT:
There's no direct public
transport link. The best
option is to travel to Kinloch
Rannoch, 5 miles from the
start of the walk. Broons
Buses and Taxis run from
Pitlochry to Kinloch Rannoch.
☎ 01882 632331

MAP
Ordnance Survey Explorer
Map 386.
Grid ref: NN 753 557

NEARBY EXCURSIONS
Glengoulandie Country Park
Foss, Nr. Pitlochry PH16 5NL
☎ 01887 830495
www.glengoulandie.co.uk
The park offers fishing and
trips to see Highland cattle
and red deer.

MORE INFO
Aberfeldy Tourist
Information Centre
The Square, Aberfeldy
PH15 2DD
☎ 01887 820276

Visit Scotland
visitscotland.com/white

Loch Ossian Highland

Distance 9 miles (14¼ km) **Type** Moderate **Time** 3-4 hours

As soon as you step off the train at **Corrour** you feel the call of the wild. This is one of the most remote spots in Britain and with the nearest road more than 10 miles away, the railway is the only way in or out. Built to serve **Corrour Estate**, the station is a gateway to one of the last remaining areas of true wilderness in the country – **Rannoch Moor**.

Covering 12,000 acres, the moor is a great morass of peat and heather. Once heavily wooded, it is now barren and blessed with a character that changes with the weather. On a good day, it is a place of striking natural beauty. On a bad day it can be dark and forbidding. In his novel, *Kidnapped*, Robert Louis Stevenson described the scene: "A wearier looking desert a man never saw". But within this desert there are some real gems and **Loch Ossian**, one of the highest lochs in Scotland, is certainly one of them.

A short walk from Corrour station, it is the perfect destination for a car-free escape. Catch the Caledonian Sleeper from London to make a weekend of it. You can tuck yourself into a bunk in the capital and wake 12 hours later in the heart of the **Scottish Highlands**.

▶ START

Film fans may recognise Corrour station from *Trainspotting*. It's the same remote station that Renton and his friends alight on a trip

▷ With no cars for miles, a trip to 3 mile-long Loch Ossian is the ideal way to escape civilisation

to the great outdoors.

Leave the platform and follow the track east towards Loch Ossian. The snaking body of water soon looms into view, the eye drawn over its wooded shores towards a cluster of 📷 Munros at the far end.

1 | 1 MILE

At the western end of the loch is **Loch Ossian Youth Hostel**, which was refurbished in 2003 as one of the UK's first eco-hostels. A wind turbine provides the power and it also features environmentally sound water and waste disposal systems.

Follow the track along the south side of the loch. It crosses open

ground, where you may spot red deer, before skirting between the shoreline and woodland, where there is a rare chance you may see pine marten.

2 | 4¼ MILES

The track curves round the western end of the loch, where estate cottages cluster. Cross the **River Ossian** and pass **Corrour Lodge**. This grand granite and glass structure is a relatively recent addition to the landscape, but the trees offer only tempting glimpses of the architecture.

A little way on a plaque commemorates the contribution of the late Sir John Stirling

Maxwell in the successful afforestation of large parts of Britain, including Corrour Estate.

At the track junction beyond the memorial, turn left and set off along the north shore. Occasional tree-lined promontories jutting into the water are great places to pause and admire the 📷 stunning scenery. From such sheltered spots you can truly appreciate the beauty of the surrounding landscape.

The track heads through forest before emerging into recently planted native woodland. Follow the track as it curves round the west end of Loch Ossian to join the main track back to Corrour station.

With no roads in or out, remote **Loch Ossian** is the perfect
destination for a car-free escape into the country

KEY

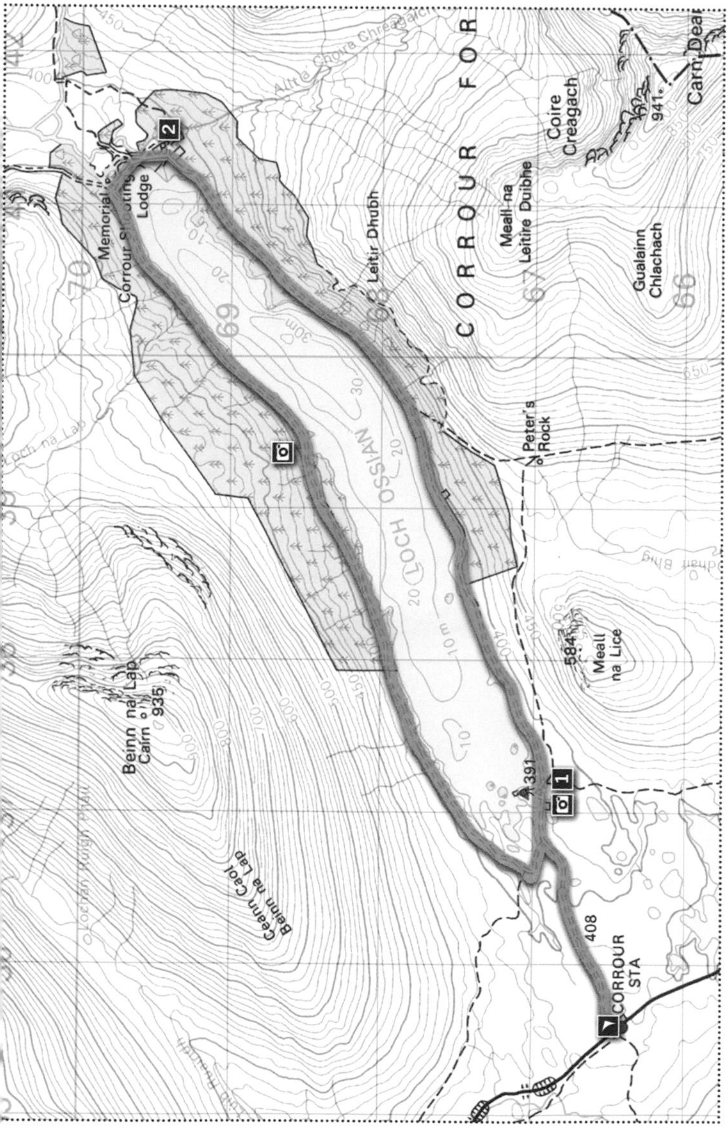

▶INFO

TERRAIN
A good track extends from
Corrour station to Loch
Ossian Youth Hostel and
continues around the loch.
Boots or walking shoes are
recommended. This part of
the country is exposed to the
elements and the weather
can change suddenly, so pack
waterproofs, warm clothing,
food and drink.

HOW TO GET THERE
BY CAR: Corrour station can't
be reached by car. The nearest
road ends at Rannoch station.
To reach Rannoch station,
head north from Perth on the
A9 to Pitlochry then follow the
B8019 west and continue on
the B846.
BY PUBLIC TRANSPORT:
First ScotRail services on
the West Highland Line stop
at Corrour. First ScotRail
Caledonian Sleeper services
running between London
Euston and Fort William also
call there on request.
☎ 0845 601 5929
www.scotrail.co.uk

MAP
Ordnance Survey Explorer
Map 385.
Grid ref: NN 355 664

MORE INFO
Tourist Information Centre,
15 High Street,
Fort William PH33 6DH
☎ 0845 225 5121
www.visithighlands.com
www.visitscotland.com

Scottish Youth Hostel
Association
☎ 01786 891400
www.syha.org.uk

Corrour Estate
☎ 01397 732200
www.corrour.co.uk

Route ———

Glencoe Highland

Distance 4 miles (6½ km) **Type** Challenging **Time** 3 hours

Kinlochleven •
Ballachulish •
•Loch Linnhe

Oban•

> The walk begins with breathtaking views of the Three Sisters

First-time visitors to **Glencoe** can't fail to be taken aback by its breathtakingly grim grandeur. The glen is 10 miles long and a mere 700m wide; imposing mountains bear down on both sides. It was in this bleak but beautiful landscape where reiving (cattle rustling) between rival clans was a way of life, and where, in 1692, the Massacre of Glencoe took place.

The journey to the **Lost Valley** traverses a steep ravine, where the Clan MacDonald allegedly drove rustled livestock. A glacial glen, created by a vast weight of ice that was blocked by a boulder avalanche, it is impossible to see until you are virtually on top of it.

It's a short, easy to navigate walk, but tough sections, scrambles and a gorge crossing make it a fun, challenging route that should take around three hours.

▶ START

Start in the upper car park on the A82. A National Trust for Scotland plaque ◻ shows the Three Sisters **Beinn Fhada, Gearr Aonach** and **Aonach Dubh** ahead.

Take a path down into the valley until you reach a track, then follow this left. The track then bears right towards the upper **River Coe**. Go down the wooden steps, which can be slippery after rain, and follow the path over a bridge above a deep

gorge. Scramble up the other side, and then bear right on a rocky path rising steeply between **Beinn Fhada** and **Gearr Aonach**, two of the **Three Sisters of Glencoe**.

1 ¾ MILE

Continue up the hillside, through a deer fence and along a narrow ledge with the burn to your left. It's probably at this point you'll find yourself wondering how on earth the clans drove their livestock along this route.

◻ Look back for views of the **Pass of Glencoe**, a phenomenal driving road that crosses **Rannoch Moor** before entering the glen, and a view of Jimmy Saville's house.

Continue to scramble up the path, tackling a few boulders and, after heavy rain, hiking up through a stream.

2 1¾ MILES

When you reach two huge boulders (if you reach a

scree slope you've gone too far), cross the burn carefully. There are a few points where a crossing is possible, but after heavy rain things are made trickier and you may have to get your feet wet – or try again another day. Once on the other side, follow the path uphill.

Climb over the brow of the hill and look down ◻ into **Coire Gabhail**, or the **Lost Valley** as it's commonly known. First-time visitors may be amazed at the size of the valley, which until now has been totally obscured from view.

It is alleged the Clan MacDonald stowed stolen cattle here (or hid their own cattle to stop neighbours rustling theirs). The valley may also have been used as a refuge for escaping clan members after the Massacre of Glencoe.

Follow the path back the way you came to return to the start point.

▶ THE MASSACRE OF GLENCOE

At 5am on 13 February 1692, troops led by Robert Campbell exacted a brutal massacre on the

MacDonalds of Glencoe on the grounds that the clan had been late in pledging their allegiance to William of Orange. Thirty-eight men were murdered as they tried to flee the glen, and 40 women and children died of exposure in the harsh winter conditions after their homes were burned. Days earlier the MacDonalds had welcomed their soon-to-be killers into their homes in the hospitable tradition of the Highlands.

Follow an unbelievable journey to the lost valley in **Glencoe** where, legend has it, local clans hid rustled livestock

KEY

▶INFO

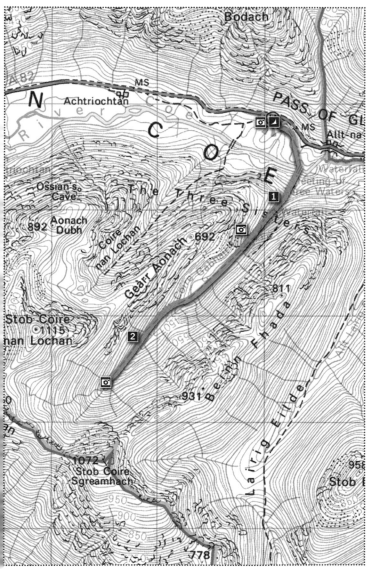

TERRAIN
Rocky, but a clear footpath runs steeply along a narrow edge. Walkers will need to scramble, climb over boulders and cross a river. May not be suitable for younger children.

HOW TO GET THERE
BY CAR: Glencoe is 16 miles south of Fort William on the A82. The starting point is the car park on the A82, 3 miles east of the Clachaig Inn.
BY PUBLIC TRANSPORT:
The National Express bus between Glasgow, Fort William and Inverness stops in Glencoe. Fort William is served by the Caledonian Sleeper Line from London Euston.
First ScotRail
☎ 0845 601 5929
www.scotrail.co.uk

MAP
Ordnance Survey Explorer Map 384.
Grid ref: NN 171 569

NEARBY EXCURSIONS
Ice Factor, the National Ice Climbing Centre – and the world's biggest indoor ice wall Leven Road, Kinlochleven, Lochaber PH50 4SF
☎ 01855 831100
www.ice-factor.co.uk

MORE INFO
Visit Scotland
www.visitscotland.com

National Trust for Scotland
www.nts.org.uk

Route ————

Glenfinnan Highland

Distance 5 miles (8 km) **Type** Easy **Time** 3 hours

› The Glenfinnan Monument sits at the head of Loch Shiel, the scene of many magical movie moments

Glenfinnan Viaduct

has featured in a string of films, but is perhaps best known by younger viewers for its starring role in the Harry Potter movies. A key crossing point on the railway journey to Hogwart's School,

the 21-arch bridge has been at the centre of some enthralling scenes. This walk takes you right to the heart of the action and there are fantastic viewpoints where young imaginations can run wild before you continue up **Glen Finnan**.

› START

From **Glenfinnan** village, head north on the surfaced Glenfinnan Estate track. The walk to the viaduct takes only a few minutes and soon you are confronted by the 📷 spectacular structure, stretching from one side of the valley to the other.

1 ½ MILE

The track passes below the viaduct, but there are a couple of short detours available. On the right a track crosses the **River Finnan**, passing through a wood yard and climbing to the eastern end of the viaduct. A short scramble on to a grassy knoll offers a great view down **Loch** 📷 **Shiel**, which featured in

The Chamber of Secrets.

On the other side of the main track, a path climbs to the western end, and here you can visualise one of the most memorable scenes from *The Chamber of Secrets*, when Harry and Ron Weasley fly through the air in a Ford Anglia, ducking in and out of the arches thanks to some clever special effects.

Back on the track, pass under the bridge and look for a plaque, unveiled in 1997, to mark the centenary of the viaduct. Follow the track beside the River Finnan, northerly along the glen to reach a bridge below Glenfinnan Lodge.

2 2½ MILES

Turn right to **Corryhully bothy**. There's a safe spot for paddling in the river here and a little way upstream there's a pool where children can swim on a hot day.

Retrace your steps to the bridge below the

lodge and head a few meters back down the track to a footbridge on the left. Carefully cross this shaky structure and go through a gate. Bear right and a woodland path curves left, climbing into the trees to meet another path marked with slim wooden posts. Turn left and, after a short but strenuous ascent, you emerge on to a forest track.

3 3 MILES

Go right and follow the track south. About 600m north of the viaduct it joins the main glen track – retrace your steps from here back to Glenfinnan. Don't forget to visit the nearby Glenfinnan Monument, erected in 1815 to mark the spot where Bonnie Prince Charlie raised his standard at the beginning of the 1745 Jacobite uprising, and to dip your toe in Loch Shiel.

An instantly recognisable feature of the Harry Potter films,
Glenfinnan Viaduct is the gateway to an enchanting Highland glen

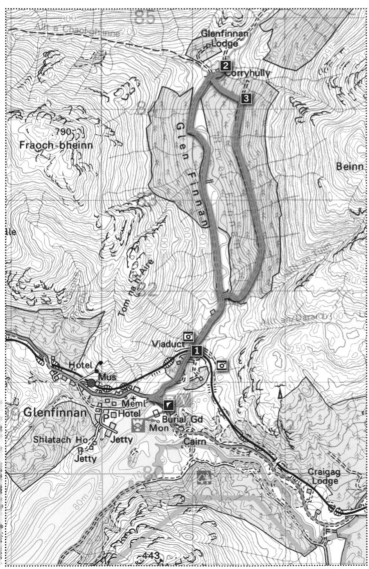

TERRAIN
Surfaced track to Corryhully bothy, suitable for buggies and bikes. Rougher forest path and track for return. The latter is unsuitable for buggies or bikes, but it is possible to return to the start by the main Glen Finnan track.

HOW TO GET THERE
BY CAR: Follow A82 north to Fort William and then A830 18 miles west to Glenfinnan.
BY PUBLIC TRANSPORT: Rail services run on the Fort William to Mallaig line to Glenfinnan station, a 10 minute walk from start point.

First ScotRail
☎ 0845 601 5929
www.scotrail.co.uk

MAP
Ordnance Survey Explorer Map 398.
Grid ref: NM 905 808

NEARBY EXCURSIONS
Glenfinnan Monument Visitor Centre
Glenfinnan PH37 4LT
☎ 0844 493 2221
www.nts.org.uk
Visitor centre and cafe open daily, 10am-5pm, Mar-Jun; 9.30am-5.30pm, Jul-Aug; 10am-5pm, Sep-Oct.

MORE INFO
Tourist Information Centre
15 High Street, Fort William
PH33 6DH
☎ 01397 703781
www.visithighlands.com

Visit Scotland
www.visitscotland.com

Route ——

217

Isle of Skye Highland

Distance 5½ miles (9 km) **Type** Moderate **Time** 3-4 hours

For those with a love of wild places, the **Isle of Skye**, with its fiercely jagged **Cuillin Ridge**, is irresistible. Scottish-born Gavin Maxwell was drawn to the island off the west coast of Scotland after the war and, characteristically (he had an exceedingly varied life), he bought the nearby small island of **Soay** where he established a shark fishery. Based on his experiences, he wrote his first book, *Harpoon at a Venture*, in 1952. The book promulgated conservation –almost unheard of at the time. When the shark business floundered, Maxwell moved to **Sandaig** on the mainland, south of **Skye**, and later to **Eilean Bán**, by the island. The writer loved Skye for its otters, whales and eagles, all of which can be seen on this walk if you're lucky.

▶ START

The south coast of Skye is one of the best places in Britain to see otters, partly because of the number of freshwater pools where these secretive creatures wash.

From the car park on the western side of **Aird of Sleat**, follow a wide track as it leads across bogland. Look for the pale green rosette of leaves and single violet flower of the insectivorous common butterwort, which uses a sticky fluid to trap and digest insects.

1 ¾ MILES

As you gain height, take

▶ The views across the Sound of Sleat to Knoydart are spectacular

stock of the superb view – the mountains of **Knoydart** stand ancient and proud across the **Sound of Sleat** and to their left is **Beinn Sgritheall**, above Sandaig. Look above for both golden and sea eagles – there are some 30 pairs of golden and nine pairs of sea eagles on this Hebridean island. Follow the track downhill.

2 1½ MILES

Bear left by a sign for the lighthouse where the track bends and follow this boggy path between

two hills. Further on there's a right turn for the point itself. Ignore this for now to continue to **Camas Daraich** – a

▶ THE REAL MIJBIL

Author and naturalist Gavin Maxwell charmed more than a million readers with his 1960 autobiographical book *Ring of Bright Water*, in which he describes life at the fictional Camusfearna with his otter Mijbil. Maxwell brought the real Mij back from Iraq, and later took him to the London Zoological Society, where he was identified as a sub-species of smooth-coated otter. Sadly this sub-species is now extinct.

beautiful sandy cove. Approach quietly for a chance to see otters. In the sea they're difficult to spot: a trailing ripple and the rounded top of their head is all you'll see in between 20-second dives. Your best chance of spotting one is on land but stay still as, despite their myopia, they will detect the slightest movement. Look for fresh spraint, the remainders of their prey and five-toed paw prints – all signs that otters live nearby.

Don't be disheartened if there's nothing – otters, which can be more than a metre in length, forage many kilometres along the coast from their base.

3 1¾ MILES

Return to the aforementioned turn and walk on to the lighthouse, which is an excellent lookout point for dolphins, basking sharks, and minke whales. And even if you don't see any of these cetaceans, the view north to the **Cuillin** is memorable certainly.

Explore the remote and wild south coast of Skye, loved by author and naturalist **Gavin Maxwell**, in search of otters

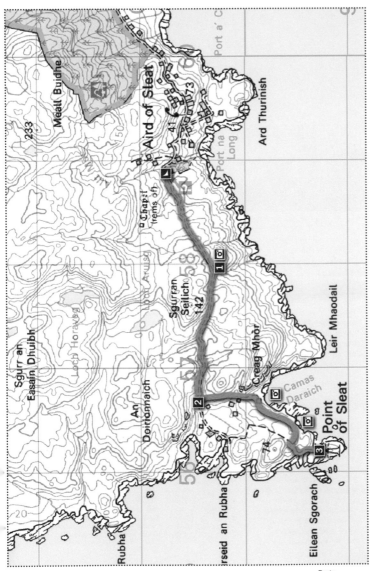

TERRAIN
Rough tracks with peaty sections. Walking boots and waterproofs are essential.

HOW TO GET THERE
BY CAR: Follow the A851/ A853 south of Broadford on Skye to its conclusion at a car park at Aird of Sleat.
BY PUBLIC TRANSPORT: The nearest bus service is to Ardvasar 3 miles east on the main road.
www.rapsons.com

MAP
Ordnance Survey Landranger Map 32.
Grid ref: NG 589 007

NEARBY EXCURSIONS
Kylerhea Otter Haven hide Kylerhea, Highland
www.forestry.gov.uk
Reached by a short walk, this hide overlooks the Kylerhea narrows. Open all year, all day.

MORE INFO
Broadford Tourist Information Centre
Main St, Broadford
Isle of Skye IV49 9AB
☎ 01471 822361
www.visitscotland.com

International Otter Survival Fund
7 Black Park, Broadford
Isle of Skye IV49 9DE
☎ 01471 822487
www.otter.org

Route ——————

219

SCOTLAND

Loch Linnhe

ISLE OF KERRERA

Inveraray ·

Argyll
Forest Park

Loch Lomond ·

Loch Fyne ·

Grennock ·

Isle of Kerrera Argyll

Distance 6 miles (10 km) **Type** Moderate **Time** 3-4 hours

The west coast of Scotland is no stranger to April showers, so a great all-weather alternative to camping is a convivial bunkhouse.

Every year thousands of tourists bypass Kerrera, in Oban Bay, as they sail from the west coast town to Mull and other Hebridean islands. But it's a mistake to ignore this small hummocky island because of its proximity to the mainland: you'll find peace and quiet here – only 30 people inhabit **Kerrera**.

A ferry plies the crystal clear **Sound of Kerrera** to the south of **Oban**. Then a 2 mile walk, or pre-arranged lift in a 4x4, will take you to the far end of the island and the bunkhouse – a stone's throw from a wild shoreline.

▶ The history of Gylen Castle is nearly as impressive as the view. It was carefully restored in 2006

▶ START

Follow a stream from the bunkhouse down to the sea at **Port a' Chaisteil**. The narrow seaweed-filled bay is a popular swimming spot where you 📷 can enjoy views out west past **Mull** and beyond to the sea. There's a good chance you'll see grey seals in the sheltered bay; a large colony lives off the northwest coast of the island.

1 ½ MILE

Follow the path round to the dramatic 16th century MacDougall tower, **Gylen Castle**, perched above the waves. Sixty years after its inception it was ransacked by the Covenanter army, who massacred all within and stole the Brooch of Lorn,

which once belonged to Robert the Bruce.

2 1¼ MILES

Retrace your steps to the bunkhouse and follow the path behind it. Where the path descends to the shore divert to the right of a house to reach pretty 📷 **Port Dubh** with views of Mull's western cliffs. Clumps of alder with newly unfurled leaves thrive here.

3 2 MILES

Back on the track continue uphill past a house, named **Ardmore**, where the path narrows and passes through richly scented bogland. Stop awhile above **Barr-nam-boc Bay** and savour the view, north over the nearby low-lying island of **Lismore** to remote **Kingairloch** and northeast to the

huge V-shaped notch that marks the start of the **Great Glen**, which transects Scotland.

4 5¼ MILES

Gird your loins for a steep climb, as the track swings inland before a long descent to the ferry slip.

From there simply follow the main track, branching right by **Upper Gylen**. Halfway along the **Little Horse Shoe Bay** makes for a good rest stop. On a warm spring day it can be just the place for a doze, before heading back to the bunkhouse.

▶ THE BUNKHOUSE

The **Kerrera Bunkhouse** is a converted 18th century stable. It's ultra cosy and has a lounge area with music system and books and games. There's spring water on tap and nextdoor is the

Kerrera Tea Gardens and a patio space, which can be a suntrap if the weather's kind. The friendly owners will ensure you have a totally relaxing stay in this secluded little hideaway.

Wake up on the enchanting **Isle of Kerrera** for a lovely day following a sinuous route among hidden coves

KEY

‣INFO

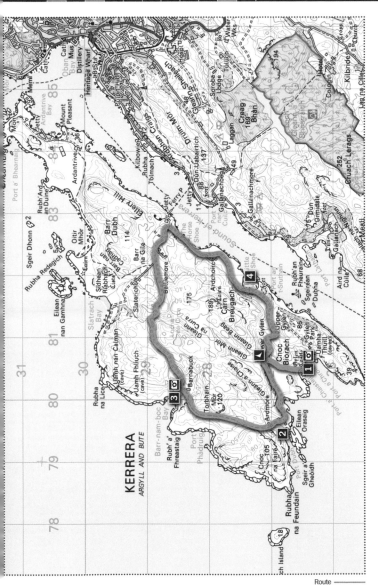

TERRAIN
Earthen path, which can be muddy. Walking boots and waterproofs are essential.

HOW TO GET THERE
BY CAR: The ferry point is 2 miles (3km) south of Oban on the Gallanach Road, signed from the town centre.
BY PUBLIC TRANSPORT: From late May the number 431 bus service from Oban connects with the 10.30am and 4pm ferries.
☎ 08705 505050
www.citylink.co.uk

Trains and buses from Glasgow serve Oban.
www.scotrail.co.uk

The ferry takes only five minutes. Departs 8.45am, 10.30am, 12.30pm, 2pm, 4pm, 5pm.

MAP
Ordnance Survey Explorer Map 359.
Grid ref: NM 806 271

MORE INFO
Oban Tourist Information Church Building, Argyll Square, Oban PA34 4AN
☎ 01631 563122
visitscottishheartlands.org
www.visitscotland.com

Kerrera Bunkhouse and Tea Gardens
Lower Gylen, Isle of Kerrera, By Oban, Argyll PA34 4SX
☎ 01631 570223
www.kerrerabunkhouse.co.uk
The bunkhouse sleeps seven. and is open all year. Advance booking recommended.

Route ⸺

Loch Fyne Argyll

Distance 3¾ miles (6 km) **Type** Moderate **Time** 3 hours

▶ START
From the **George Hotel** head towards the harbour. Follow the road round and head for **Inveraray Castle**. The third Duke of Argyll moved Inveraray to its current location so he could build on the original site and enjoy some privacy. Although the

▶ THE PUB

Inveraray was Scotland's first planned town and the **George Hotel** is one of its finest buildings. Originally two private houses, it was amalgamated into a hotel in 1866 by the Clark family, who still own it today. An elegant building, with roaring fires and flagstoned floors, the George shows an impressive commitment to malt whisky, real ale and locally sourced produce.

castle is shut in winter, the grounds are open all year round.

1 ¾ MILE
Inveraray Castle is an architecturally complex building combining Baroque, Palladian, Gothic and Gallic influences. Sir John Vanbrugh, architect of Blenheim Castle, made the original design, which was then developed by architects Morris and Adam. The current duke grew up in the castle and achieved a certain celebrity for leading Scotland's Elephant Polo team to victory in the 2004 and 2005 World Championships. To the far side of the castle car park is a signpost suggesting a choice of three walks: yellow, brown or blue. The blue route is the longest and takes you to the summit of **Dun Na Cuaiche**. All routes are well signposted. Head

▶ **Top: Inveraray Castle; Above: The view of Loch Fyne from Dun Na Cuaiche is wonderful**

away from the castle, over the elegant **Frew's** or **Garden Bridge**, designed by John Adam, and leave the path as directed. The path gently climbs into woodland, passing through the **Pinetum**, which includes some impressive red cedars. Soon after, the yellow path diverges and the brown and blue paths curve to the right.

2 1¼ MILES
The blue path then turns left, climbing steeply up the hill, but for tantalising glimpses of the town and castle follow the brown signs until you reach a brown marker labelled

'E' and a blue one marked '17'. Then head up the hill, taking care as it climbs steeply as it can be soggy. The trees thin as you reach the summit, 248m (813ft) up, and then take a left to the tower.

3 1¾ MILES
This unusual, oriental-style building was constructed in 1748 for the sum of £46. Its purpose was decorative, although it is an ideal place in which to enjoy the view without being assaulted by the weather. Although squat and square on the outside, it has a circular interior.

▣ **Loch Fyne**, Scotland's longest sea-loch, stretches before you. Although it has been known to play host to dolphins, seals, otters and basking sharks, it is more likely that its inhabitants will, for the most part, be seafood. Still, Loch Fyne oysters are famous worldwide. To the east and south rise snow-capped hills, including some Munros. For the descent, either take the left fork just below the summit and follow the path back to the Pinetum by a circuitous loop, or retrace your steps to blue marker 17 and continue down to the **Sweetie Seat** and back to the castle through the seed orchard. Thoughts of warm fires and good food waiting for you at the George Hotel should help sustain you.

Enjoy a ramble to the summit of **Dun Na Cuaiche**, where the views
of Inveraray and Loch Fyne are Truly spectacular

KEY

▶INFO

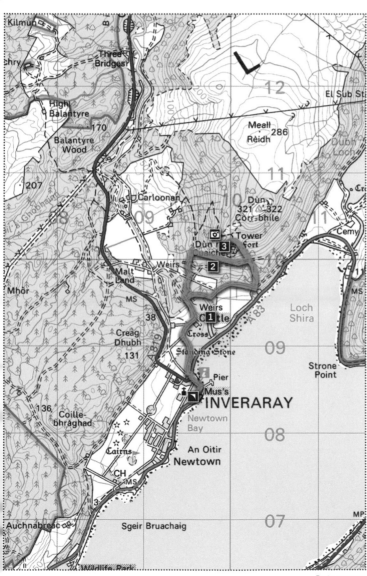

TERRAIN
Woodland and well
signposted paths.

HOW TO GET THERE
BY CAR:
From Glasgow take the A82
and then the A83 at Tarbet.
Inveraray is on the west shore
of Loch Fyne and the George
Hotel is on Main Street East.
There is a pay and display car
park – as you enter Inveraray,
take the first right after the
A819 turning.
BY PUBLIC TRANSPORT:
Inveraray is served by Citylink
bus from Glasgow.
Buchanan Street Bus Station
☎ 0871 200 2233

MAP
Ordnance Survey Explorer
Map 360.
Grid ref: NN 095 085

NEARBY EXCURSIONS
Inveraray Jail
Argyll PA32 8TX
Open all year: Apr-Oct,
9.30am-6pm; Nov-Mar,
10am-5pm.
☎ 01499 302381
www.inverarayjail.co.uk

MORE INFO
Inveraray Tourist Information
☎ 01499 302063

The George Hotel
Main Street East, Inveraray,
Argyll PA32 8TT
☎ 01499 302111
www.thegeorgehotel.co.uk

Route ⎯⎯

NORTHERN IRELAND

The **Giants Causeway** is a phenomenon in the truest sense of the word. Some 38,000 hexagonal columns of basalt stretch out before you, almost daring you to think that they are too perfect, too geometric, to ever have been created by sheer chance. Surely this isn't just a case of lava cooling when it met the sea? Perhaps there is something in the legend that it was constructed so that warring giants from Scotland and Ireland could nip over the sea to battle without wetting their great clod-hopping feet.

The thing is, the Giants Causeway is so spectacular that it overshadows Northern Ireland's other rural delights. In these happier post-Troubles days, Northern Ireland is finally able to take its rightful place as one of the real highlights for every kind of walker in the British Isles.

While hill-walkers and climbers make a beeline for the honeypots of Snowdonia and Cumbria, those in the know head for the **Sperrin Mountains** in **County Tyrone**, one of the least explored mountain ranges in the United Kingdom. Although the Sperrins can look barren, even uninviting, in bleak weather, when the yellow gorse blooms the mood changes and the fresh, lush foothills teem with life.

County Fermanagh is another tourist magnet waiting to happen. It's the lake district of Northern Ireland, dominated by **Lough Erne**, a 50-mile (80-km) waterworld, dotted by over 300 pleasantly wooded islands. The character of the county, small in size, but large in natural splendour, has been shaped by its water. Indeed, the locals often quip that for six months the lakes are in Fermanagh, and for the rest of the year Fermanagh is in the lakes.

Other comparisons with England can be made. If Kent is the garden of England, then **County Down** is Northern Ireland's counterpart, with countless orchards and strawberry fields that seem to stretch forever and while the **Mourne Mountains** form a compact range they easily rival the majesty of the Peak District. After all, it was the 'kingdom of Mourne' that inspired C. S. Lewis to create the world of Narnia.

With delights like these on offer, it can't be long before the rest of the world cottons on and starts arriving in this tip of the **Emerald Isle** in their droves. Beat the rush, and experience the magic for yourself while the going is good.

Glenariff Forest Co Antrim

Distance 3 miles (4.8 km) **Type** Moderate **Time** 2 hours

Glenariff Forest Park is located in **Glenariff Glen**, one of the famous Glens of Antrim. Glenariff, also known as the Queen of the Glens, consists of a U-shaped valley, and is considered to be the most stunning of all nine glens. Glenariff Forest Park covers a total of 1,185 hectares, and is bisected by two beautiful rivers, the **Glenariff** and the **Inver**. The forest contains tree species such as ash, oak, beech, Scots pine and hazel.

▶ START

Glenariff Forest Park is situated on the main Ballymena to Waterfoot road. The walk begins in the large main car park of the forest (fee charged). Before setting off, have a look at the In Touch information kiosk located at the top end of the car park (on the path which takes you to the cafe) to familiarise yourself with the area.

Starting from the car park, follow the red trail arrows, which lead back out towards the entrance of the car park. The path quickly descends away from the road towards the Glenariff River. Look to your right for stunning 📷 views down the glen towards the sea. This is also an excellent high vantage point to appreciate the vibrant natural colours all around you. Follow this path as it then veers right and you will shortly come to an information board, with another route which forks off to your left.

▶ The Ess-na-Larach waterfall is an incredible highlight of the walk

1 ½ MILE

The main waterfall walk leads you past this and further down into the heart of the forest, however, time permitting, it is worthwhile to head left for 50m or less to view the newly constructed **Rainbow Bridge** that crosses the Glenariff River. Continue past the information board, and follow the path, keeping the river on your left. This section descends further through Glenariff, with well-maintained steps and fences, and suitably positioned wooden benches – ideal locations to stop and take in the area's beauty and to breathe in the fragrance of the forest.

2 1 MILE

Eventually the steps bring you to the side of the impressive **Ess-na-Larach** waterfall, the largest waterfall in the forest. At the foot of this waterfall, cross the wooden bridge. From this point, you have fantastic views looking back up into the face of the fall. After heavy rain, this bridge can be quite wet and slippery, so take extra care.

Follow the wooden pathway as it twists along the left-hand side of the river. Again, the colours here are stunningly beautiful as they blend against the rockpools and smaller waterfalls of the Glenariff River. The path eventually reaches Laragh Lodge, a pub restaurant. Opposite the lodge, a small wooden bridge crosses you back over the Glenariff River. From here, you will have great views of both the Glenariff and Inver rivers as they meet and continue downstream through the glen.

3 1½ MILES

On your left, a small path leads down to one of the highlights of the walk, the beautiful **Ess-na-Crub** waterfall. After visiting the waterfall, follow the main path uphill until you come to a clearing where the path forks in several directions. Turn right and follow this path as it begins a gradual ascent through the forest and towards the main car park. There are several clearings with stunning views down the glen towards the seaside village of **Waterfoot**. A cafe is located just beside the car park at the end of the walk.

Enjoy the beauty and tranquillity of **Glenariff Forest** and discover the many waterfalls and pools on its Waterfall walk

KEY

INFO

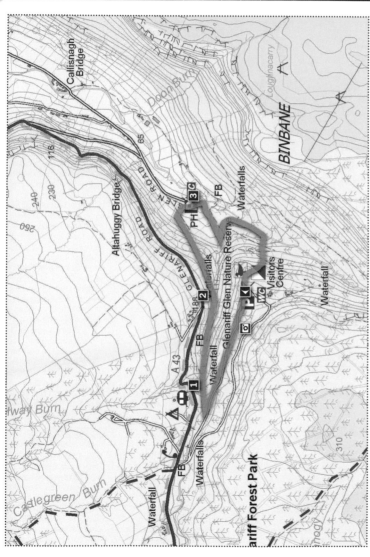

TERRAIN
Broken surface material, steps with steep gullies, overhanging branches in places. Well-marked trail with rest areas at irregular intervals.

HOW TO GET THERE
BY CAR: Glenariff Park is signposted of the A43 Ballymena-Waterfoot road 22km north east of Ballymena.
BY PUBLIC TRANSPORT:
Ulster Bus runs daily between Ballymena and Waterfoot.

MAP
OSNI Glens of Antrim Map.
Grid ref: D204211

NEARBY EXCURSIONS:
Giants Causeway, Whitepark Bay Beach, Dunluce Castle, Murlough Bay

MORE INFO
Open all year round, although closing time varies with sunset time.

Forest Service NI, 6 Forest Road, Garvagh, County Londonderry BT51 5EF
☎ 028 29 556003
www.forestserviceni.gov.uk

Ballycastle Tourist Board, Sheskburn House 7 Mary Street, Ballycastle BT54 6QH
☎ 028 20 762024
www.moyle-council.org

Walk Northern Ireland
www.walkni.com

Discover Northern Ireland
discovernorthernireland. com

Route ———

Lough Neagh Co Armagh

Distance 3 miles (5 km) **Type** Easy **Time** 2 hours

> **Above and below:** The bogs that inspired Heaney's work

> Derryhubbert Bog in Peatlands Park is home to an array of birdlife

Seamus Heaney, Ireland's Nobel Laureate poet known affectionately as Famous Seamus, was born and brought up a few miles north of **Lough Neagh** in mid-Ulster. The rush-dotted fields, peat bogs and endless tasks of smallholders might seem like mundane scenes but are honed to great beauty by the sharp eye and pen of this great poet. A walk in County Armagh's **Peatlands Park** near Lough Neagh lets you tap into some of the scenery and wildlife, which inspired and continue to captivate Heaney.

▶ START

Peatlands Park is just off junction 13 on the M1, 34 miles west of Belfast. There are several walks available, up to 5½ miles in length.

This 3-mile route, like the others, starts at the information panel beside the car park. Follow the bog walk signs.

1 ¼ MILES

Mullenakill Nature Reserve gives you your first glimpse of open bog. The peat here has been forming for 8000 years

and is 9m deep. The bright russet and fawn shades of winter give way to green in late spring.

Continue to the larger **Derryhubbert Bog**. The small brown birds flitting about are meadow pipits and reed buntings, and herons lurk in ditches waiting for a passing fish. Former owners planted isolated Scots pines on the bog and the dead trunks and branches show that many were not happy living in this very wet and acidic environment.

2 1¼ MILES

The route takes you through the edge of woodland at **Annagarriff Nature Reserve**. An excursion into this wood

reveals large mounds of plant debris, made by wood ants, and this is the only place in Ireland where this species occurs. Back to the bog trail, don't miss the zigzag track (on your right just after crossing the mini-railway) to the turf-cutting displays. Heaney's poem *Digging* explores the poet's fond memories of his grandfather, who could cut more turf than any other man on Toner's Bog. He recalls the squelch and slap of the peat, the smell of potato mould and the way his granddad would heave the cut turf over his shoulder.

Peat bogs are able to preserve things incredibly well, and the history of the landscape is revealed in plant pollen, buried casks of butter, remains of giant elks and even 2000-year-old human bodies in remarkably intact condition. Heaney's poetry preserves the landscape in the same way: digging with his pen to present readers with wonders found from within the peat bogs.

3 2¾ MILES

Follow the circular walk around the bog garden to see extraordinary insect-eating plants and find out about boggy nappies and moss bandages used in the First World War. Then it's a short and leisurely stroll back to the visitor centre and nearby car park

Explore beautiful peat lands and wildlife at the edge of **Lough Neagh** to discover the landscape captured in the work of Seamus Heaney

KEY

INFO

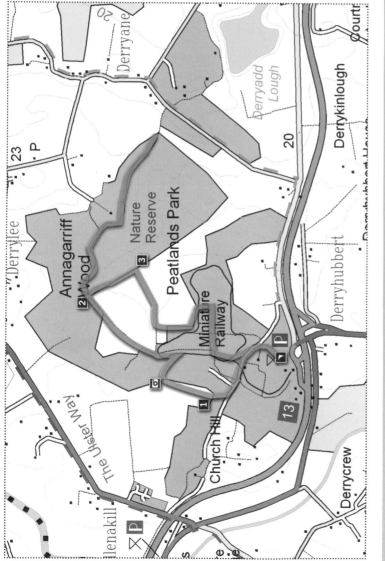

TERRAIN
Paths through woodland and across bogland. Hard surface, woodchip covering and raised wooden trackways over the bogs. Stout shoes and outdoor clothing should be worn.

ACCESS
Most paths are suitable for disabled access.

HOW TO GET THERE
BY CAR: Peatlands Park is 34 miles west of Belfast on the M1. Leave M1 at J13 (Loughgall) and follow signs to Peatlands Park.
BY PUBLIC TRANSPORT: There are no bus or train services to this site, but it is on Sustrans Route number 94. No cycling is permitted in the park.

MAP
OSNI Discoverer Series Map 19.
Grid ref: H 896 603

NEARBY EXCURSIONS
To see Lough Neagh visit Lough Neagh Discovery Centre at Oxford Island, 21 miles west of Belfast, signposted off J10 on the M1.

MORE INFO
Peatlands Park
33 Derryhubbert Road, Dungannon BT71 6NW
☎ 028 38851102
www.ni-environment.gov.uk/ peatlands

Craigavon Borough Council Civic Centre, PO Box 66, Lakeview Road, Craigavon, County Armagh BT64 1AL
☎ 028 38312400
www.craigavon.gov.uk

Route

The Granite Trail Co Down

Distance 3 miles (4.8 km) **Type** Moderate **Time** 2 hours

▶ START

From the **Harbour Bar**, cross over the main road and turn left. After 50m, turn right at a sign for the **Granite Trail**, and climb steps that rise above the harbour. At the top of the steps cross **King Street** and follow the concrete path between the houses. You will notice the granite tram lines symbolising the old Bogie Line. An interpretation panel marks the start of this historic walk.

Follow the granite steps uphill under the red brick arch. You will pass a model bogie, a low truck on four wheels, used on the narrow gauge railway to bring quarried stone to the harbour below.

After 20 minutes of steep climbing, you reach a shoddy hut where men working the stone would have sheltered from the elements. These huts got their name from the pieces of granite shoddy left after dressing the stone. Pause to admire the view over the harbour and the Irish Sea.

At the fence line climb the stile and continue for 20m uphill. Follow the grassy track, cutting through the heather. The track is uneven and rocky with muddy sections. After 10 minutes you will reach a stile and gate. Cross over and your uphill effort will be rewarded ◉ with spectacular views across the towns of Newcastle, Dundrum and Castlewellan, and to

▶ The Mourne Mountains rise impressively behind the small seaside resort of Newcastle

the iconic landmarks of **Scrabo Tower** and Slieve Croob. On a clear day, you can glimpse the Isle of Man and the Mull of Galloway in Scotland.

A short walk uphill leads to **Thomas's Quarry**. Then continue downhill, back into the trees on a wide forest track leading into **Donard Wood** until you reach a bridge over the **Glen River**. Turning left uphill leads towards **Slieve Donard**, the tallest peak in Northern Ireland at 852m (2,795ft).

1 1¾ MILES

Cross the bridge and turn right along one of several tracks leading downhill along the left-hand side of the river. These tracks are narrow, steep and uneven with rocky outcrops and exposed roots. At the next stone bridge track right over the bridge and then turn left along the Glen

track, passing waterfalls and large clear pools ◉ brimming with chilled mountain water. After passing a huge oak tree, descend along a cobbled path before reaching another granite bridge. Track right along a small dirt path through the mixed woodland. Donard Lodge once stood in these grounds, a bathing villa built by William Annesley, 3rd Earl, in 1830. This large house was used in the Second World War by the 11th infantry of the US army as a headquarters prior to the D-Day landings. A fire at the time left the building unsafe and it was demolished in 1966.

The path continues through the woodland before joining the road opposite the school. Turn right, passing the gate lodge and continue along King Street. After about 200m turn left down

Bath Lane, following the steep steps down towards the sea. When you reach Main Road once more, cross over and turn right, following the footpath along the sea wall. A short 400m walk takes you back to the Harbour Bar.

▶ SCRABO TOWER

Stretching to over 600 feet above sea level, Scrabo Tower is an impressive focal point in the skyline above Strangford Lough. Built in 1857, the tower is open 7 days a week in the summer months to those who wish to climb its 122 steps, but only on Sundays during winter.

Starting at the foot of the **Mourne Mountains**, this walk offers spectacular views and an insight into the local mining history

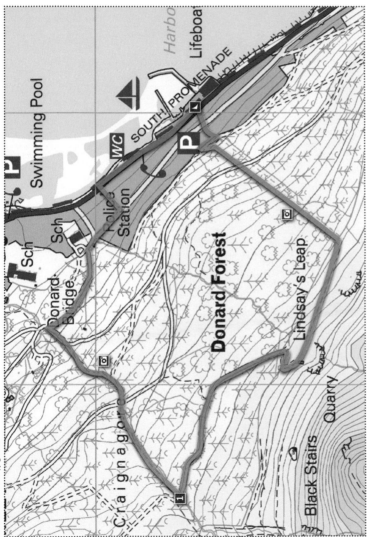

TERRAIN
The route is challenging at first as you climb from near sea level to around 600ft in just over ½ mile. After this the path levels out. Terrain ranges from steep steps to uneven rocky tracks.

HOW TO GET THERE
BY CAR: From Newcastle take the A2 towards Kilkeel. After passing the police station at the southern end of town look out for the yellow Harbour Bar on the left-hand side of the road, just before the harbour. Some parking is available behind the pub.
BY PUBLIC TRANSPORT:
The start is 1 mile from Newcastle Bus Station following the main street south through the town towards Kilkeel. The yellow Harbour Bar is located on the left just before the harbour.

MAP
OSNI Discoverer Series Sheet 29.
Grid ref: J 381 296

MORE INFO
Tollymore Forest Park
www.forestserviceni.gov.uk

Newcastle Tourist Information Centre
The Promenade, Newcastle
BT33 0AA
☎ 028 4372 2222

Walk Northern Ireland
www.walkni.com

Discover Northern Ireland
discovernorthernireland.com

Route ————

Ring of Gullion Co Armagh

Distance 8 miles (12.5 km) **Type** Moderate **Time** 5½ hours

The **Ring of Gullion** is a rugged range of heather-covered hills in south Armagh, the remains of a circular ring dyke volcano which erupted 50 million years ago. From the summit of Slieve Gullion (573m, 1,880ft), the highest point in **County Armagh**, you can cast your eye over a wild landscape that's brimming with myth and dark legend.

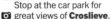

▶ START

The walk begins and ends at the car park next to the courtyard of **Slieve Gullion Forest Park**. Climb a path at the top left of the car park beside an interpretive panel. Walk up the path's gentle slope through woodland for ½ mile to a bench opposite a marker post. Turn right on to the forest drive and continue uphill through mature beech trees for 800m. Turn right on to a short section of forest track to the upper forest. Turn left on the forest drive and continue along the southern slopes of Slieve Gullion until you reach a car park.

1 2½ MILES

Stop at the car park for great views of **Croslieve**, **Slievebrack** and **Mullaghbane**. Turn right a short distance past the parking area up the mountain path. This short, steep incline is the most demanding part of the walk.

Climb a stile and continue until you reach a stone shelter. Views

> The Ring Dyke structure formed when a volcanic caldera collapsed

open to include the peaks of **Slievenacapple** and the **Ring of Gullion**. An interpretive panel at the shelter illustrates the legends of the area. Keep to the right of the shelter across areas of peaty and rough ground.

2 4 MILES

The path arrives at the summit of Slieve Gullion and the Neolithic **South Cairn Passage Grave**.

The tomb, the highest remaining passage tomb in Ireland, can be entered from just below the summit. Enjoy panoramic views from the summit to the **Mourne Mountains**, **Carlingford Lough**, the **Cooley Peninsula**, the **Armagh Drumlins** and beyond. Continue northwest along the summit until you reach the eerily still **Calliagh Berra's**

Lake. The lake is named after a sorceress who, according to folklore, bewitched the giant Finn McCool. Tricked into diving into the lake, Finn was transformed into an old man with silver hair. The spell was reversed, with the exception of his silvery mane, and legend has it that a head of white hair awaits anyone who falls in.

After the lough you reach the **North Cairn**, a Bronze Age burial chamber. Continue on the path and descend the north side of the mountain for a mile, where captivating views will continue to open out in front of you, to **Ballard Road**. Turn right and follow the lane as it curves through the striking landscape. Keep right after 1½ miles where the road forks.

3 6 MILES

You soon reach **Killevy Old Churches**, an ancient convent dating from the fifth century. St Moninna, also known as St Bline, is buried in the churchyard near the well named after her.

Continue along the country lane, past **Clonium South Cairn Portal Tomb** on the left and **Killevy Castle** on the right for a further 1¼ miles, then turn right at a crossroads. Continue through gateposts on to the exit drive from the courtyard centre to return to the car park.

Wonder at the grandeur the **Ring of Gullion**, where craggy, heath-covered hills offer an insight into unique geology

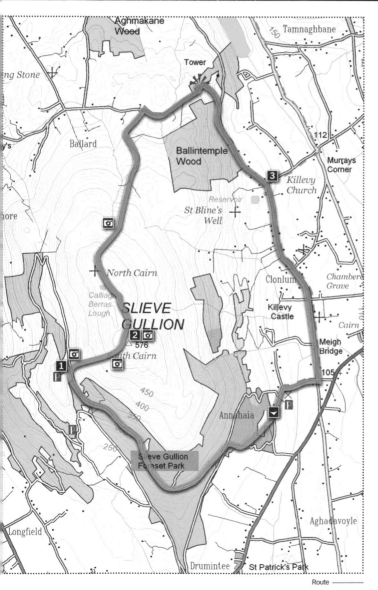

TERRAIN
Forest track followed by sometimes muddy mountain paths and minor roads. As mountain ground can be muddy, wear sturdy shoes or boots. Wear waterproof, warm clothing.

HOW TO GET THERE
BY CAR: From Newry take the Dublin Road until the Cloghoge roundabout. Travel on the B113 towards Forkhill for 3½ miles, past Meigh, until the sign for Slieve Gullion Forest Park on the right-hand side of the road just before Drumintee. Follow the drive past the courtyard centre to the car park.
BY PUBLIC TRANSPORT:
Frequent trains and buses between Belfast and Dublin stop at Newry. From Newry bus station, take number 43 bus to Forkhill, which stops at the forest park entrance.

MAP
OSNI Discoverer Series Sheet 29.
Grid ref: J 042 196

MORE INFO
Newry Tourist Information Centre, Town Hall, Bank Parade, Newry BT35 6HR
☎ 02830 268877

Walk Northern Ireland
www.walkni.com

Discover Northern Ireland
discovernorthernireland. com

Route ⎯⎯⎯⎯

233

Cuilcagh Way Co Fermanagh

Distance 4.6 miles (7km) **Type** Challenging **Time** 6 hours

Marble Arch Caves Global Geopark, the world's first International Geopark, covers an expanse of 18,000 hectares within Fermanagh and Cavan. The brand new 33km **Cuilcagh Way** is almost entirely off-road and stretches from the low lies of the **Cladagh River** to the blanket bog summit of **Cuilcagh Mountain**. The waymarked walk can be walked in six sections, and this linear stretch heads up to the summit of the Cuilcagh Mountain for phenomenal views over six counties.

▶ START

Start at the **Cuilcagh Mountain Park** car park and head south along the stone track. This runs parallel with the **Owenbrean River**, one of three rivers on the northern flanks of Cuilcagh Mountain, which sinks underground to form the **Marble Arch** cave system. You are now in the distinctive limestone landscape where you will see surface features such as limestone pavement and surface depressions known as dolines and shakeholes – evidence of cave systems in the area. After crossing the bridge, the landscape notably changes to blanket bog. As the track starts to climb, take a moment to stroll along the boardwalk. This conservation site was once bare peat after previous commercial peat

▶ At 665m (2,182ft) Cuilcagh Mountain is the highest point in the county and affords superb views

extraction stripped the surface vegetation and the drainage system dried out the peat. By damming the drains the water table returned to its natural level, allowing the rare and diverse ecosystem to regenerate.

1 2½ MILES

Leaving the track, the waymarked trail winds its way over the blanket bog on the middle slopes of Cuilcagh. As you look west, you can see an obvious bite out of the middle of the ridge; this is called the **Cuilcagh Gap**. Littering the slopes, are gigantic sandstone

boulders, which were deposited by melting glaciers about 13,000 years ago. The climb up the waymarked path is steep and rocky in parts but well worth the effort. Standing at 665m (2,182ft), Cuilcagh is the highest point in Fermanagh. The distinctive ridge summit is made up of horizontal layers of Lackagh sandstone, formed more than 320 million years ago, when this area would have been covered by a huge river delta probably similar in size to the Amazon River today.

Follow the route

east, heading to a large summit cairn.

2 4¼ MILES

The summit cairn is in fact a Neolithic burial chamber. Once on top you will discover magnificent 360° sweeping views that, on clear days, can reach to counties Tyrone, Donegal, Cavan, Leitrim, Sligo and Roscommon. Once you've had your fill of fresh mountain air and your head is awash with the spectacular vista, you can turn back and retrace your steps down this delightful route to the car park.

Be one of the first to walk the **Cuilcagh Way**, an exciting new long distance path across blanket bog and stunning limestone scenery

KEY

▶INFO

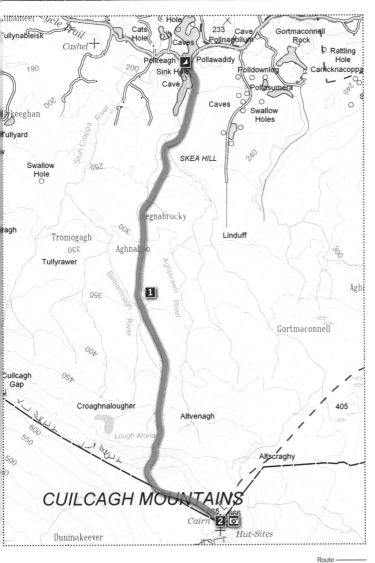

TERRAIN
Paths through farmland and across blanket bog. Hard surface stone tracks over the bog and stony sections. Stout footwear is essential.

HOW TO GET THERE
BY CAR: From Enniskillen take the A4 Sligo Road for 3 miles then branch off on the A32 Swanlinbar Road. Follow signs to Marble Arch Caves, pass the entrance and continue along the road to the Cuilcagh Mountain car park.

MAP
OSNI Discoverer Series Map 26.
Grid Ref: H 121 335

NEARBY EXCURSIONS
Marble Arch Caves
Marlbank, Florencecourt
BT92 1EW
☎ 028 6634 8855
marblearchcaves.net
globalgeopark.com
Open daily, mid Mar-June, 10am-4.30pm, Jul-Aug 10am-5pm, Sept 10am-4.30pm. The caves may close for safety reasons following heavy rain, so call before setting out in bad weather.

MORE INFO
Fermanagh Tourist Information Centre
Wellington Road, Enniskillen
☎ 028 6632 3110

Blacklion Tourist Information Centre, Main Street, Blacklion, Co Cavan
☎ +353 7198 53941

Walk Northern Ireland
www.walkni.com

Discover Northern Ireland
discovernorthernireland. com

Route ———

Robbers Table Co Tyrone

Distance 9 miles (14.5km) **Type** Moderate **Time** 3½ hours

The **Sperrins** are one of Northern Ireland's most beautiful yet least explored mountain areas. Easily accessible from Belfast and Londonderry, this dramatic landscape of upland bogs and lush forested valleys is a world away from the city lights. The route takes you over blanket bog uplands, where turf cutting has been practised for centuries to a stunning vantage point, where remarkable views over the **High Sperrins** and **Omagh Plain** await.

▶ START

Park at **Gortin Glen Forest Park**, an Area of Outstanding Natural Beauty with red squirrels. Exit the car park and follow a forest track to the B48 Glenpark Road. Turn left, then after 50m take a right down Lisnaharney Road. At the crossroads of Lisnaharney Road and Castleroddy Road you'll find the former **Castleroddy Old National School**, built in 1832. In the 19th century Irish culture underwent a huge change. The Irish language went into decline after the Great Famine and in the 1820s, national schools were set up to encourage literary, but they only provided lessons in English.

Look out for the carved stone near the gable saying 'Castleroddy NS', with the N backwards. After ½ mile, turn right up a track marked

> On a clear day views from the Curraghchosaly Mountain stretch out over the Sperrins to Donegal

'**Lisnaharney Public Right of Way**', then carry straight on at the fork, following waymarker posts alongside evergreen woodland, over the western slopes of **Curraghchosaly Mountain**. At the summit take in incredible 📷 views over the **Central Sperrins**, the **Bluestack** and **Derryveagh Mountains** to the west, while the **High Sperrins** stretch out ahead.

1 3½ MILES

Climb a stile, and then head downhill on the path, passing over several stiles and gates. On the mountainside to your right you can see great chunks cut from the peat. In the 17th and

18th centuries, peat was the main source of fuel in the country.

Blanket bog harbours many unique and interesting plants, from orchids to heather and bog cotton, and cutting turf for fuel has been the main reason for the decline of peatlands in Northern Ireland. With souring fuel prices there has been a recent revival of turf cutting across the country.

2 4¼ MILES

Turn left at Liscabble Road. After ½ mile turn left at a tracked marked '**Eskeradooey Public Right of Way**', an old drover's road on which tarred geese were once driven to

Omagh, and climb over the **Ballynatubbrit Mountain**. As you near the summit take a detour right to the **Robber's Table** – a refuge where local highwaymen, who terrorised the carriageway in the 17th century, came to divide their spoils.

Continue along the path over the brow of the hill, where the path becomes a grassy track and passes through a gate. Go through another gate at farm buildings, then turn right down to Lisnaharney Road. Follow the road left all the way back to the main road, turn left then right and head back to Gortin Glen Forest Park.

Enjoy phenomenal views over the **Sperrin Mountains** on a route
once used by highwaymen and 17th century drovers

KEY 🦦 🍴 🚻 📷 🎣 🐎 🏞 ⛴ ⛺ 🔭 ♿

▶INFO

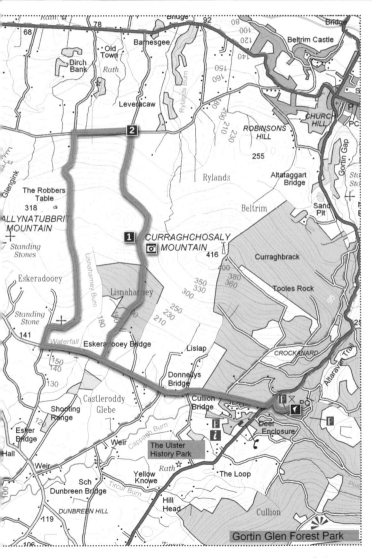

TERRAIN
Moorland paths, which can
be boggy, and quiet roads.

HOW TO GET THERE
BY CAR: Gortin Forest Park is
located on the Gortin Road.
Park at Gortin Glen Forest
Park, where there are toilets
and waymarked forest trails.

MAP
OSNI Series, Sheet 13.
Grid ref: H 485 822

NEARBY EXCURSIONS
An Creagan Visitor Centre
An Creagan, Creggan
BT79 9AF
☎ 028 8076 1112
www.an-creagan.com
The visitor centre offers a
range of cultural activities,
from traditional storytelling
to archaeology tours, a
craft shop, self-catering
accommodation and
a restaurant.

MORE INFO
Walk Northern Ireland
www.walkni.com

Discover Northern Ireland
**discovernorthernireland.
com**

Omagh Tourist Information,
Strule Arts Centre, Townhill
Square, Omagh BT78 1BL
☎ 028 8224 7831
www.omagh.gov.uk

Sperrins Tourism
www.sperrinstourism.com

Walk on the Wild Side
☎ 028 8075 8452
www.walkwithmarty.com

Route ⸺

INDEX

ACKNOWLEDGEMENTS

10 9 8 7 6 5 4 3 2 1

Published in 2010 by BBC Books,
an imprint of Ebury Publishing.
A Random House Group Company

Foreword © Julia Bradbury 2010
Main Text by Cavan Scott
Walks copyright © Bristol Magazines Ltd 2010
Editorial arrangement and contribution
© Woodlands Books 2010

The Random House Group Limited Reg. No. 954009

Addresses for companies within the Random House Group
can be found at www.randomhouse.co.uk

A CIP catalogue record for this book is available from the
British Library.

ISBN 978 1 846 07883 5

The Random House Group Limited supports the Forest
Stewardship Council (FSC), the leading international forest
certification organisation. All our titles that are printed on
Greenpeace approved FSC certified paper carry the FSC logo.
Our paper procurement policy can be found at
www.rbooks.co.uk/environment

Commissioning editor: Muna Reyal
Project editor: Joe Cottington
Copy-editor: Stephanie Evans
Designer: Alison Fenton
Production: Helen Everson
Walks originally commissioned by Jo Tinsley

All the walks in this book originally appeared in BBC
Countryfile Magazine and were written by the editorial team
and by contributors to the magazine.

While every effort has been made to provide the most
accurate route information, it is essential to take the
appropriate map with you on the walks. You can buy
detailed versions of the maps in this book online at
www.ordnancesurvey.co.uk/mapshop (for Great Britain)
and www.lpsni.gov.uk (for Northern Ireland).

Colour origination by: Alta Image
Printed and bound in Singapore.

To buy books by your favourite authors and register for offers,
visit www.rbooks.co.uk

Where possible, a blue grid is displayed on the maps used
throughout this book. Please note that each tile is 1km wide.

BBC Books would like to thank the following individuals and
organisations for providing photographs and for permission
to reproduce copyright material. While every effort has been
made to trace and acknowledge copyright holders, we would
like to apologise should there be any errors or omissions.

AA World Travel Library/Alamy 216 (bottom); Hannah Adcock
222 (all); Angela Batty/Alamy 40; Sarah Baxter 68; Andrew
Beaven 206, 210; Mark Blackmore 32 (bottom), 44 (bottom);
Blackwater Valley Partnership 66; Sean Burke/Alamy 116;
Adam Burton/Alamy 13; Margaret Canning 232; James
Carron 208 (bottom), 212; Neil Coates 15, 18, 110 (both),
112, 124 (top), 154; David Cheshire/Alamy 118; Roger Clegg
11, 190 (top); Ben Cleuch/Alamy 204 (top); Coolcamping.
co.uk 58 (bottom), 168 (bottom); David Cordner 08/Alamy
230; Roger Coulam/Alamy 186, 196; Mick Coulson 17,
74; Michael Cowton 94; Dartmoor National Park Authority
32 (both); Stephen Dorey ABIPP/Alamy 122; Dual Aspect
Photography/Alamy 6-7; Cody Duncan/Alamy 220 (top);
Katharine Eastham/Alamy 156; Patrick Eden/Alamy 50;
Darrin Jenkins/Alamy 70; Explore Kent 2, 64 (both); Ian
Foulis/Alamy 30; Cyril Francis 9 (right), 90 (bottom); Richard
Hammerton 54 (bottom); Steven Hanna 226; Robert Harding
Picture Library Ltd/Alamy 34 (top); Emma Harvey 100
(bottom); Dorothy Hamilton 140, 142, 146; Brian Harris/
Alamy 214 (bottom); Nick Heasman 56 (both), 58 (top); Lisa
Heaton 236; Holkham Estate 90 (top); Nigel Housden 78,
80, 88, 92; International Photobank/Alamy 138 (top); Chris
Laurens/Alamy 62; Alistair Laming/Alamy 76; Tom Mackie
82; Andrew McCloy 102, 184 (all); Simon McEachran 220
(bottom); Fergal McErlean 204, 218 (top); Dave McFadzean
200 (top right and bottom); Anna McKibbin 60; Tor McIntosh
138 (bottom); Robert Morris 108; The National Trust
Photolibrary/Alamy 84, 86 (top), 114; Christopher Nicholson/
Alamy 52; Kevin Oates 136; Eli Pascall-Willis/Alamy 152; Ian
Patrick/Alamy 44; Photoshot Holdings Ltd/Alamy 86 (bottom);
Simon Price/Alamy 208 (top); Anne Karin Purkiss 54 (top;
Quantock Hills AONB 38; Scottish Viewpoint 9 (left), 200 (top
left), 202, 216 (top), 218 (bottom); Michelle Shannon 234;
Shutterstock 42, 120, 124 (bottom); Skyscan Photolibrary/
Alamy 46; Steve Smith 1 (left), 130; Jon Sparks 162; Chris
Sperring 40 (top); Anna Stowe Landscapes UK/Alamy 14;
Jane Swale 19, 26 (all); Jo Tinsley 1 (middle and right), 98
(top), 100 (top), 134, 194, 214 (top); Anthony Toole 188,
192 (both); Sue Viccars 36 (both); Visit Cornwall/John Such
28; Visit Wales 128, 132, 144, 148; John Warburton-Lee
Photography/Alamy 230; Sebastian Wasek/Alamy 158; Phillip
S Watson 228 (all); Robin Weaver/Alamy 106; Sue White 22
(both); Dave Willis 160, 164, 166, 168 (top), 170, 172, 174;
David Winpenny 178, 180, 182; Ian Woolcock/Alamy 24

Special introductory offer

SAVE 30%

when you subscribe to *Countryfile Magazine* today

Subscribe to *Countryfile Magazine* for **just £14.25 every 6 issues** by convenient Direct Debit** and get the **best of the British countryside** delivered to your door every month.

Don't miss out on this very special offer

OFFER ENDS 30 JUNE 2011 *Sorry, 30% saving only available to UK residents. Your subscription will start with the next available issue. **Direct Debit saving is calculated by 12 issues x cover price, non-Direct Debit saving is calculated by 13 issues x cover price.